A Hug From Afar

One family's dramatic journey through three

continents to escape the Holocaust

Claire Barkey Flash

Edited and compiled by Cynthia Flash Hemphill

Translated by Morris Barkey

Dedicated to the Barkey and Capeluto families

PRAISE FOR *A HUG FROM AFAR*

"This book is an amazing example of a Jewish family's immigration story before, during and after WWII that's beautifully preserved in the detailed letters written by a young Sephardic girl to her uncle in the United States. It's a must-read for anyone trying to understand the global immigration story, especially in light of the continued controversy over immigration to the United States that we still face today."

-- Lisa Kranseler, Executive Director of the Washington State Jewish Historical Society

"The author has taken a box of family letters and melded it with history to illuminate a slice of World War II through a deeply personal and fascinating lens."

-- Diana Brement, editor

"*A Hug from Afar* reads like a suspense novel–only it's a true story, and it feels as though it's your family caught up in a tale of hope and fear, frustration and happiness, family ties that reach across continents and over decades, and an American immigration bureaucracy working to make family reunification as difficult as possible. Cynthia Flash Hemphill has done a wonderful job of compiling family letters and official documents to make the story of her immigrant family come alive, not only for those whose families share similar histories, but also for everyone else wanting to understand from the inside a suspenseful immigrant story full of resourceful characters, and a happy ending in the U.S."

-- Paul Burstein, Professor Emeritus of Sociology and Political Science, and Stroum Professor Emeritus of Jewish Studies, University of Washington

"The Sephardic Jewish story is rich with history and culture. This book illustrates in great detail what it was like to be a Sephardic Jew on the Island of Rhodes before the Nazi occupation and the tragic ramifications felt by the community afterward. Fortunately for all of us, this is a story of triumph demonstrated by extreme determination on the part of the letter writer, Claire Barkey Flash."

-- Stuart Eskenazi, award winning journalist and curator

"Although this book focuses on one family's story, it is an excellent example of the larger immigration story. It illustrates with personal letters and plenty of official documents just how complicated the whole issue of immigration is. It was complex in the 1940s, and it continues to be that way today."

-- Joel Benoliel, University of Washington Regent and Co-Founder of the Seattle Sephardic Network

"This book shows how the Holocaust impacted a vibrant Jewish community on a distant Aegean island, wiping out this community near the end of World War II. Letters isolate and share personal stories without looking through the lens of time. To see the impact of the Holocaust as it affected a community and one family's tale of perseverance, escape and triumph, read this book."

-- Dee Simon, Baral Family Executive Director, Holocaust Center for Humanity

"Within the first pages, you will find yourself instantly smitten with this story. Cynthia Flash Hemphill has invested an incredible amount of love and research to bring her family's journey to life. What begins with a sweet letter from a 9-year-old girl quickly turns into a life and death struggle to find shelter in a new country. It puts a human face on today's immigration debate and reminds us of what the promise of starting a new life in America means to so many. Anyone interested in a rich, compelling immigrant story, will find themselves unable to put this book down."

-- Stephen Sadis, Sadis Filmworks

"The person who coined the phrase 'Don't judge a book by its cover' obviously didn't see the cover of 'A Hug From Afar.' This brilliantly designed book is a fascinating and inspiring must-read for anyone who wants to tell the heroic stories of their families, and that's most of us."

-- Bill Kossen, Seattle-based historian and writer

A Hug From Afar
One family's dramatic journey through three continents to escape the Holocaust

Copyright © 2004 (first edition) © 2016 (second edition) by Claire Barkey Flash and Cynthia Flash Hemphill

ISBN (Printed): 978-0-9973088-0-8
ISBN (Mobi ebook - for Kindle): 978-0-9973088-1-5

Published by Cynthia Flash Hemphill,
Flash Media Services, 13239 SE 51st Pl., Bellevue, WA 98006

Library of Congress Cataloging-in-Publication Data
Type of Work: Text

Registration Number / Date:
TXu001178019 / 2004-01-20

Title: A hug from afar : one family's immigration story / by
Claire Barkey Flash ; edited and compiled by Cynthia
Flash Hemphill.

Description: 352 p.

Copyright Claimant:
Cynthia Flash Hemphill, 1962-

Date of Creation: 2004

Previous Registration:
Preexisting material: letters of Claire Barkey Flash,
documents, translation.

Basis of Claim: New Matter: some text, editing, compilation.

Copyright Note: C.O. correspondence.

Names:Flash, Claire Barkey, 1921-1991
Hemphill, Cynthia Flash, 1962-

Contents

FOREWORD

A Hug from Afar is not only one family's immigration story. Through the unusually rich collection of letters and documents assembled and/or translated here, A *Hug from Afar* gives voice to a now lost Jewish community on the verge of annihilation, to a Jewish family seeking asylum, and to one young woman who initiated a thread of correspondence with relatives in the United States that would ultimately solidify her family's escape from the Nazis.

The story itself is not only captivating and powerful on its own, but is also of great historical and cultural significance. Too seldom do we have access to the perspectives of women in history, even fewer with regard to young women, and very few when it comes to the Sephardic Jewish world. While we know of Anne Frank and her diary, we have almost no sources composed by Sephardic Jewish girls or young women describing their experiences regarding the rise of fascism and the onset of the Second World War. While not a diary and not focused as much on the period of the war itself, Claire Barkey's letters, which form the first part of the present book, nonetheless offer the reader a glimpse into a young woman's world on the cusp of unimaginable rupture and impending doom.

In the letters that she began writing to her relatives, especially her uncle Raphael Capeluto in Seattle, in 1930, remarkably at age nine, Claire Barkey reveals insights into her everyday experiences and impressions of life on the island of Rhodes and the changes afoot in her society as across the globe. Part of the Ottoman Empire since the 16th century and home to a small but important Jewish community, Rhodes became, in 1912, an Italian colony along with the other Dodecanese islands. These very changes, along with other factors, compelled some of the island's Jews to seek out new lives elsewhere during the early 20th century. A wide-spanning *Rhodesli* diaspora emerged with hubs reaching from Brussels to Cape Town, New York to Seattle.

Claire's initial letters nonetheless reveal the strong imprint of the local cultural milieux. Not only did Claire's father come from mainland Turkey and hold Turkish citizenship—signifying a continuing link to the old Ottoman world—but Claire's writing, ostensibly in the local Judeo-Spanish language of the Sephardic Jews, is peppered with vocabulary drawn from the Italian she encountered at school and on the street. She often renders her Judeo-Spanish with Italian spelling conventions. While many of these nuances are unable to be translated, despite the faithful English renderings undertaken by her brother, Morris, they still can be gleaned in the originals, some of which have been reproduced in this book, or explored in more depth in digital form via the Sephardic Studies Program at the University of Washington or through the Washington State Jewish Archives at the University of Washington Libraries.

While clearly embedded in the Italian cultural environment that shaped the dynamics of Jewish life on Rhodes during the 1920s and 1930s, Claire and her family experienced a heart-wrenching rupture first with the imposition of fascist laws and ultimately the oncoming Nazi occupation that separated the family, sending members first as refugees to Tangier, Morocco, and then ultimately to be reunited in Seattle with relatives there. The documents offer a rare window into the entire experience, the bureaucratic and diplomatic processes involved in getting the family to Tangier, and then ultimately, after years in limbo, to Seattle in the wake of the war. Along the way, they discover the fate of friends and family they left behind on their native island.

It was thanks to the correspondence that young Claire initiated with her uncle in Seattle, well before the onset of the war, that her rescue and that of her family became possible—indeed a reality.

As much as the tale that unfolds in the pages that follow reveals a powerful "hug from afar"—the embrace between relatives stretching from the Aegean Sea to the Puget Sound—it also represents a set of missives from afar, letters from a bygone world, documents that reveal aspirations and anxieties shared by Jews all throughout Europe on the eve of World War II. For every story of a successful escape, like the one documented here, there were many more attempts that never came to fruition.

Finally, as much as A *Hug from Afar* is a tale of immigrants, it is also a tale of exiles and refugees. Today, in an era in which the plight of refugees preoccupies us anew, the story about Claire and her family revealed in this book gains new vitality and relevance. The members of the family that played a role in bringing their story to light for us in the 21st century should be applauded. They remind us how much we have learned—and how much we haven't.

Devin E. Naar

Isaac Alhadeff Professor in Sephardic Studies

University of Washington

INTRODUCTION

Immigrants enter the United States every day, creating an international collage that makes this country unique. These immigrants—from Europe, Asia, Africa, South America, and the former Soviet Union—come here by boat, by foot, and by plane to start promising new lives they could only dream about in their native lands.

In fact, most Americans came from immigrant families. At one point in their history they came from somewhere else.

While all of us have immigrant ancestors, few of us know the detailed stories of how these family members came to America. But many of them have a difficult and often times heroic story to tell.

This is the story of one of those families—the Barkeys of the island of Rhodes in the Aegean Sea. The Barkeys came to America after World War II, refugees from Rhodes, which was ruled by Italian dictator Benito Mussolini and ultimately invaded by the Nazis.

This story is told mainly through letters written by Claire Barkey, the eldest of the family's six children. Claire, through these letters to her Uncle Ralph and Aunt Rachel Capeluto in Seattle, Wash., takes you on the roller-coaster ride that the Barkey family went through to come to America.

This book, compiled after their deaths, is dedicated to Claire Barkey and Ralph and Rachel Capeluto. Claire was the driving force that led her family to America and Ralph and Rachel offered the financial support and political connections to bring the family to their new adopted homeland.

Special thanks are also given to Regina Amira, Michele Erdrich Gidley, Morris Barkey, Philip Flash, editors Diana Brement, Rabbi Allison Flash and Edward Flash, and designer MeshCreative. Regina, Claire's sister, helped edit and type this book. Michele, Claire's niece, helped organize distribution of this book. Morris, Claire's brother, spent many hours translating the more than 100 letters to English from Ladino, the ancient language spoken by Sephardic Jews from southern Europe. Translation help also came from Molly FitzMorris and Paola Pinto. The translations—which remained faithful to the originals—made it possible for Claire's words to be understood by the relatives in America. And Philip, Claire's husband, had the foresight to realize that the letters were more than just words on paper, but the makings of an important family heirloom and historical document.

Please note that the spelling of names varies throughout the document. That is because the names (first and last) have been translated from various languages (Spanish, Ladino, French, Italian, Hebrew, Turkish, etc.) into English and there is no common English spelling. Sincere apologies for any confusion that may arise. Also, any bracketed items [ ] were added by the translator. The full collection of original letters are stored and can be accessed at the University of Washington Libraries Jewish Archive Collection.

WHO'S WHO

Beginning with the first chapter in order of appearance, people appearing in the story are only listed the first time they appear.

CHAPTER ONE – FAMILY TREE

Clara (Claire) Barkey: Author of most of the letters, oldest daughter of Abraham and Mazaltov (Mathilda) Barkey

Ralph Capeluto: Claire's uncle, Mathilda's brother, who emigrated to Seattle in 1920, married to Rachel [Alhadeff]

Lea Levy: Claire's first cousin, daughter of Marie and Sadik Levy

Marie Levy: Mazaltov's second oldest sister, married to Sadik Levy, parents of above mentioned Cousin Lea Levy and Lea's sister, Rachel Levy

Grandpa: Musani Capeluto with his wife, Rachel, were Mazaltov's parents

Papa and Mama: Avraham and Mazaltov [Mathilda] Barkey, Claire's parents

David and Behora Capeluto: Behora, "oldest," is Tamara Capeluto, the oldest sister of Mazaltov. Although she and her husband shared a last name, they were unrelated

Uncle Sadik: Sadik Levy, married to Marie Levy

Chelibon Maiche: Married to Mazaltov's sister Gioia

Aunt Esther: Mazaltov's youngest sister and the only one still a minor when their parents, Musani and Rachel, died, rendering her a ward of Mazaltov and Abraham

Sarina Maish: Mazaltov's younger sister, married to Chelibon Maish

Gioia Levy: Mazaltov's younger sister, married to Nissim Levy

Clara Barkey: Abraham's mother, maiden name Alagem

Mathilda Cherez, Rachel Israel, Vida Alhadeff, Rosa Franco: These four sisters (listed here with their married names) are the daughters of David and Behora (Tamara) Capeluto

Claire Barkey [Barchi] Flash: Daughter of Mathilda and Avraham Barkey, author of most of these letters

Rachel (Alhadeff) Capeluto: Ralph's wife. Parents were Rahamim Alhadeff and Mazaltov Hasson

Marie and Jacob Mayo: Family friends

Uncle Jacob Capeluto: Mazaltov's relative

Abraham Piha: Family friend

Moshe (Morris) Capeluto: Ralph and Rachel's first born son

Jacob Surmani: A cousin to the Barkey siblings

Heskia (Harry) Benatar: A cousin living in New York who was a great help to the family when they were able to emigrate

Jamila Almelech, then Hunio: Mazaltov's next-youngest sister, already living in Seattle. She was married twice, to Shelomo Almelech and then to Abraham Huniu

CHAPTER TWO – THE JEWS OF RHODES

Mazaltov and Abraham's children:

Clara (Claire) Barkey

Rachel Barkey

Haim (Victor) Barkey (twin of Morris)

Morris Barkey (twin of Victor)

Gaico (Jack) Barkey

Regina Barkey

Shelomo Almeleh: Aunt Jamila's first husband, who died in a car accident

Abraham Huniu: Aunt Jamila's second husband

Rebecca [known as Betty] Capeluto: Ralph and Rachel's second child

"Sister" Zimbul Surmani: A relative of Rachel's

CHAPTER THREE – RALPH CAPELUTO IMMIGRATES TO AMERICA

Marlene and Mimi Capeluto: Ralph and Rachel's third and fourth children

Abraham Capeluto: Mazaltov's older brother

Rahamin Alhadeff: Rachel's father

Leon Levy: Mazaltov's nephew, son of Marie and Sadik Levy

Bension Hanan: Identity uncertain

"In-law Bollissa": Identity uncertain

Rahamin Hasson: Identity uncertain

Nissim Israel: Father of Ralph's business partner Morris Israel

Nissim Alhadeff and Salomon Alhadeff: Rachel's uncles

Joseph Alhadeff: Identity uncertain

Nissim Levy: Husband of Aunt Gioia

Haim Barchi and Lea "Clara" Alagem: Avraham's parents; Claire's grandparents

Bohor Capeluto: Haim D. Capeluto, known as "Bohor," son of Aunt Behora (Tamara) Capeluto and cousin to Claire

CHAPTER FOUR – LEAVING RHODES

Witnesses to Avraham Barchi's declaration of birth:

Heskia Buenavida: Family friend who worked with Abraham in Rhodes

Nissim Levy: Gioia's husband

Behor Cadranel: Identity unknown

Aronne Coen: Identity unknown

CHAPTER FIVE – ARRIVING IN TANGIER

Maurice Hasson: A cobbler who gave Morris and Victor some work

Charles B. Alhadeff: Rachel (Alhadeff) Capeluto's cousin, son of Nissim Alhadeff

Salvator Levy: Brother of Rahamin Levy of Toronto, cousin to Claire

Rizula and David Levy: Parents of Salvator; this branch of the family was in Africa

CHAPTER SIX – RALPH AND RACHEL CAPELUTO IN AMERICA

Dave Amato: Ralph's friend and an attorney in Washington, DC, and a great help to the family

Rebecca and Moshe Hasson, Mazaltov and Jacob Pasha, Mlle. Mathilda Taranto: All former Rhodeslis in Tangier and Seattle. Mlle Taranto was the Barkey children's French teacher in Rhodes and taught Italian in Seattle

Mary Israel: A Seattle pen-pal of Claire's, daughter of Ralph's business partner

Eliezer Jacob Surmani: Son of Jacob Surmani and grandson of "Tia Tamar," Mazaltov Barkey's aunt

Moshe Levy: Lea Levy's brother, who died at Auschwitz

Rosa Capeluto: Daughter of Behora and David Capeluto

Vida Capeluto: Daughter of Behora and David Capeluto

Rachel Levy: Daughter of Marie and Sadik Levy

CHAPTER SEVEN – THE REALITY OF WAR

Mathilda Capeluto Cherez: Daughter of Tamara (Behora) and David Capeluto, and Claire's cousin, married to Albert and living in Egypt before the war

Joe Fintz: Family friend

Mardoche Menashe, Nissim Mussafir, and Marco Franco: All former Rhodeslis

Marie Israel: Mary Israel, Ralph's business partner's daughter

Mazaltov and Jaco Pasha: Identity uncertain

Hugh De Lacy: Congressional representative from Washington, see footnote in text

CHAPTER EIGHT – FINALLY - THE USA!

Victor Amira: Regina Barkey's husband

EPILOGUE: THE BARKEYS IN SEATTLE

Philip Flash: Claire's husband

Cynthia and Edward: Claire and Philip's children

Merle Erdrich: Rachel's husband

Roberta, Harry and Michele: Rachel and Merle's children

Ruth Druker: Victor's wife

Myrna: Victor and Ruth's daughter

Flory Gabay: Morris' wife

Illana, Sarina, Avraham and Yemina: Morris and Flory's children

Susan, Marcelle and Rozanne Amira: Regina and Victor's children

Jewel Capeluto: Morris Capeluto's wife, Ralph's daughter-in-law

Joseph Huniu: Esther's husband (no relation to Jamila's husband Abraham Huniu)

FAMILY TREE

Abraham Capeluto

Haim Capeluto
Tamar Menasei

Jiuseppe Capeluto
Miriam Capeluto

Moshe "Musani" Capeluto
b. 1855 Rhodes, d. 1935 Rhodes

Rachel Capeluto
b. 1865 Rhodes, d. 1927 Rhodes

Tamar (Berhora) Capeluto
b. 1882 Rhodes, d. 1944 Auschwitz
David Capeluto
b. 1876 Rhodes, d. 1944 Auschwitz

Marie Capeluto
b. 1883 Rhodes, d. 1944 Auschwitz
Sadic Levi
b. 1888 Turkey, d. 1944 Auschwitz

Avraham Capeluto
b. 1885 Rhodes, d. Argentina
Reina

Mazaltov (Matilda) Capeluto
b. 1895 Rhodes, d. 1977 Seattle
Avraham (Abraham) Barkey
b. 1891 Aidin, Turkey, d. 1981 Seattle

Jamila Capeluto
b. 1896 Rhodes, d. 1965 Seattle
Shelomo Almelich (1st husband), **Abraham Honeo** (2nd husband) d. 1966 Portland

Rafael (Ralph) Capeluto
b. 1898 Rhodes, d. 1984 Seattle
Rachel Alhadeff
b. 1907 Rhodes, d. 1994 Seattle

Yaakov Capeluto
b. 1899 Rhodes, d. 1908 Rhodes

Sarina Capeluto
b. 1899 Rhodes, d. 1968 Montevideo, Uruguay
Shabtai "Chelibon" Maiche
b. Aidin, Turkey, d. 1970 Montevideo, Uruguay

Unnamed twin sister of Sarina
(Died in infancy)

Esther Capeluto
b. 1909 Rhodes, d. 1994 Seattle
Joseph Huniu
b. 1899, d. 1959 Seattle

Gioia Capeluto
b. 1910 Rhodes, d. 1973 Israel
Nissim Levy
b. 1896 Turkey, d. 1949 Israel

Claire Barkey
b. 1921 Rhodes, d. 1991 Seattle
Philip Flash
b. 1918 Victoria, Canada, d. 2015 Seattle

Rachel Barkey
b. 1923 Rhodes, d. 1968 Seattle
Merle Erdrich
b. 1918 Seattle, d. 1987 Seattle

Victor (Haim) Barkey
b. 1925 Rhodes, d. 2004 Seattle
Ruth Druker
b. 1919 Iowa, d. 1998 Seattle

Morris (Moshe) Barkey
b. 1925 Rhodes
Flory Gabay
b. 1944 Morocco

Jack Barkey
b. 1928 Rhodes, d. 2006 Seattle

Regina Barkey
b. 1932 Rhodes
Victor Amira
b. 1931 Seattle

Rodi 24 Marzo 1930.

Carrissimo Tio Rophael Capelouto.
Con grande plaser ti ago esta cica letra por
acerti saver como grazias al diò ià stamos mui
buenos de la salut de miesmo speramos sa=
ver de su parte amen esta semana ricevi=
mos una cica letra suia i mos alegrimos
moi muncio tuvimos riscivo de su letra che
mi alegri mui muncio cumu che risiviera
particolar para mi cherido Tio es che il tiempo
no mi promete che cada semana le chero escri
vir porchè l'estudio tinemus muncio aguera
porchi stamos asiendo lo che estavan asiendo
antis nellas classas altas. Cada Viernes tinemus
gimlastica l'otro Viernes mos foto-grafimos con
el mixiv di gimlastica che es un Italiano
i si ama Pacello. I merchè ena stampica
che no costa nada, se chero conoserme es mas xxx
che me dixio il cherido Papa che meta un

Claire's first letter, written in Ladino.

TRANSLATION

Letter dated March 24, 1930[1]

My dear Uncle Raphael Capeluto,

It is with great pleasure that I write this short letter in order to let you know that, thank God, we find ourselves in good health; likewise, we hope you are. This week we received a short letter from you and were very glad to receive news from you.

Dear Uncle, time does not allow me to write every week because our studies are those done previously by higher grades. Every Friday we have gymnastics. Last Friday they took a picture with our gymnastics teacher, who is an Italian by the name of Paoselli. I bought a photo which hardly cost anything. If you want to recognize me, at the suggestion of my father I put a dot on my forehead. If you want to know, Lea of Aunt Marie is in my class; that is the third grade. I am trying to finish school fast so that I could help Mama. Dear Grandpa, when he took the letter [in his hands], started to cry from joy.

Dear Grandpa says hello and gives you a big hug from afar. Regards from dear Papa and dear Mama. Regards from Uncle David and Aunt Behora and daughters. Uncle Sadik, Aunt Marie and family send you their regards. Also Chelibon [pronounced Che-li-bon], Aunt Esther, and Aunt Sarina and family, Aunt Gioia, Grandma Clara, and all the relations send you their regards.

Bye, your very dear niece, Clara Barchi, who sends you regards and a tight hug from afar. I beg you to answer me.[2]

---

[1] Claire, born on March 14, 1921, was nine years old when she wrote this first letter to her uncle Ralph Capeluto in Seattle, Wash.

[2] The information in most of the footnotes has been provided by Morris Barkey, Claire's brother, who translated the letters from Ladino (Sephardic Spanish) to English.

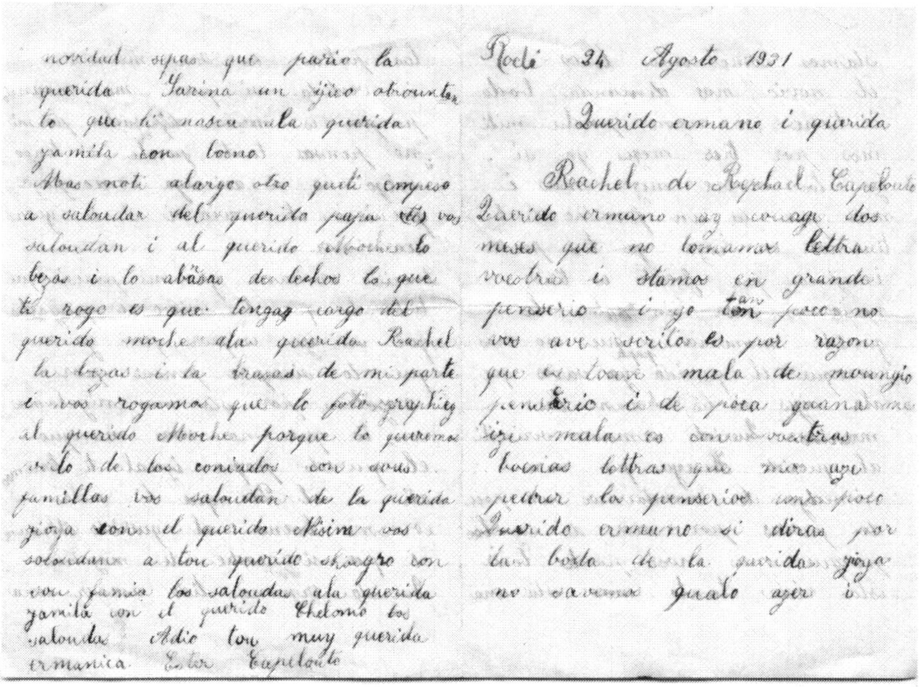

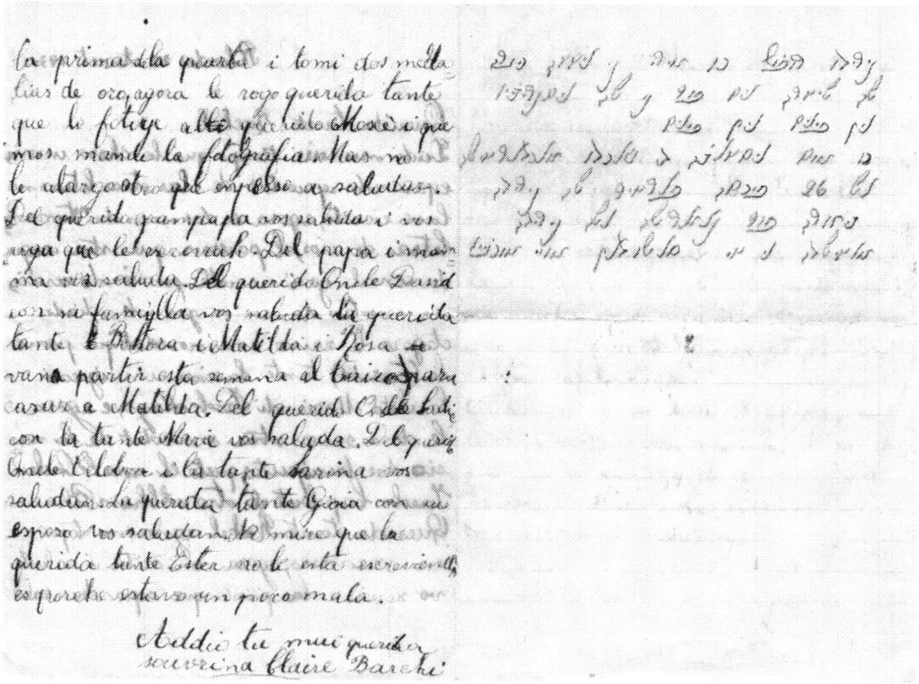

Rashi text

TRANSLATION

Letter dated August 23, 1931

Dear Aunt Rachel,

I wanted to write to you for a long time, but because I was waiting for answers to the other letters, I did not write. It has been two months without a letter from you. It seems that you are busy with your son and are unable to write, but we are worried.

Now, I give you the news that Aunt Sarina gave birth to a boy and the godmother was Marie, wife of Jacob Mayo. And now other news: twins were born. The godfather was Uncle Jacob Capeluto for one, and Abraham Piha for the other.

Dear Aunt Rachel, I am now on vacation, and God willing, will go to the fifth grade. I want to let you know that I was the top in the fourth grade and received two gold medals. I beg you to take a photo of Moshe [Morris] and send it to us. I do not want to stretch this letter.

Dear Grandpa sends you his regards and begs you to write. Mama and Papa send you their regards. Uncle David and his family say hello. Dear Aunt Behora, Mathilda, and Rosa will leave for Cairo for Mathilda's wedding. Uncle Sadik, Aunt Marie send you regards. Uncle Chelibon, Aunt Sarina, Aunt Gioia and her husband also send you regards. Aunt Esther did not write because she was a little sick.

Goodbye, your dear niece,

Claire Barchi[3]

---

[3] This letter was not written by Claire, but dictated to someone, possibly by Esther. The twins were born to Jacob Surmani—a cousin of Esther and her siblings—and his wife. Some of the words in this letter are undecipherable. The person who wrote it is apologizing for writing the letter while standing, and is also repeating the news that Aunt Behora is leaving for Cairo on the 26th to marry off Mathilda (her eldest).

This letter was written in the Rashi cursive form favored by the Ladino-speaking people. It is difficult to read, especially when accounting for styles of individual handwriting. The printed form is much easier to read and was developed by the renowned Biblical commentator Rashi in the 11th Century (1040 to 1105) to transcribe his interpretations. It is sometimes used as a guide to certain prayers, but the words in this case are Hebrew, not Ladino.

TRANSLATION

Letter dated August 24, 1931

Dear brother Raphael and dear Rachel Capeluto,

Dear brother, it has been almost two months that we do not receive a letter from you, and we are greatly worried. I have not written likewise because I was sick from worry and it is your letters that bring a little relief.

Dear brother, if you ask me about Gioia's wedding, we do not know what to do and are going crazy. The fiancé wants a wedding.[4] We thought we would be having it in three months, but it has been nine months already. It is even more difficult as he is a stranger [from out of town], and we have him in the house with dear Mama. And Papa, may God preserve him, is old, and old people do not change their ways. Dear brother, write to Heskia to find a way to send us some money in order to allow us to marry them. We can't stand this life any longer. We need to provide her clothes as she is a fiancée. I do not need any myself. If I have them, I go out. It is not like Gioia who has to go out with her fiancé.

Dear brother, I know that what I am writing are demands, and we all know how much you think of us. We think of you as a father, may God preserve our father, and may God cause you to have a good heart and think of us.

Dear brother, I will give you the good news that Sarina gave birth to a boy. Similarly we hope God will grant Jamila an offspring.

Dear Papa sends you his regards. Please kiss Moshe [Morris] and take care of him. Send our best to dear Rachel, and we beg you to send us pictures of Moshe. All the brothers-in-law and their families send you regards.

Gioia and Nissim send you regards. Give our best to your in-laws and their families, to dear Jamila and Shelomo.

Goodbye, your dear sister,

Esther Capeluto

---

[4] At the fiancée's family's expense.

THE JEWS OF RHODES AND THE CAPELUTO FAMILY

The Jews of Rhodes lived a happy and proud existence, one that had changed little since traveler Rabbi Benjamin of Tudela, Spain, first referenced a Jewish community there in the 12th century. The rabbi, who visited about 300 cities, found a community of some 400 Jews in Rhodes, though it's not known how they arrived on the remote island in the Aegean sea.

The Jewish community, descendents of the Jews of Spain who fled during the Inquisition, flourished even as the Island came under the rule of various nations.[5]

Rhodes, one of the Dodecanese Islands that lies between Greece and Turkey, was first settled sometime during the 15th Century B.C.E. Over the next six centuries the 540-square-mile Island fell into the hands of the Achaeans, the Dorians, the Romans, the Persians, the Seldjuks and the Byzantines. The Byzantines fortified the city with a brick wall in 1261 A.D., and in 1309 the Knights of St. John of Jerusalem settled in the city after returning from the Holy Land.

The Turks captured Rhodes from the Knights of St. John of Jerusalem in 1522, making it part of the Ottoman Empire. But they lost the Island to the Italians during the Italo-Turkish war of 1912. At the time the Italians annexed all the Dodecanese Islands to the Italian Empire. After World War II, on March 31, 1947, the Dodecanese were annexed to Greece.

The Jews of Rhodes grew from a community of 400 to 5,000 before World War II. They led a vibrant Jewish life that centered around the *Collegio Rabbinico* (rabbinical college), the *Alliance Israelite Universelle* school sponsored by the Rothschild Foundation, and five synagogues, each with its own special liturgy.

The Capeluto family lived on Rhodes well before the 1800s, with records successfully tracing the family back to Abraham Capeluto (dates of birth and death unknown). He was the grandfather of Mussani Capeluto, who was born in 1851 and married Rachel Capeluto, born in 1865. They died in 1935 and 1927, respectively. The couple had 10 children: Tamara (known as Behora for "first born"), Avraham, Marie, Mazaltov (Mathilda), Jamila, Yaakov, Raphael (Ralph), Sarina, Gioia, and Esther.[6]

---

[5] References to a Jewish community on Rhodes are found in ancient Roman documents, but details are unclear until later centuries. (jewishrhodes.org and Wikipedia.org, referencing Marc Angel's book)

[6] Tamara (Behora)married David Capeluto; Avraham married Reina; Marie married Sadik Levi; Mazaltov married Avraham Barkey; Jamila married Shelomo Almelech and then Abraham Huniu; Yaakov did not marry; Refael (Ralph) married Rachel Alhadeff; Sarina married Chelibon Maiche (Sarina had a twin sister who lived just a short time); Gioia married Nissim Levi and Esther married Joseph Huniu. - CFH

This story centers on Claire Barkey Flash, the author of most of the letters printed here, and the oldest child of Mathilda (Mazaltov) Capeluto Barkey and her husband Abraham Barkey. Claire's dogged correspondence with her Uncle Ralph, Mazaltov's brother and an early immigrant to the United States, and her determined efforts to secure a free and unencumbered life for her family is the inspiration for this book.

Ralph Capeluto emigrated to the United States in 1920 at age 20, following in the steps of his sister Jamila. They in turn were following the first Rhodesli, who immigrated to Seattle in 1904. By the time Ralph Capeluto moved from New York to Seattle in 1930, the Seattle Sephardic community already had more than 800 members, mainly Jews from Rhodes and Turkey.

The same year that Ralph left Rhodes, Mathilda Capeluto ignored the suitor chosen for her by her parents and married Abraham Barkey (also spelled Barchi or Barki).

Abraham, who was born in Aidin, Turkey in 1891, fled the city in 1918 during the Turko-Greek conflict. Aidin was destroyed and burned by the advancing Greeks, who had landed at Smyrna. In fleeing, Abraham lost all his worldly possessions, and entered Rhodes. He became an ambulant merchant and when he eventually made it to Seattle, found a job as a salesman in a department store owned by the wealthy Alhadeff family.

Abraham and Mathilda Barkey had six children: Claire (1921), Rachel (1923), Haim (Victor) and Morris (twins, 1925), Jack (1928) and Regina (1932). In 1927 Mathilda's sister Esther Capeluto (1909), who was the youngest of the Capeluto children, was orphaned and moved into the Barkey home.

In 1930 life on the Island was quiet for this family living in the Jewish quarter, "La Juderia," but it had its challenges. They were not wealthy. They were not powerful, but they suffered little as they lived each day the way the Jews did back then. The children went to school and played with their friends. The women prepared for the holidays and tended house. The men, who worked during the day in the shops that surrounded the main thoroughfare of La Kay Ancha, socialized at night with their friends, drinking Raki (a licorice liqueur), smoking a "narguileh," or water pipe, and playing backgammon in the cafes that lined Mandraki harbor or in the Piazza Del Fuoco (square of fire), also known as "Lo Kemado" in Ladino.

La Kay Ancha, "The Wide Street," was the main thoroughfare and center of commerce in La Juderia, the one-mile square area that comprised the Jewish quarter of the walled city. The Jews of Rhodes rarely ventured beyond the narrow streets and ancient homes in their small corner of the Island, enjoying a quiet and cultured Jewish life of peace and tradition. Rather than completely assimilating and taking on the customs of their countrymen of Turkish, Italian or Greek descent, the Jews of Rhodes lived by the same laws and rules of their Southern European ancestors.

The family lived in several houses in the Jewish quarter, all within a quick walk of cousins, aunts, uncles, and of course, the synagogue. The houses were tiny, one- and two-story block buildings of cut stone, most constructed in the Middle Ages. In one house, the children slept in one room and their parents slept in another. A bedroom at night was converted into the eating and studying area during the day. Before their deaths in the late 1920s, Rachel and Mussani Capeluto, Mathilda Barkey's parents, slept on a wooden platform with the family.

Behind each house was a hole in the ground—the toilet. Every few years someone would come and clean it out. The family boiled water outside so everyone could have a warm bath on Friday night, the beginning of Shabbat. (Occasionally, the women would go to the public baths to bathe and socialize.)

There were very few cars on the balmy, tropical island. Most people either walked or rode in a horse-drawn carriage.

For entertainment, the children would walk along Mandraki harbor—which according to ancient lore was home to the Colossus of Rhodes—one of the Seven Wonders of the World. They would stand by the governor's palace and watch the Fascist governor parade by, ordering all residents to salute him. During Fascist holidays, the children stood dutifully, essentially forced to listen to his speech.

The twins, Morris and Victor, would often sneak into the opera house or movie theater to see the latest film or opera production, and every June the family would take a picnic to the harbor docks to watch the Italian fireworks display.

Even as they enjoyed the sunny isle, unrest was erupting on the European continent. Adolph Hitler, who became chancellor of Germany in 1933, began his reign of terror on all the Jews and pursued his quest to conquer Europe. By 1936 he had initiated anti-Jewish regulations through the Nuremberg Doctrine. Italian dictator Benito Mussolini followed suit, instituting them throughout Italy. Sensing that Rhodes would no longer be a welcoming place to live, the Barkey family knew they should leave and turned to Uncle Ralph in Seattle for help. - CFH

TRANSLATION

Rhodes, June 18, 1933

Dear and esteemed sister-in-law Rachel Capeluto,

With this letter I inform you that, thank God, we are in good health; likewise we hope to hear from you good news, amen.

Dear Rachel, you cannot imagine the great anxiety we felt not hearing from you, especially in regards to Morris. We were very glad to have the good news. Hope everything goes smoothly and may he bring good luck to everyone and bring success to Uncle Raphael's business.

Dear Rachel, I had several reasons for delaying my writing. We did not have a mind to write as we had Claire with a severe illness called meningitis. It affected her head, and we had the best doctors attending her in an effort to cure her, and we were giving her four or five baths a day. You can imagine the unrest and expense. Thank God, she came out without permanent injury and without harm as the doctors had lost hope. Now, thank God, she goes to school. When she got on her feet, we passed out candy to all the relatives. All the teachers never failed to ask about dear Claire, and the students would come, taking turns in order not to make noise. And we thankfully and joyfully can write about it now. I don't want to make it long, and send you regards.

Dear Papa, brothers-in-laws and their families, Mazaltov and Abraham and sons send you regards. Dear Rachel, you will receive two wedding pictures; one is for dear Jamila[7] and the other one for you. We were going to send you some apricot paste, but seeing that the postage is so expensive, we changed our minds. Next letter will be longer.

Goodbye, your dear sister-in-law,

Esther Capeluto

---

[7] Jamila was Mathilda's sister who emigrated to the U.S. about the same time as Ralph or soon after. She was married to Shelomo Almeleh, who lived in Seattle. Shelomo died in a car accident in which Uncle Ralph was driving. Jamila later remarried Abraham Huniu from Portland.

TRANSLATION

Second part of letters dated June 18, 1933

Dear Aunt Rachel,

From my part, Claire Barkey, I embrace you and give you my regards and wish very much to see you. Aunt Esther wrote to you regarding the tough moments I spent. I write to you now only a couple of lines so that you may rejoice as I don't have the time. And the exams are here, and I am weak from the illness. You can't imagine the joy I felt seeing the picture of Morris with dear Uncle Raphael and to receive a letter so long awaited, and we rejoiced at the great news.

Send my regards to dear Uncle Raphael with dear Morris, Uncle Shelomo, and dear Jamila and all the relatives in general.

I kiss you and embrace you.

Your dear niece,

Clara Barchi[8]

---

[8] At that time, when meningitis was hardly known, and the small island of Rhodes lacked proper equipment and medical facilities, it is a miracle that Claire survived. In later years she recalled family members putting ice packs on her head all day, and people visiting.

TRANSLATION

Undated[9]

Dear Aunt Rachel,

I send you my greetings and my congratulations on the birth of your daughter. We pray that she brings you luck and success to Uncle Raphael in his business so that sometimes we may see each other.

You write that you would have liked if I were near so that I may play with your children, and I wish it so and that someday we will meet in good health.

Dear Aunt Rachel, I am not going to add anything else as I have a lecture at school, Saturday.

Dear Papa and Mama send you regards. Regards from grandpa [Mussani] and all the relatives in general. Give kisses to dear Moshe and dear Rebecca [Betty]. Regards to Aunt Jamila and Uncle Shelomo.

Bye, your dear niece which wishes very much to see you.

Claire Barkey

Dear Sister-in-Law Rachel Capeluto,

I was very glad to receive your dear letter. You can't imagine our worry because you sent the other letter where you wrote that you were seven months pregnant and we were awaiting month after month your good news.

Dear Rachel, we were glad you had an easy childbirth. We pray God that it will bring us good luck and bring success to Ralph. Dear Rachel, I was sorry that I could not send anything because the custom duties exceed the value of the thing [gift]. Sarina and Gioia will follow your footsteps; one is six months pregnant, and the other one five months. You write that dear Rebecca is pretty. It gives us great desire to be near and see them. I hope dear Jamila will also be a full-fledged mother like you.

Dear Rachel, after we received the letter, Sister Zimbul Surmani [honorable title given usually to an elderly woman] passed by and told us that she received a letter from your grandmother and that you brought to life a male twin and a female twin. Please clarify it. May it bring us luck. I can't find anything else to write.

Dear Papa [Mussani] sends you regards. Regards from dear David and family, Sadik and family, Abraham, Mazaltov and the kids, Chelibon and family, Nissim and family. Regards to your dear father and mother and family. Kisses to dear Raphael and the kids, as well as dear Shelomo and dear Jamila. Regards to your dear grandmother.

Bye, your sister-in-law,

Esther Capeluto

---

[9] Most likely around 1934, as Claire was still in school, Ralph's daughter Betty was born, and her grandfather Mussani was still alive (he died around February 1935).

RALPH CAPELUTO EMIGRATES TO AMERICA

One of the biggest fears among young men in Rhodes was being drafted into the army. To them, it felt like going to prison and they would do anything to escape.

Ralph Capeluto, seeing no financial opportunity on the island and wishing desperately to avoid being drafted, decided to leave. So in 1920, at about age 20, he said goodbye to his parents and his siblings, bought a ticket in steerage and sailed to New York.

He had been planning for the trip for quite some time and was able to save a substantial sum of money for an immigrant from Rhodes, but almost as soon as he disembarked the ship, someone saw the sum he was carrying and stole it from him.

Ralph was left to find a job as quickly as possible to be able to support himself in this new land. He took a job as a window washer, and because it was dangerous to climb so high on the buildings of New York, the job paid a premium, allowing Ralph to land more quickly on his feet.

One night he was washing the skylight in a bra factory, which was empty except for a mechanic working on some of the machines. Needing some help, the mechanic motioned for Ralph to come down from the skylight and give him a hand.

The mechanic was so impressed with Ralph's work that he offered him a job right there on the spot. That got Ralph out of the window-washing business and led him to subsequent mechanic jobs at a hat factory and a curtain manufacturer.

By 1930, Ralph's family in Rhodes became anxious to have him back. The family summoned him and arranged for him to marry someone in Rhodes. He planned on his return to bring his parents to the United States with him.

Before returning to Rhodes, he journeyed west to visit his sister Jamila in Seattle. Jamila and her husband Shelomo had left Rhodes years earlier and had settled in that western city where many other Jews from Rhodes had landed.

Jamila strongly objected to Ralph's plans to return to Rhodes for an arranged marriage. People in America do not marry that way, she told him. Instead, she offered to introduce him to Rachel Alhadeff, a woman from Rhodes who had come to Seattle when she was a young child.

Ralph and Rachel met. Within a week he proposed, and within a month they married on June 30, 1930.

As it turned out, Ralph's parents did not want to leave their native Rhodes, where they felt settled and secure.

As the young Ralph and Rachel started their new life together, the couple had to decide how to support themselves. Ralph thought they should open a candy concession at a movie theater. Ralph's cousin Harry Benatar had a successful candy business in the theaters of New York and tried to convince Ralph that was a business he should pursue.

Rachel, however, did not want to sell candy in the theater. She asked her new husband if he could do anything else.

Ralph mentioned that he had worked at a curtain factory and that he was good with the machines. Rachel, meanwhile, had gone to business school and had bookkeeping skills. There was no other curtain factory in Seattle, and Rachel liked the idea of starting a curtain manufacturing business from scratch. Rachel said she could run the business end if Ralph did the rest.

The two of them met with buyers from three large Seattle department stores—Frederick & Nelson, Sears, and The Bon Marché—to see if they were interested in buying curtains locally. The buyers were thrilled to be able to order curtains in town, rather than wait weeks for them to arrive from New York.

With that vote of confidence, Rachel and Ralph went to New York to buy some sample bolts of fabric and two tiny sewing machines. They returned home and opened Seattle Curtain Manufacturing Co. at Prefontaine Boulevard, at the south end of the city's downtown.

Ten months after they wed they had their first child, Morris. Over the next nine years they had three daughters, Betty, Marlene and Mimi. - CFH

TRANSLATION

Letter dated April 28, 1935

[Written by Claire for her mother, who could not write in Latin characters.]

My dear brother Raphael Capeluto,

I am writing this letter to let you know that, thank God, we are in good health; likewise, we pray you all are.

Dear brother, we have sent you five or six letters without receiving an answer. We wonder what is the cause as we are worried. The second day after dear Papa died, we sent you a telegram and we did not receive an acknowledgement or a salutation. And two months and a week have already elapsed since he died, ample time to receive letters from you. This delay causes great worry, and if we had money, we would send a telegram with paid reply just to find out how you are.

Dear brother, I beg you to answer right away as it weighs heavily on my soul. Esther is sad and anguished. She is with me, and I feel sorry seeing her that way. I entreat you to write to her in order to give her solace.

Dear Avram [Abraham], our sisters send you their regards. Please hug dear Rachel and the kids. Give our regards to your father-in-law and mother-in-law, to Jamila, Shelomo. Again, dear Raphael, I beg you to answer me. Don't do as usual when my letters or my dear Avram's letters go unanswered.

Bye, your dear sister,

Mazaltov[10]

---

[10] In 1935, distances from Rhodes to anywhere in the world were relatively considerable. People—and communication— traveled only by boat, and slow boats at that.

TRANSLATION

Letter dated January 4, 1936

[Written by Claire.]

Dear brother:

I wanted to write for a long time, but I was waiting for your letter. Five or six months have elapsed without news from you, and we are concerned. Dear brother, please write often as we want to know how you are and to make dear Esther forget. If not you, who would bring her some relief?

Dear Abraham did not even send a condolence word about the death of dear Papa. I wrote him a letter this week. We will see if he will remember to answer.

Dear Ralph, please give dear Jamila and Shelomo my regards and write to us how they are. Give my regards to dear Rachel and please tell her to write. Kiss the kids for us.

Regards to your father-in-law and mother-in-law. Behora and David, Marie and family, Sarina and family send you regards. Similarly dear and sons. Dear Esther sends you regards.

Dear brother, when you send money, I hope you send it in dollars. I repeat, dear brother, do not leave us without a letter.

Goodbye, your dear sister,

Mazaltov Barki[11]

---

[11] The Abraham mentioned here is her brother in Argentina. He passed away a long time ago, leaving an invalid daughter and a son, Moshe.

The spelling of "Barkey" varies with the country, but the phonetics are the same. Barchi in Rhodes, Barki in Morocco, and Barkey after we acquired citizenship.

porke quero ver a los ijos
que mos los alavaron de ser
muy ermosos. Queria top<del>eme</del> toparme
seria i verlos.
Querido oncle Raphael le rogo
que mos escriva al coriente
porke la mamma sta el
tino en vosotros
Vos abrasso de todo me corason
                    Claire Barchi
———————
Querida tante yamila
De me parte Claire l'abrasso
i la rengrasio del por el
codiado que tuvo de mi.
Cuando me visto la blusa
la enmombro muy munchio.
Al querido oncle Selomo lo
saludo. El papa i la mamma
vos saludan. Yo vos abraso
                    Claire Barchi

Rhodes 4 /1/ 1936

Querido ermano
Disde munchio tiempo que quero
escrivirte, esperando tomar de vuestra
parte, es dia de oy que ay
como 5 o 6 mezes que no
savemos nada de vosotros i
estamos en grande codiado.
Querido ermano te rogo que
mos escrivas al coriente porke
queremos saver qualo vos topach,
i por azer olvidar un poco a
la querida Ester.
Cuando vosotros no le vas afalagar
chen es i el querido Abraam
nou mando ni por saludar
de la muerte del querido papa
esta semana le ise lettra,
veremos si se arecodrara a

Letter from January 4, 1936. Written in Ladino.

TRANSLATION

Letter dated January 4, 1936

Dear Aunt Rachel and Uncle Raphael:

On my behalf, I, Claire, greet you and hug you. You'll excuse me for not having written until now. The reason is that I finished school and I am learning dressmaking and I am very busy. Papa sends you regards. Enclosed you will find some small snapshots of our family. I pray to take some pictures of all of you and send them to us because I want to see your kids whom they have been lauded as being beautiful. I would like to find myself near you and see you.

Dear Uncle Raphael, I hope you write often because Mama has always all of you in her mind. I hug you with all my heart.

Claire Barki

Dear Aunt Jamila,

I send you big hugs and thank you for your concern toward me. When I put on the blouse I think of you very much. Give regards to Uncle Shelomo. Papa and Mama send you regards. Big hugs!

Claire Barki

TRANSLATION

Undated[12]

Dear Jamila:

I send you my regards and pray that you will write because you have been in America so many years and have not written. Now, I hope you will write and we will send and receive joyful letters from all sides. I hope your Shelomo is in good health, and I pray you will send some help for Esther. It is a *zehut* [merit] toward an orphan. What can we do? A little from each one, and we will be ready to marry her off.

Give regards to dear Shelomo. I will write later on in detail.

Bye, your dear sister

Mazaltov Barchi

[Letter addressed to Uncle Ralph, written by Claire.]

Undated, assumed written at the same time as above letter

It isn't that we have many complaints. You have sent enough [money] for dear Sarina and Dear Gioia.

Dear brother, many times dear Esther is very upset and to see how I worry, she says that she would go to do housework for someone. Now, dear brother, you don't see any young girl who goes out to earn money. You see only Greek housemaids, and besides, our honor does not allow her to go to work. For this reason, I again request that you send us whatever you can. And if you cannot, make out the papers, bring her to your side, and perhaps she will change. Please answer me concerning what I write, and do not forget.

Nothing else to add. Regards to dear Rachel and ask her to write. Give kisses from the kids and tell us how are dear Rebecca's [Betty's] eyes. Regards to dear Jamila and Shelomo. Tell us how is Shelomo's health. Regards to the in-laws Rahamin [Alhadeff] and family. The two daughters of dear Behora are in Rhodes. They came with their husbands to spend the summer.

Regards from dear Sadik and family, Chelibon, Nissim, Esther, Avraham and the kids. Please answer without fail.

Bye, your dear sister,

Mazaltov Barchi

---

[12] Probably prior to 1938 because Shelomo Almeleh, Aunt Jamila's first husband, was still alive.

TRANSLATION

May 30, 1937

[Letter from Leon Levy from Sassari, Italy]

To my dear and esteemed Uncle Raphael Capeluto,

I am writing this short letter to let you know that I am well and enjoy perfect health. Likewise, I hope you all do.

Dear Uncle, I was idle, and not having work, I was compelled to enlist in the Army. The hard times that my family went through were not enough and I had to leave them to suffer more and to waste my youth in the military life at a great distance from my family. I never thought I would suffer so much. They give me work I never thought I would do in all my life, and the pay is two dimes a day, not enough for a cigarette, even though I do not smoke. Somehow, I manage with the little they give me. From the day I left to the present, I have only tears in my eyes because I left them suffering. I would like to send a picture home and to all the relatives, but I have no money for a photo. When I save enough, I'll do my best to send a picture so that you'll recognize me.

Regards to Aunt Rachel and the kids.

Your dear and esteemed nephew,

Leon Levy[13]

---

[13] Leon was the oldest son of Mary [Marie] (Claire's mother's sister) and Zadik Levy and the brother of Rachel and Lea of Milan, Italy, later survivors of the concentration camps. Another brother, Moshe, died in a concentration camp at around 19 years old. As an Italian soldier, Leon was sent to Spain during the Spanish Civil War. He returned to Rhodes for a year or so until he decided to leave for Tangier, although he could have remained as the rest of his family unfortunately did. He stayed in Tangier during World War II, and subsequently emigrated to Israel. He was not very communicative, but is believed to have married there and settled on a kibbutz.

Sassari is on the Island of Sardinia.

TRANSLATION

June 30, 1937

[Unsigned letter in Claire's writing]

My dear brother Raphael Capeluto:

I write this letter to let you know about our good health; similarly, we hope to hear from you.

Dear brother, you can't imagine how worried we are without a letter from you. We have not written because we are going through hell with sick people. Esther has been sick for the last two years and not receiving your letters adds to it. Dear brother, there is no end to the doctors' expenses. The least you can do is write to her a letter of consolation. What dear Abraham does for her not even a brother can do. Let's leave that aside, just write to her. From time to time she wants to go out and she needs clothes to save appearances. If we could, we would do more for the memory of dear Papa and Mama.

Now, dear brother, please do not fail to send a little money because we have a bridegroom-to-be in sight, and we need ten thousand lire. Now that she is okay, we'll finish this business because as the years pass, the more likely she is to become an old maid. And I, dear brother, have two girls my size, making it three ladies at home. I pray God that He may bring someone first for Esther and then my girls. I hope you do not let us bang our heads against the wall and do answer us.

I feel ashamed in front of Abraham who takes care of all of us and our sisters. If Gioia is married today, it is through the efforts of dear Abraham and me. I have pawned things for something for Gioia's wedding for a debt of 1,000 lire. You will not recognize me on account of the anguish I suffer for my sisters, but we do everything for "*zehut*." Everything will be over when we marry off Esther. Since you have no monthly support payments for Papa and Mama for they are no more, may God help you so that you can marry off Esther from your earnings. Besides you and us, there is no one who would take care of her.[14]

---

[14] One or more pages appear to be missing as there are no salutations, etc.

TRANSLATION

September 14, 1937

[Typed on letterhead from the office of sales representative Saul M. Habib where Claire worked.]

Dear Uncle Raphael and Aunt Rachel:

The purpose of this letter is to let you know that we are in good health; similarly we hope you are.

Dear Uncle and Aunt, it appears you have forgotten that you have an orphan girl in Rhodes, and if it were not for us, she would be "dragging in the sewer." But now life is not like before, prices are astronomical and Papa can barely make it to support us, so much that I, at the age of 17, when one has fun, am compelled to work in order to help the household.

You'll say that it is one more mouth to feed, but the matter is not the food but the fact that Esther is close to 30 and this worry is driving Mama crazy.

Dear Uncle and Aunt, I have been thinking of writing to you for a long time, but not having the time, employed by a sales representative, I have a lot of work, and my boss is on a trip to Italy and I have the responsibility of the office. Another employee and I share the correspondence and accounting. Now that I have more time, I am writing, but do not let this letter unanswered. I work 10 hours a day, and they pay me a miserable amount of 120 lire a month, which only suffices for my expenses.

Dear Uncle and Aunt, we received your package and we thank you a lot. But dear Esther fell sick that day, and it would have been better not to have received it because when we received a notice from the post office, we thought it was a registered letter. But a package with a letter caused her great grief. Thinking that you wanted to get rid of her with a few things, she didn't even fix the dresses, so perturbed she was. The only one who suffers the blows is Mama, so pale from what she is going through. At least answer her for she is tired of writing.

Haskia Benatar[15] is now in Rhodes and is very grateful for what you did for him (I am kidding) so much that he does not talk to her when he sees her in the street. He does not seek her nor has he come to our house after so many invitations. He thinks himself as a prince.

A little bit of this, a little bit of that, Esther is gradually losing her health and again the burden falls on Mama. No other sister thinks of her as every household has its worries. But, it does not matter; everything comes from above and hopefully for good.

---

[15] Haskia Benatar, a first cousin to Claire's mother, lived in New York and was helpful to Uncle Ralph when he was living there.

Dear Aunt and Uncle, Mr. Bension Hanan[16] came from America and told us that he went to Seattle and saw you. And we were glad to know you are all well.

I am writing this letter without Mama's knowledge and to let out my feelings. But I hope you do not leave my letter unanswered. Kiss the kids for me, and please let me know how are Rebecca's eyes. Everyone from Rhodes sends you regards. I kiss you and hug you.

Your dear niece who wishes you a good year.

Claire

Please answer me at the address below:
Miss Claire Barchi
C/o La Ditta Saul M. Habib
Via Gran Maestro Di Naillac No. 23
Rhodes (Aegean)

Page 2—September 14, 1937

You'll excuse me that I am writing in this manner, but it is from seeing dear Esther cry so much, not having received an answer for a year. Regards to Aunt Jamila and Uncle Shelomo and tell them I will write another time.

---

[16] It's uncertain who this is.

NOVEMBER 1937

———

BENITO MUSSOLINI ALLIES WITH
HITLER, REINFORCING THE
ROME-BERLIN AXIS AGREEMENT
OF 1936.

TRANSLATION

Rhodes, February 15, 1938

Dear Uncle Raphael and Aunt Rachel,

This is to inform you that we all enjoy good health; likewise, we hope you all do.

Dear Uncle and Aunt, I hereby confirm my letter of four months ago that you did not deign answer. I do not know the reason, although according to the last letter, you told us that you derived great pleasure by reading our letters.

I see days transpiring without receiving your news and waiting to receive one letter from you for each 10 of mine; but nevertheless, I take advantage of my boss's absence to steal a couple of minutes to bring you up to date about our situation.

As busy as you may be, you cannot compare it with my whole busy day. I go home from work at nine in the evening and what awaits me? Annoyances and the kids' homework as, "*mashala*,"[17] they are now grownups and in secondary grades and they need help. You can imagine the disposition of things in the house at night, one here, one there with his homework, and dear Papa, not being able to make ends meet with his day work, having to work at night instead of resting.

But what goes on does not matter as we have hope of your keeping the good promises you make. When you find Mama sad and crying, the reason is so evident, we do not need to explain. How many promises made to Esther when she is sad, to give her great help and a well-deserved dowry, but alas, it will be too late.

Now, I beg you not to dismiss this letter and do answer it without fail. If Uncle Raphael cannot, then let Aunt Rachel write two lines even in bed, if you do not have time, as you say.

As dear Mama relates, when you went to America and would write letters, you would send money for stamps in order to get an answer. Now, do not get upset. I would like to send not money but stamps in my letters to get an answer, but they do not sell stamps here and not knowing how much it costs, I am not doing it.

I think you will understand my distress and my wish to receive news. And I am sure you will answer and renew our cordial relationship. Please acknowledge receipt of this letter and answer in detail. Let me

---

[17] "May God preserve you from the evil eye." A typical expression of Jews of all cultures, and many others in the Mediterranean basin, reflecting the belief that sharing good news or stating someone's age is an invitation for bad luck and precaution must be taken.

know how are the kids as I would like so much to have them at my side and love them as my own brothers as you loved Mama. I am enclosing a little picture of me taken a year ago and entreat you send for my album one of you and include Marlene as we do not know what she looks like and if she is as beautiful as Morris and Rebecca [Betty].

Dear Morris must be a young man, and you must prepare a bride for him as well as a groom for Rebecca.

I again pray that you will not ignore my letter and answer it because we keep on saying that America alienates one if there is no correspondence, as we can prove it with Uncle Avraham about whom we know nothing. On your answer, please let us know if you have any correspondence with him; thus we will know about him indirectly.

Hoping my letter will find you in good health. I kiss you and embrace you. Your little niece who remains with the hope of receiving your letter.

Claire

P.S. you can write directly to me at this address:
Miss Clara Barchi
c/o Saul M. Habib
Via Gran Maestro Di Maillac No. 23
Rhodes, (Aegian)[18]

---

[18] Claire is referring to Uncle Avraham (Capeluto) who emigrated to Argentina (Buenos Aires). The family stopped hearing from him after a while. It is known that he had two children, one—named Moshe after Claire's grandfather—who had polio.

TRANSLATION

Rhodes, April 29, 1938

Dear Aunt Rachel and Uncle Raphael,

I received your long-awaited letter of March 2nd, and was very glad to read its contents. Dear Aunt Rachel, the mailman brought your letter on a Saturday when I was leaving to go to the movies. I was so overjoyed that I started to read it during intermission and was not satisfied to read it five or six times, so much that my friends, sitting at my side would say, "Aren't you through with that small portion?"

You can't imagine the joy in the house, especially that of Esther when she read the part addressed to her. The first one to read it was Aunt Esther as she was at the home of Aunt Sarina. Aunt Sarina was in the hospital due to a fall and remained there for a month. You must realize that the burden of the family fell on Esther, although the [other] sisters would give a hand once in a while. But being the Passover season, everyone is busy in her own house.

Now, dear Uncle and Aunt, I beg you to answer me over this matter and not ignore this paragraph of my letter as was done in my preceding letters, and be very kind and help us as much as possible, save your younger sister and sister-in-law who unfortunately has remained without any support of parents.

I thank you for the pocket money you sent for her small expenses, and pray that from now on God may grant you a long life and success so that you may attempt to bring her some relief, as she deserves it, having suffered so much.

I congratulate you regarding the house you bought and hope you enjoy it, and perhaps one day we will see it. It must be very beautiful as you described it in detail, and I believe I can find the house without a guide.

I have run out of things to say and start my greetings. Send my regards to all your relatives. From Rhodes all the uncles and aunts greet you, particularly Aunt Esther. My Papa and Mama and brothers send you regards. Kiss your son for me. Say hello to Aunt Jamila and Uncle Shelomo.

Bye, your niece who wishes you well and hopes to receive your news.

Claire

Rhodes, April 29, 1938

Dear Aunt Jamila:

I have been wanting to write to you, but was unable for lack of time. Writing to Aunt Rachel takes all my time. As you may know, I work for a sales representative and have a lot of work. I get home at nine in the evening. Now, it is Saturday and [I] have time to write a couple of words.

Dear Aunt Jamila, I thank you for your concern toward Aunt Esther by sending her a little of your savings. May you be paid in health and long life. Please let me know how is Uncle Shelomo's health. Being the first time I write to you, I do not know what to write. I pray my letter finds you in good health. I kiss you and hug you from afar. Your dear niece who wishes to see you.

Claire

Envelope that contained letter dated April 29, 1938, sent from Claire Barkey in Rhodes to Ralph Capeluto in Seattle, Wash. Claire was employed by Saul M. Habib.

TRANSLATION

Rhodes, June 23, 1938

Dear Uncle Raphael and Aunt Rachel,

I am holding your welcomed letter dated May 19th, and am reading its contents with my most undivided attention. I found enclosed two other letters, one addressed to the in-law Bollissa, the other to "*ermano*" [brother] Rahamin Hasson, which I promptly handed over to them.

Dear Uncle Raphael, I realize that I am becoming boring, but it is my duty to tell you that here when a girl reaches her 25th birthday, she is considered to have passed her marriageable age. It is not as in America where you find a lot of old maids who do not want to get married because they work or are rich heiresses who lead a better life than the married ones. As you well know, Aunt Esther is not like the aforementioned girls. She is, as one may say, living under our roof and losing her health, being that she is about to pass the marriageable age and is full of worries about her sisters, especially Aunt Sarina who has been the most unfortunate of all the sisters. She [Sarina] has seven children and all of tender age, having no maid to look after them, and all of this is on her shoulders [Esther's]. As I wrote to you on another letter, she [Sarina] fell, and who got the brunt of it all? The month when she was in the hospital, who had the responsibility of the household? Everything fell on Esther.

It would have been another matter was she settled in her own house. It is true that Sarina's sisters wanted to go once in a while to give a hand with the kids, but they all have their chores, and the husband [Chelibon] should have engaged a person to look after the family, and he thus felt a bit the absence of his wife.

All of this, dear Uncle Raphael, I believe will not please you to hear but I feel the duty to bring it out so that you may harder than you intend to get your dear sister out of her present condition and send whatever you have in mind right away before the years fly.

Dear Uncle Raphael, to you it would appear to be the same, but rather better, to send on time, whatever amount you have in mind, for as years go by, dowry increases. Alas, this is becoming a market where one speculates in merchandise. Dear Uncle, do not think that I am dissipating all that I earn. Although I am helping my family, whatever remains I am saving for Aunt Esther's dowry.

Now, thank God, my boss has recognized my worth and increased my salary to 250 lire a month, committing himself to increase it further at his return from a trip, as you may understand from my delay in answering your letter, and I hope you excuse that and my monotonous repetition.

Dear Uncle Raphael, returning to the question of Aunt Esther, I must tell you that after the joy I felt by receiving your letter, which I longed for, I felt bad that I could not see a single word addressed to Aunt

Esther. One can't imagine how left out she felt when I told her we received a letter and that there was nothing for her. I beg you that even if you do not write to me, write to her, if only to console and to make her recover a little. Please consider the contents of this letter and answer me about every detail, not failing to write to Aunt Esther as soon as possible. I thank you in advance.

Now, dear Uncle Raphael, I would like to thank you with all my heart for the care of sending money for the graves of the departed. May God reward you with life and health and may think of marrying off your dear sister. Here, dear Uncle, the young men were always very few, and more so now that they are all emigrating to Africa to look for a future. Of all those who have remained most of them have hopes of emigrating and wait for a girl to turn up and be asked for. If the girl has a brother or a relative in Africa who will bring them over, they will accept; otherwise, they will refuse, preferring to remain single without the burden of supporting a family. The reason is that the girls of Rhodes are trying to go to Africa or America where they have relatives who take pity on them and bring them over. It is this way that many have left to find their good fortune. As the proverb says, "help yourself and God will help you," meaning that you aim for success and success comes to you.

Dear Uncle Raphael, I was glad to know that you have taken pictures and will have the pleasure of receiving them as well as those of Aunt Jamila and Uncle Shelomo. I am, therefore, waiting for them and hope you will send them without fail. Dear Uncle and Aunt, the daughter of Aunt Behora, Rachel, arrived from Cairo to spend the summer here.

I have run out of things to say, and give you regards from the uncles and aunts, Mama and Papa, Aunt Esther. Say hello to all our relatives, Aunt Jamila, and Uncle Shelomo.

Goodbye, your dear niece who yearns to see your faces and all in a good state.

Claire

Dear Aunt Jamila:

I hereby confirm sending a previous letter and hope to get an answer. I thank you for the care shown and may God grant you all your wishes. Say hello to Uncle Shelomo. From Rhodes, all the uncles and aunts send their regards, particularly Aunt Behora, Uncle David and family.

Mama, Papa, Aunt Esther send their regards. I kiss you and hug you from afar. Your dear niece who wishes to see you,

Claire

TRANSLATION FROM FRENCH

Rhodes, September 1, 1938

Dear Uncle and Aunt,

I hereby confirm my letter dated June 23, 1938, to which I have not received any answer so far.

First of all, I let you know that, thank God, we are all feeling well. Similarly, I wish to hear from your side.

Now, I must tell you that Mr. Heskia Benatar has sent $25 to Aunt Esther and $10 to Aunt Sarina through one of his aunts. He did not want his mother to know because God knows what she might say. From this you understand what she must have told Heskia during his stay at Rhodes to the point that he would not talk to Aunt Esther. In spite of this, Aunt Esther sent him something for the newborn baby girl through his partner who happened to visit here.

I find nothing else to write since I have not received any news from you. How are the children? A kiss to all from me.

Aunt Esther sends you hugs. Mama, Papa, my brothers and sisters greet you. Please give my regards to Aunt Jamila and Uncle Shelomo. Lots of hugs from all my heart.

Your niece who wishes to receive your news.

Claire

United States of America
State of Washington   )
City of Seattle   ) ss.
County of King   )

I, RAPHAEL CAPELUTO, age 38, being duly sworn, depose and say:

I reside at 807—30th Avenue South, Seattle, King, Washington.

I am a Native-American or Naturalized Citizen of the United States as evidenced by my certificate, Naturalization Certificate No. 2393226 issued on February 21, 1927 by Southern District of New York Court at New York, New York.

I am married and dependent on me for support are my wife and three children.

I am partner (one-half owner) Seattle Curtain Manufacturing Co., address: 304 Prefontaine Bldg., Seattle, King County, Washington. My income from this business is $200.00 per month or more.

In addition, I have assets consisting of residence, cost $5,500.00, subject to mortgage $4,000.00—my equity $1500.00. My one-half interest in Seattle Curtain Manufacturing Company is conservatively worth $15,000.00.

I am the brother of Esther Capeluto now residing at Island of Rhodes, Italy, who desires to come to the United States to join me and others of the family, and whom I am most anxious to bring over.

I do hereby promise and guarantee that I will receive and take care of my sister who is applying for an immigration visa, and will at no time allow her to become public charges to any community or municipality. I do further promise and agree that those of my relatives covered by this affidavit within school age will attend public school, and will not be permitted to work until they are of age.

I make this affidavit for the purpose of inducing the United States Consular authorities to grant the visa to my said relative, and herewith submit corroborative proof as to my personal standing.

I, Christine Weiss, a Notary Public, duly commissioned, do hereby certify that this affidavit was sworn to before me this 17th day of September 1938, and that affiant herein mentioned has exhibited to me the naturalization certificate above-mentioned.

Christine Weiss, Notary Public   Raphael Capeluto
[signed]   [signed]

TRANSLATION FROM FRENCH

Rhodes, October 9, 1938

Dear Uncle Raphael and Aunt Rachel:

We have received your esteemed letter, and we greatly rejoiced reading its contents and to learn that, thank God, you all enjoy good health. We received enclosed in your letter pictures you sent and enjoyed seeing the kids. May God keep them away from the evil eye for they are something to behold.

Now, dear Uncle and Aunt, I thank you for the little check you sent for Aunt Esther and of the good news you informed us about. You cannot imagine the joy we felt by reading that you are trying to bring Esther to your side, all the more that she may escape from this poverty in Rhodes and because, following what is happening, we will not know what would become of her.

Since the 1st of September of this year, new laws have been enacted and are as follows: whoever came to Rhodes after January 1st, 1919 must leave it within six months, and those who do not leave will be forcibly chased out. And in this situation Papa finds himself, for he came to Rhodes after the date appearing on this decree, that is on April 1919. Therefore, you can see that we must leave and do not know where.[19]

We cannot enter Turkey because Papa had escaped and has no documents from there. We have nobody anywhere who would bring us because in any place, especially Africa[20] where Papa wants to go at any cost, one needs to receive a work contract. Scores of people have been leaving, but we are compelled to wait six months and be chased away like dogs and until wait and see where the boat will take us. In this situation are Aunt Gioia and Aunt Sarina and their families who do not know where to go as their husbands are alien. You can imagine the worry we are experiencing these Moadim [High Holidays], not knowing what will become of us. Aunt Behora, perhaps, will go to Cairo with her daughters. As for Aunt Esther who could remain here, we do not know where to leave her. You can have an idea of the joy we felt to read your letter. Now, we are waiting for the papers you promised us in order to do immediately the necessary before we leave who knows where.

Dear Uncle and Aunt, it is with tears in my eyes that I am writing this letter, but only to tell you that we were born to suffer. If we could only send Aunt Esther, it would be a great relief for Mama. Being expelled,

---

[19] This decree dictated that all foreign-born Jews who emigrated to Italy after a certain month of 1919 had to leave Italy and its possessions, but the families could remain. The Barkeys did not want to split the family and be without father and his support, and with no chance for continued education, as the secondary schools were closed to Jews. As it turned out it was a blessing for all whose parents were foreign-born. A large contingent from Rhodes went to Tangier, Morocco, and the rest will be referenced by Claire in subsequent letters.

[20] Meaning South Africa, Rhodesia or Belgian Congo.

you can't imagine what life we lead without being able to do anything to save ourselves. This only happens to the Jews who have the bad luck of not having a country where we could seek refuge in time of distress. They can do nothing to the Greeks and the Turks because they have their governments to defend them. To top it all, the schools have been closed for the Jews, and the kids are in the streets until we leave. After studying so many years, they will remain half-educated. Poor kids, they had such a will to learn!

Dear Uncle Raphael, I beg you to read carefully my letter so that you may realize that who knows when we will have some rest. And to try to send us somewhere without squandering your money. Alhadeff [Department Store] will provide the fare for the trip as Papa was employed with them during his stay at Rhodes. We have no one to help us for we are unique in that Papa is the only son whereas the others have brothers, sisters, grown-up sons who can claim them. Papa is in despair and thinking more than anyone for he already experienced the flight from a city without a destination. We are going crazy not knowing what to do, especially Mama who is in such a bad state since the decree.

Dear Uncle Raphael, please give us an idea (as to what we can do) and answer us as soon as possible because you are the only hope we have from anywhere.

I cannot continue writing because every time I think about the situation I start crying, especially at the thought that they are debasing us in the newspapers from everywhere. They call us crooks and trouble-makers and accuse us of stealing their bread by taking all the money out of Rhodes. There is no end to what they are doing, and we cannot say anything. They say they will send us to hell and for that purpose, they will give us castor oil to speed it up and other things too numerous to mention. I wanted to cut a few items from the newspaper, but I do not want to worry you.

Please, dear Uncle, I beg you to answer and give me a ray of hope if only as a mitzvah, for we find ourselves in an impasse. Regards from Aunt Esther, Papa, Mama, and the kids.

I thank you in advance, certain that you will answer immediately, giving us some consolation. And I hope you will forgive me for all the stress I am causing you. I kiss you and hug you.

Your niece who hopes to hear from you and to see you.

Claire

Please answer right away and do find some remedy as we are really lost. Mama does not want to write in order not to worry you. But I write because if we do not try in time, I can foresee the end.

United States of America
State of Washington   )
City of Seattle   ) ss.
County of King   )

I, RAPHAEL CAPELUTO, age 38, being duly sworn, depose and say:

I reside at 807—30th Avenue South, Seattle, King, Washington.

I am a Native-American or Naturalized Citizen of the United States as evidenced by my certificate, Naturalization Certificate No. 2393226 issued on February 21, 1927 by Southern District of New York Court at New York, New York.

I am married and dependent on me for support are my wife and three children.

I am partner (one-half owner) Seattle Curtain Manufacturing Co., address: 304 Prefontaine Bldg., Seattle, King County, Washington. My income from this business is $200.00 per month or more.

In addition, I have assets consisting of residence, cost $5,500.00 subject to mortgage, $4,000.00—my equity $1500.00. My one-half interest in Seattle Curtain Manufacturing Company is conservatively worth $15,000.00.

I am the brother-in-law of Abraham Barchi, now residing at Island of Rhodes, Italy, who desires to come to the United States to join me and others of the family, and whom I am most anxious to bring over.

I do hereby promise and guarantee that I will receive and take care of my brother-in-law who is applying for an immigration visa, and will at no time allow him to become public charges to any community or municipality. I do further promise and agree that those of my relatives covered by this affidavit within school age will attend public school, and will not be permitted to work until they are of age.

I make this affidavit for the purpose of inducing the United States Consular authorities to grant the visa to my said relative, and herewith submit corroborative proof as to my personal standing.

I, Christine Weiss, a Notary Public, duly commissioned, do hereby certify that this affidavit was sworn to before me this 4th day of November 1938, and that affiant herein mentioned has exhibited to me the naturalization certificate above-mentioned.

Christine Weiss, Notary Public   Raphael Capeluto
[signed]   [signed]

COMMITTEE FOR THE ASSISTANCE

OF JEWISH REFUGEES

Via Degli Amedei #3 Tel. 17-672

MILAN

Milan, November 10, 1938

Mister

Abramo Barchi

Rhodes

Dear Mister Barchi:

    I acknowledge receipt of your letter of 11/25/1938—XVII. We regret very much to have to answer that we do not have the least influence on the decisions of the Consulate General of the United States which proceeds at any rate only according to the laws concerning the immigration.

    Our best regards

Committee for the Assistance

of the Jewish Refugees

[signed]

TRANSLATION

Rhodes, November 11, 1938

Dear Uncle Raphael and Aunt Rachel,

I hereby confirm my letter of October 9 and write this to let you know that we all enjoy good health.

Dear Uncle, we have received the guarantee papers that you sent us for Aunt Esther, and we in turn sent them to the Naples Consulate to have them signed since there is no American Consulate here. To speed up things, we dispatched them through a friend of Papa, an important person of rank in the Rhodesian Government and who is a good friend of the Consul, advising him that we are dealing with an orphan who has no one to take care of her and due to the fact that her sister would have to leave in two months and that her brother wants her at his side to prevent her from being homeless. Indeed, dear Uncle, to prevent her from being homeless, because unfortunately we are in a desperate situation and with no hope of escape.

I do not know what was our sin to find ourselves this way. And to imagine that we have less than two months as by the end of the year, we must leave Rhodes without knowing how. Here, everyone is striving to leave, some for Africa, some for America, and other places where they have relatives. Perhaps we are the only ones with hands tied. All the governments to which the Community of Rhodes have appealed to accept some Jews have responded that regretfully they cannot, none of them, as they are overburdened with population. And we are going crazy only to think that after being, good or bad, in our niche with all our relatives, who knows until when and after so many perils and sorrows we will find a nest of refuge.

We do not have the least idea where we will be going, what kind of place and no one to protect us. We have no choice but to await the events. Heaven will decide our fate and will see where we will end up, except that, dear ones, if you have pity on us and show us a way of escape.

Indeed, dear Uncle, I throw myself at your feet and beg you to do your utmost to save our lives. Imagine that what may happen to us is what happened once in Spain, and to think that we have only two months at our disposal drives us out of our minds.

In our despair, the only help that we can expect is from you. We wrack our brains to find ways of escape. We see no one but you. Unfortunately, we have no one to lend us a hand. No relative is left to Papa for he does not have brothers and, I repeat, we have no one. How can you abandon home and move toward who knows what danger? Many families have started to take the necessary steps because they have received the papers from America, and I cannot explain how everything comes easy to some people.

Dear Uncle, they are punishing not only us but those who will remain at Rhodes. No more circumcision of babies, no more slaughtering for kosher meat, no more synagogues, and everything is getting dark for the Jews of Rhodes. What haven't they forced us to do? To open on Shabbat and to close on Sunday, their day of rest.

The situation got more serious due to the fact that in France a young Jewish boy of 17, a refugee from Poland whose parents had been killed, wounded the Secretary of the German Ambassador the other day. One day later he [the Secretary] died, and Germany demanded they hand over the Jew. But France refused, first because he was a minor; secondly, because in the presence of the Court, he answered frankly, "Why are you surprised that I assassinated one when day after day, without any cause, they are murdering so many of my innocent brethren?" The newspapers constantly insult us, especially the one from Rhodes, closely allied to Germany, which is the cause of what is happening to us.

Dear Uncle, every night as soon as the newspaper comes out, we run in order to read "our sentence" as we are the only topic. Everything is gloomy for us; the kids will remain ignorant and will not stop cursing us.

Dear Uncle Raphael and Aunt Rachel, I am surprised at not having received an answer to my letter of a month ago, and I am waiting anxiously your news. In the meantime, I have received your letter of October 1st, and took note of its contents. And I am not in position of going over every detail because, dear Uncle, the only thing in our minds is to save ourselves in time. The allocated time has elapsed and they are going to chase us like dogs. I have nothing else to write, but you now have an idea of what is happening to us. Not even Cairo would admit anyone. The daughters of Aunt Behora made an application to bring Uncle David and Aunt Behora and her two daughters [Vida and Rosa], and they answered that even if they deposited all the money in the world, no Jew can enter Cairo. We are thrown out like the plague.

I hope your next letter will bring us good news, and please do your utmost to save us.

Kisses and hugs from your niece who expects nothing but good from you.

Clara

TRANSLATION

Rhodes, November 19, 1938

Dear Uncle Raphael and Aunt Rachel,

We received your letter of the 2nd of November, and paid much attention to its contents.

Unlike what you wrote about our brothers, we were informed here that three young men from Rhodes were sent to Seattle without reaching the age of 15 or finishing school in Rhodes and they were schoolmates of my brothers.

It is even easier now because the new decrees affect the whole family and not only Papa, as you interpreted it. It is possible to go to America with only an Act of Recall[21] meaning that by appearing before the Dept. of Immigration and detailing facts upon facts and stating that you can be guarantors for us, they can from there [the U.S. in this instance] send signed documents to the Government of Rhodes. And without the need of sending them to the Naples Consulate with a simple passport and ticket, we can be at your side and even quicker than Aunt Esther. Here they stamp at the bottom of the passport "Expelled" so that with a simple Act of Recall that can be sent from here to Milano to the Association in Amedo St. No. 7, we can go to all kinds of places such as Holland, Rhodesia, and America. Since we do not have anyone in those places but only you, it behooves you to try to save us.

We are starting to apply for passports and will write "America" as destination because we are more than certain to be at your side being that you will endeavor to act.

As far as money is concerned, we can manage to pay for the trip ticket. Also, your partner's father, brethren Nissim, who has some money, and not being able to take more than 350 lire per passport, wants to rid himself of the money and offers to lend it to us, who later, in Seattle, will reimburse his son.[22]

I beg you, dear Uncle, to do your utmost because at the synagogue today they said that they received a letter from the Government which stated that they want all of us out of Rhodes by the beginning of the year and for us to write to everyone so that they may come to our aid. I beg you not to let us die for if we do not go, they will condemn us to prison and to stray like dogs. You will not regret it if you do us the favor because we are not ingrate and do not forget so easily, and we will pay you to the last cent. I am rushing these few lines and await your answer by AirMail.

Kisses,

Clara

P.S. I am enclosing a note from brethren Nissim Israel for his son stating that he agrees to give us the money that he has in Rhodes and that he awaits for an answer from his son to do the necessary.

[21] Atto di richiamo, in Italian.

[22] Nissim Israel's son's name was Morris. Morris' daughter was likely a very good friend of Claire's.

TRANSLATION

Rhodes, November 22, 1938

[Written by Claire for her father.]

Dear brother-in-law Raphael:

For a long time I wanted to write but the new consternations that have befallen on all of us leave us with no mood for anything and for this reason I have not written.

Dear Raphael, here everyone is in good health; likewise, we hope to hear from you, amen. But concerning everything else, we are here in a bind. As Claire wrote to you, and according to what she told me, you must be up-to-date as to what concerns our family and find a need to talk in this regard. Now dear Raphael, what I am writing in this letter must require your utmost attention, and I believe that in your answer you must not miss any detail. Dear Raphael, according to the new decrees announced last night on the radio, the immigration to the United States will be open shortly but only for the Jewish refugees expelled from Italy and for those having means of support there, that is, that a person having a relative in that country, and this guarantor offering a certificate of recall, that is a guarantee to the local Immigration Department, it is easy to bring them over.

Now, dear Raphael, regarding our situation, by showing good will from your side, and neglecting somewhat your business for a little while, you will succeed in bringing us over. If not for a relative, do it for *zehut* because we have only one month at our disposal. To make you understand better, I am writing clearly as to what the facts will be after you file your certificate of recall to the department (Immigration) of Seattle. This document must be sent from there to the Jewish Refugee Committee of Milan at Amedeo Street, No. 3, legally drawn. And after receipt, this office will send it to the Government of Rhodes. And if everything is accurate, they will authorize us our departure.

I believe, dear Raphael, you will understand very well what I wrote and what needs to be done, and trust you will try to do the utmost. There is no need to say what we intend to do in the future for, as you well know me, I do not forget anything. In order to gain time, I am writing here the necessary steps to take over there, details of birth, etc., in case they require them.

Again, I trust you as much as myself, and hope to hear from you by telegram. I kiss you.

Your brother-in-law,

Abraham Barchi

TRANSLATION

Rhodes, November 27, 1938

Dear Uncle Raphael,

I received your letter of the 8th and instantly I read with great care its contents.

Dear Uncle Raphael, Mama's talk praising your kindness was substantiated by the facts. I did not ever think having an uncle like you and wish more than ever to see your face and speak with all my heart. I think that Heaven could not have given you a better companion than Aunt Rachel. She must be like you. Dear Uncle Raphael, I don't know how to thank you for what you are doing on our behalf. May God reward you with everything that is good and grant you good health for the kind of heart you have. I received the papers you sent Papa. And since their receipt we have been frantic, especially Mama, because, dear Uncle, the decrees affect the whole family, not only Papa. The same as you, I thought how can Papa go by himself and leave us by ourselves to be sent wherever they want. It is always easier when there is a man in our midst. Even under these conditions we were encouraged to send the papers to the Naples Consulate and at the same time we sent a letter to the Jewish Refugee Committee of Milan, stating that they should be signed quicker in order to receive them in time for him to leave Rhodes before being sent elsewhere. It is difficult to have the papers signed at the Naples Consulate as they require a strong guarantee. Two persons left Rhodes this week for America, and after having received from Naples the signed papers and once in Italy, they were not allowed to go beyond and were compelled to return to Rhodes. But in the case of Papa, I believe it will be easier to let him go for he has been expelled. In spite of all this, I beg you to try to bring in more guarantee, even from the community of Seattle and satisfy these greedy ones; you will save us from a deep abyss. We found out here that your uncles Nissim Alhadeff and Salomon are very rich. Please entreat them to help us, as Jews that they are. Time is short and you need to try very quickly to do what is necessary. I beg you to do all you can and as fast as possible because, I repeat, the hours are short.

Regarding what you wrote to me about the husbands of Aunt Sarina and Gioia, they fall in the same category as ours. Uncle Chelibon has two brothers in America, while Nissim has many brothers but knows nothing about them, if they are alive, or where they are. He only has a sister, Victoria Capuano, in New York, and he sent a letter a month ago but has received no answer from her. As I thought he would do, Nissim sent a letter to his sister last week, giving her your Seattle address and advising her to communicate with you. And at the same time he sent you a letter giving his sister's address and requesting you write to her in order to do something for him too.

After reading your letter he wrote you yesterday at length anew. I have no other news and have no more time. I hope to get an answer without fail and as soon as possible for you are our only hope. Everyone from Rhodes greet you. To Aunt Rachel, kisses and hugs and thank her for what she is doing for us. To the family, kisses from us. And I believe that Maurice [Morris] is at the level of writing a few lines to cheer us up. Kisses and hugs from your dear niece who wishes to see you.

    Claire

Page 2

November 27, 1938

Abraham Barchi	born at Aidin	2-20-1891
Mazaltov Barchi (Capeluto)	born at Rhodes	3-05-1895
Claire Barchi	born at Rhodes	3-14-1921
Rachel Barchi	born at Rhodes	3-05-1923
Haim and Moshe (Victor & Morris)	born at Rhodes	3-27-1925
Jack Barchi	born at Rhodes	3-03-1928
Regina Barchi	born at Rhodes	1-09-1932[23]

---

[23] Note the coincidence that the majority of the family was born in March.

COMMITTEE FOR THE ASSISTANCE

OF JEWISH REFUGEES

Via Degli Amedei #3 Tel. 17

MILAN

Milan, November 30, 1938

Mister Abramo Barchi

Rhodes

Dear Mister Barchi:

I acknowledge receipt of your letter of 11/25/1938—XVII. We regret very much to have to answer that we do not have the least influence on the decisions of the Consulate General of the United States which proceeds at any rate only according to the laws concerning the immigration.

Our best regards,

Committee for the Assistance

of the Jewish Refugees

[signed]

F

SAUL M. HABIB

Filiale in CAIRO (Egitto)
19, Rue Manakh, 19
Telefono N. 42562

RAPPESENTANZE · COMMISSIONI · CONSEGNE

23, Via G. M. di Naillac, 23

RODI (EGEO)

Telegr.: SAUL HABIB - RODI

Codici : Bentley's
A. B. C. 5th Edition

N/ Ref. **Clara Barchi**
V/ Ref.

RODI, li___ **9 Dicembra 1938 XVII°**

Queridos oncle Raphael i tante Rachel,

Con la presente vos ago saver como grasias a el Dio todos ya mos
encontramos muy buenos de la salud i de mismo speramos saver de
vuestra parte siempre bueno, amen.—

Queridos tios ay tres letras que vos escrivimos i dinguna vuestra
avemos tomado en repuesta a eias.— Aqui todos estamos como unos locos
i estamos asperando una vuestra letra onde salir un poco de codiado.—
Agora sepac como los papeles del querido papà ya los mandimos a
Naples, ma sicumu el Consul de ay es muy negro, està mandandolos atras
sin firmarlos.— Aqui ya recevieron atras muncia gente, ma los muestros
no aven venido de ainda.— Esto todo es para los que son nacidos en
Turquie como el papa i dicheron que cale que los papeles seian mandados
al Consulat de Smirne o al de Athènes.— Ma el papa no puede entrar
en Turquie porquè es fuido i a Athènes no dechan entrar Jidios.— No
ay que una via de scampo para aremediarmos.— Esto es que el, querido
oncle se va presentar personalmente al Ministero de ay i va rogaldes
a què escrivan al Consulat de Naples i lo uvlighen a accettar los
papeles del querido papa antes que mo los retorne.— Bel mismo tiempo
ase todo su possible para bochear mas garansia, ayudandose magari de
sus parientes, i percurar tambien por mosotros que es mas facil porchè
somos nasidos en Rhodes.— Esto se deve aser a lo mas presto que puede
porchè la ora està curta i se no vamos percurar por tiempo i presto
quen save preda de que ondasmarinas vamos ser.— Querido oncle lo
supplico de aser esto todo sin piedrita de tiempo por salvarmos de
este abisso sin puerta para salir.— Se esto todo que le esto escriviendo
va ver que es impossible i que el Consulat de Naples no va querer
accettar bujca de asermos ir para otro logar serca de vosotros onde
no ay tantas difficildates para entrar, come por exempio Cuba i otros
logares, i duspues a poco a poco mos jieva a su lado; como es su deseo.—
Ya me està paresiendo querido oncle un atagantamiento de escrivile
tanto, ma que se ase? estamos en unas oras de diperation.— No le
paresca que mosotros estamos aqui inactivos.— Esta semana fuè la
mamma ande el Federale de Rhodes, come desir el segundo Governador,
con el qual la mamma tiene conossensia porquè se lo presentò el
ijo de Mr. Joseph Alhadeff quando vino a Rhodes i la bujcò a la
mamma, i el Federale le dicho a la mamma de esr una lettra al
Governador mismo i que el se la ia presentar.— Pichin asimos la
lettra disiendo que tenemos de irmos entre dos mese i que tenemos
un tio que mandò papeles para el papa i que estan ande el Consulat di
Naples i que percure para aserlos accettar i asermos ir a toda la
familia an Seattle onde tenemos parientes que garantisan por mosotros.—
El Federale topò la lettra ecia muy buena i la rimittiò al Governador
i mos assigurò que el tambien va percurar por mosotros por riguardo
al ijo de Mr. Joseph que es su intimo amigo i que la raccomandò muncio
a la mamma.— Agora estamos asperando repuesta a esta lettera i pechin

Letter from December 9, 1938. Written in Ladino on letterhead from Claire's employer.

SAUL M. HABIB
RODI (Egeo)

Seguito foglio N. 2   Rodi, li 9 Dicembre 1938

per oncle Raphael i tante Rachel Capelouto

./.

no vo mancar de tenervos al coriénte.-

Mas querídos tios no se qualo escrevirvos i repeto en cuâto que
lo que queremos de vosotros es que vos arecojgaj unos quantos
jidios de ay i vos presentej ande al Minitero de ay i que vos
quechej por las vengansas que está asiendo a todos los jidios
el Consulat de Napkes que no quere firmar dingun papel de queios
que son nasidos en Turquie.-

Ya creygo no vaj pedrer tiempo a aser todo lo menesteroso i
espero una vuestra respuesta immediacta sin falta.-

Aqui todos estamos muy buenos i todos vos saludan.-

Rogo saludar a todos los parientes,a los ijos besaj de mi
parte,vos beso i vos abrasso vuestra querida suvrixa que vos
roga todo bueno;

Claire

TRANSLATION

Rhodes, December 9, 1938

Dear Uncle Raphael and Aunt Rachel,

We thank God that everyone is in good health. We hope you are too. Dear Uncle, we have written three letters without receiving an answer. Here we are all going crazy and hoping to receive your news to reassure us. We have sent Papa's papers to Naples, but since the Consul[24] is a bad fellow, he is returning them without a signature. This has happened to a lot of people here, but we have not received ours. This affects those who were born in Turkey, like Papa, and they suggest they be sent to the Smyrna or Athens' Consulate. But Papa cannot enter Turkey because he escaped [as a young man], and Jews are not allowed to enter Athens. There is no way of helping the situation. But, if you appear yourself in front of the Ministry [Immigration Department] and beg them to write to the Consul of Naples and force them to accept Papa's documents before they are returned to us.

Meanwhile, do try your best to increase the guarantee with the help perhaps of your relatives and try to do something for us, which would be easier since we were born at Rhodes. You must do it as quickly as possible as time is running short; otherwise, who knows what kind of sea waves we will be prey to. Please do it without wasting time to save us from this abyss without exit. If you see that what I am writing about is impossible and that the Naples Consul does not accept, try to send us some place near you where there are not so many difficulties to emigrate, as, for example, Cuba, and other countries, and later, gradually, you bring us over as you may desire. It seems to me that I am imposing on you with so much writing, but what can one do? We are desperate; don't think that we are inactive here.

This week Mama went to the "Federale" of Rhodes, who is like a second Governor [second in command] and to whom Mama was introduced by the son of Mr. Joseph Alhadeff when the latter came to Rhodes and looked for Mama. The "Federale" told her to address a letter to the Governor himself and that he would hand it to him. We immediately wrote the letter stating that we had to leave within two months and that we have an uncle who sent papers to Papa and these are in the hands of the Naples Consul and to make him accept us and let the whole family go to Seattle where we have relatives who are our guarantors. The "Federale" found the letter well written, he handed it to the Governor, and assured us that he himself would help us out of consideration for the son of Mr. Joseph, his intimate friend who recommended highly Mama.

We are now awaiting an answer and immediately will bring you up to date. I find nothing else to add. And what we want you to do is meet with some Jews over there and go to the Ministry [Immigration] and complain about the punishment inflicted upon the Jews by the Naples Consul who does not want to sign

---

[24] This apparently refers to the American consul.

any papers for those born in Turkey. I believe you are not going to waste any time and will do the necessary without fail.

Regards from everyone. Give regards to the relatives, and embrace the kids. Kisses from your niece who wishes you well.

Claire[25]

---

[25] Claire and her family, it seems, were not aware of the quota of Turkish citizens allowed into the U.S., which was probably less than 100 a year.

TRANSLATION

Rhodes, December 10, 1938

Dear Uncle Raphael,

I keep wondering why I have not received a letter in answer to the many I have sent. Perhaps you are too busy working for us and for that I don't blame you for it. What I repeat is that until now we have not found a place to go and that we are off our minds as little time remains.

Now, dear Uncle, I let you know that the consul of Naples finally got around to answer regarding Aunt Esther's papers. They ask that we fill in the papers as follows:

1) Report from the information agency "Dun & Bradstreet" about your business, yearly gross, and profit.
2) Letters from the bank where you have your savings.
3) Tax receipts on your house and business.

I beg you, dear Uncle, to try sending them as fast as possible, informing yourself from others who also have sent papers there. The Consul has also sent a questionnaire to complete, requesting all kinds of things. This questionnaire will be sent together with the papers that are missing after we receive them from Seattle. And after that nothing remains but to sign them. I believe you'll do everything quickly.

Aunt Esther is not writing because she is very busy as Gioia gave birth to a boy. She asked me to greet you on her behalf. Mama also sends her regards. Papa sends his regards and you can imagine his anxiety. All the relatives from Rhodes send their regards. Kisses to Auntie Rachel and the kids. I hug you and kiss you.

Your dear niece who wishes to see you.

Claire

I am enclosing a photo of the whole family that we took for the passport, and it came out okay. Send your answer to our home address:

Via G. Maestro Heredia No. 4

Rhodes (Aegean)

because my boss is leaving on January 10 for Africa. He also came to Rhodes after 1919. And I quit my job.

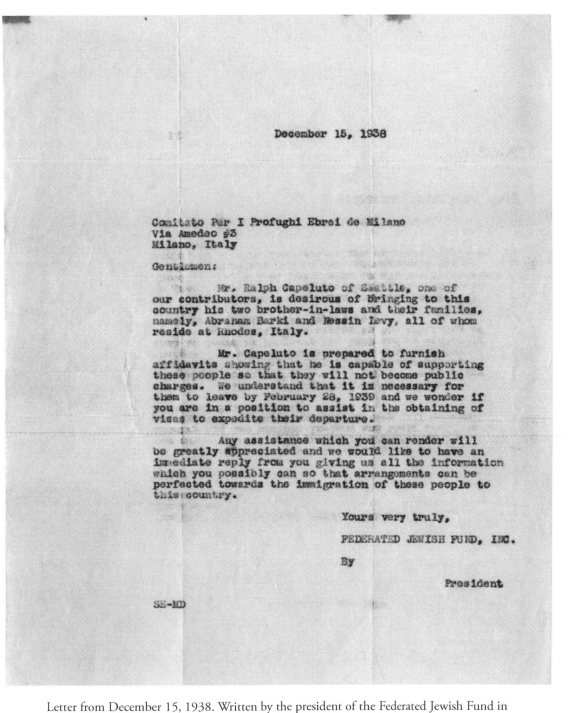

December 15, 1938

Comitato Per I Profughi Ebrei de Milano
Via Amedeo #5
Milano, Italy

Gentlemen:

Mr. Ralph Capeluto of Seattle, one of
our contributors, is desirous of bringing to this
country his two brother-in-laws and their families,
namely, Abraham Barki and Nessin Levy, all of whom
reside at Rhodes, Italy.

Mr. Capeluto is prepared to furnish
affidavits showing that he is capable of supporting
these people so that they will not become public
charges. We understand that it is necessary for
them to leave by February 28, 1939 and we wonder if
you are in a position to assist in the obtaining of
visas to expedite their departure.

Any assistance which you can render will
be greatly appreciated and we would like to have an
immediate reply from you giving us all the information
which you possibly can so that arrangements can be
perfected towards the immigration of these people to
this country.

Yours very truly,

FEDERATED JEWISH FUND, INC.

By

President

SE-MD

Letter from December 15, 1938. Written by the president of the Federated Jewish Fund in
America to the Committee for Jewish Refugees in Milan, Italy.

December 15, 1938

Comitato Par I Profughi Ebrei de Milano

Via Amedeo #3

Milano, Italy

Gentlemen:

Mr. Ralph Capeluto of Seattle, one of our contributors, is desirous of bringing to this country his two brothers-in-law and their families, namely, Abraham Barki and Nessim Levy, all of whom reside in Rhodes, Italy.

Mr. Capeluto is prepared to furnish affidavits showing that he is capable of supporting these people so that they will not become public charges. We understand that it is necessary for them to leave by February 28, 1939, and we wonder if you are in a position to assist in the obtaining of visas to expedite their departure.

Any assistance which you can render will be greatly appreciated. And we would like to have an immediate reply from you giving us all the information which you possibly can so that arrangements can be perfected towards the immigration of these people to this country.

Yours very truly,

FEDERATED JEWISH FUND, INC.

By
[signed]
President
SE-MD

ABF : xgc = Abramo Barchi

AMERICAN CONSULAR SERVICE

Consulat General at Athens

December 22,1938

Mr. Abraham Barchi,

__Rhodas .Egeo__

Dear Sir :

Reference is made to your letter of November 25 1938, addressed to the American Consulat General at Naples, concernig your desire to proceed to the United States for permanent residence.— You letter has been referred to this office inasmuch as the Italian Islands of the Aegean are now within the Athens consular district.

The Consulate General wishes to point out that each alian who calls to file application for a visa does so on his own responsibility.— The commitments he makes beforehand and the expenses he incurs in the journey from his home to this office, should be undertaken with a knowledge that a visa may be refused and that he may not be adle to go to the United States.—

In view of the extensive unemployment in the United States it is more difficult for an alien to establish his admissibility now than in former times.— In order to receive a visa, an applicant must prove, among other things, that he will have assured shpport for an indefinite period and must present conclusuve evidence that there will be at his disposal a margin of income adequate to preclude the likelihood of his becoming a public charge.—

If in spite of the above warning you wish to make application for an immigration visa, you may procure all the documents noted on the enclosed list and present yourself at the Consulat General. It is necessary for you to appear in person to execute your application, and no assurance can be given in advance that a visa will be issued.—

Very truly yours,

For the Consul General

Andrew B. Foster

American Vice Consul

Letter from December 22, 1938. Written on behalf of the American Consul General in Athens, Greece, to Abraham Barkey.

<u>Documents to be submitted with visa application</u>

I°) Passport valid for immediate travel to the United States,or a
statement from the governmental authorities that such a passport
will be issued to you if you qualify for a visa fort the United States

2°) 3 copies of your birth certificate.-

3°) 3 copies of your certificate of identity issued by the local authorities,
bearing your photograph.-

4°) 3 copies of your penal record issued by the police of the place where
you reside.-

5°) 3 copies of your marriage certificate (il married),from the Metropolis,
bearing its official seal and your photograph.-

6°) 3 copies of a statement (if unmarried),to the effect that you are
unmarried,from the Metropolis,bearing its official seal and your photograph

7°) 4 photograph ,6 centimeters square ,on thin paper,with light background,
and not in group.-

8°) $ IO.OO in American currency,or its equivalent in Greek drachmas.-

X 9°) Birth certificate or certificate of identity of the child who is calling
you to the United States.-

IO°) Documentary evidence to establish that ,if admitted to the United States
for permanent residence ,you will not be likely to become a public charge

N.B. Under the law,no specific documents can be required to establish this,
but it is suggested for your guidance that you present the following :
An affidavit,in duplicate,from the relative in the United States morally
and / or legally obligated to support you,and setting forth in detail
his financial position and number of present dependents.- The statements
in this affidavit relative to his employment,income,property,bank
account,and other financial resources,must be corroborated by documentary
evidence from absolutely disinterested persons.- This corroboration
might take the form of (in duplicate).- :

— I°) Photostat copy of the sponsors latest federal income tax retourn,
or copy certified by Collector of Internal Revenue where retour
was filed.-

2°) Letter from employer on his business letterhead,stating salary
received and length of employment/-

X 3°) Statement from bank showing date deposit was opened,average balance
and present sum.-

4°) Statement from bank or brokerage house regarding security holdings.

5°) Letter from insurance company regarding face and cash value of policy

— 6°) Statement from tax collector showing real estate holdings.-
— 7°) Statement from County Clerk's office showing whether real estate is
clear or mortgaged,and amount of mortgage.-

8°) Statements from certified public accountants and commercial credit
investigators,in addition to the above listed documents.-

ABF: gc = Abramo Barchi

8II.II ABF:xgc—Barchi, Abramo.

AMERICAN CONSULAR SERVICE

CONSULATE GENERAL AT ATHENS

December 22, 1938

Mr. Abraham Barchi

Rhodes, Egeo.

Dear Sir:

Reference is made to your letter of November 25, 1938 addressed to the American Consulate General at Naples concerning your desire to proceed to the United States for permanent residence. Your letter has been referred to this office inasmuch as the Italian Islands of the Aegean are now within the Athens consular district.

The Consulate General wishes to point out that each alien who calls to file application for a visa does so on his own responsibility. The commitments he makes beforehand and the expenses he incurs in the journey from his home to this office should be undertaken with a knowledge that a visa may be refused and that he may not be able to go to the United States.

In view of the extensive unemployment in the United States, it is more difficult for an alien to establish his admissibility now than in former times. In order to receive a visa, an applicant must prove, among other things, that he will have assured support for an indefinite period and must present conclusive evidence that there will be at his disposal a margin of income adequate to preclude the likelihood of his becoming a public charge.

If in spite of the above warning you wish to make application for an immigration visa, you may procure all the documents noted on the enclosed list and present yourself at the Consulate General. It is necessary for you to appear in person to execute your application, and no assurance can be given in advance that a visa will be issued.

Very truly yours,
For the Consul General:

[signed]
Andrew B. Foster,
American Vice Consul

Enclosure:

List.

Documents to be submitted with visa application

1) Passports valid for immediate travel to the United States or a statement from the governmental authorities that such a passport will be issued to you if you qualify for a visa for the United States.

2) Three copies of your birth certificate.

3) Three copies of your certificate of identity issued by the local authorities bearing your photograph.

4) Three copies of your own record issued by the police of the place where you reside.

5) Three copies of your marriage certificate (if married), from the Metropolis, bearing its official seal and
your photograph.

6) Three copies of a statement (if unmarried) to the effect that you are unmarried, from the Metropolis,
bearing its official seal and your photograph.

7) Four photographs, six centimeters square, on thin paper, with light background, and not in group.

8) $10 in American currency or its equivalent in Greek drachmas.

9) Birth certificate or certificate of identity of the child who is calling you to the United States.

10) Documentary evidence to establish that if admitted to the United States for permanent residence, you
will not be likely to become a public charge.

Under the law, no specific documents can be required to establish this, but it is suggested for your
guidance that you present the following: An affidavit, in duplicate, from the relative in the United States
morally and/or legally obligated to support you, and setting forth in detail his financial position and number
of present dependents. The statements in this affidavit relative to his employment, income, property, bank
account, and other financial resources must be corroborated by documentary evidence from absolutely disinterested persons. This corroboration might take the form of (in duplicate):

1) Photostat copy of the sponsor's latest federal income tax return, or copy certified by Collector of Internal
Revenue where return was filed.

2) Letter from employer or his business letterhead stating salary received and length of employment.

3) Statement from bank showing date deposit was opened, average balance, and present sum.

4) Statement from bank or brokerage house regarding security holdings.

5) Letter from insurance company regarding face and cash value of policy.

6) Statement from tax collector showing real estate holdings.

7) Statement from County Clerk's office showing whether real estate is clear or mortgaged, and amount of
mortgage.

8) Statements from certified public accountants and commercial credit investigators in addition to the
above listed documents.

TRANSLATION

Rhodes, January 3, 1939

Dear Uncle Raphael and Aunt Rachel,

I received your letter and thank you for what you are doing for us. We pray that God rewards you as you deserve and that the steps we are taking are not in vain. Unfortunately, we stumbled across very bad consuls and a time of strict laws. We finally conclude that the Consul of Naples is interested only in those born in Rhodes and the Consul of Athens in those outside of Rhodes, as, for example, Papa. As we wrote you, we sent Papa's papers to Naples, but the Consul, not being concerned with the Turkish-born, sent them to Athens from where we received an answer as shown on the copy we are enclosing together with a list of what needs to be done in order to obtain a visa.

I therefore request that you read attentively this list and send us immediately what is expected of you, not only regarding Papa's papers but also ours in order to save time. Meanwhile, we are going to prepare all the papers required from us and send them as soon as we receive yours.

We hope these are not steps made for naught as we are becoming aware that the Consuls are very bad and take their time to answer, and there is not much time. I repeat, if you endeavor to send us immediately what concerns you, perhaps we get things done in time.

Now, dear Uncle and Aunt, there is the favorable aspect that the Milan Committee of Jewish Refugees to whom you wrote received several permits recently, and they, in turn, sent some to Rhodes. And here, the Community [leaders] got interested and called a few people, among whom was Papa who has a "protector" in America, and they [leaders] made note of all the details such as number of offspring, ages, et cetera, and they sent it all to the Committee to have them completed and then have the Consul sign [approve] them for the purpose of entering the U.S.

The Committee is now acquainted with Papa's name from the papers you sent to Naples as well as your letters and also upon the recommendation of the Community as to his honesty, having worked for Alhadeff. We have hope that everything will be easier and we will emigrate to America and escape these persecutions. We are trying without losing hope, and with God's help everything will turn out all right.

Besides all this, all the Jewish men, until from those who must leave Rhodes by the 28th of February '39, who have a trade, have registered with the Community for the purpose of emigrating to Rhodesia. Papa also registered because he is very handy as a carpenter, chest maker, et cetera, and that would help to give us some hope.

I wish to be at your side, but we cannot. What can we do? God will open for us doors to other places, and from somewhere we will try in time to join you and doing it at leisure. What is tormenting us is the lack of time as we have less than two months. Meanwhile, Mama is abed with pneumonia, and we are wondering how can she tolerate such a restless trip. What can be done? Everything comes from God and it will be for the good.

I don't want to prolong it, but pray for your answer as soon as possible and your sending me what I am requesting as well as the papers for Aunt Esther as mentioned on my letter dated December 30, 1938.

Everyone from Rhodes sends you regards, particularly Aunt Esther, Mama, Papa, and the kids. Kiss your kids for me. I kiss and hug you from afar.

Your niece who wishes to see you and send you excuses for annoying you,

Claire

TRANSLATION

Rhodes, January 11, 1939

Dear Uncle Ralph,

As I wrote you on the previous letter in reference to the papers you are preparing for the whole family and for Uncle Nissim, the Community of Rhodes received a letter from the Committee of Milan stating that the "Society," I do not recall which one, from Seattle wrote to said Committee, advising that Mr. Ralph Capeluto wishes to bring to his side two families from Rhodes, Mr. Abraham Barchi and Nissim Levy, and that the Committee is waiting for the affidavits in order for them to have the Naples Consul sign them. And meanwhile for the Community of Rhodes to give them information about these two families as to the number of people, place of birth, and amount of money available for the tickets. The Community meanwhile had already sent from Rhodes the necessary information about all those who have sponsors in America. And I believe by now the Committee has it in its hands. Now it remains for them to receive the affidavits and have them signed as quickly as possible. I think you have sent them by now. If not, I beg you not to send them to Rhodes, but to the "Committee for the Aid of Jews from Italy," Via Amedo No. 3, Milan, which will busy itself to have them signed as they have more influence on the Naples Consul. For the better, they have appointed a Vice-Consul who, unlike the previous one, is easier to deal with.

We wait for a letter from you as well as what I requested concerning the papers of Aunt Esther and ours.

Nothing else to add. Everyone sends you regards, including Mama, Papa, and the kids, and Aunt Esther who has not written because this week we are exhuming the departed and are spending whole days in the cemetery. [26]

Regards to Aunt Jamila, Uncle Shelomo. Kisses to Aunt Rachel and the kids. Hugs and kisses from your dear niece who wishes to see you.

Clara

[26] In reference to the exhuming of the deceased either for building a road to the beach or to provide the marble for a building.

January 19, 1939

Seneca Textile Corp.
91 Franklin Street
New York, New York

        Attention Mr. Maurice E. Bretzfield

Dear Mr. Bretzfield:

        I would like to ask a personal favor of you in the
form of a letter of recommendation.

        I have sent for my youngest sister from Italy. In
doing so I have filed affidavits with the American Consul at Naples, but he wants to recheck my business standing. I would therefore appreciate it greatly if you
would write a letter of recommendation to the American
Consul in Italy and mail it to me in order that I may
send it along with the other letters that I will get
here in Seattle.

        Thanking you in advance and trusting that I will
receive an early air mail reply, I am,

                Very sincerely yours,

                Ralph Capeluto
                SEATTLE CURTAIN MFG.CO.

RC

Letter from January 19, 1939. Written by Ralph Capeluto to Seneca Textile Corp. New York,
NY, asking to write a letter of recommendation to the American Consul in Italy.

January 19, 1939

Seneca Textile Corp.

91 Franklin Street

New York, New York

Attention: Mr. Maurice E. Bretzfield

Dear Mr. Bretzfield:

I would like to ask a personal favor of you in the form of a letter of recommendation.

I have sent for my youngest sister from Italy. In doing so I have filed affidavits with the American Consul at Naples, but he wants to recheck my business standing. I would, therefore, appreciate it greatly if you would write a letter of recommendation to the American Consul in Italy and mail it to me in order that I may send it along with the other letters that I will get here in Seattle.

Thanking you in advance and trusting that I will receive an early air mail reply, I am,

Very truly yours,

Ralph Capeluto

SEATTLE CURTAIN MANUFACTURING COMPANY

RC

W. O. ATWOOD

CERTIFIED PUBLIC ACCOUNTANT

White Building

Seattle

January 20, 1939

TO WHOM IT MAY CONCERN:

I have known Mr. Ralph Capeluto, partner of the Seattle Curtain Manufacturing Company, Seattle, Washington, for the past nine years, and have found him to be a man of high ethical and moral standards, as well as a very capable businessman.

He has a very fine family of exceptionally good character.

Yours very truly,

[signed]

CERTIFIED PUBLIC ACCOUNTANT

January 23, 1939

Pickwick Draperies

45 Leonard Street

New York, New York

Attention: Mr. S. J. Bush

Dear Mr. Bush:

I would like to ask a personal favor of you in the form of a letter of recommendation.

I have sent for my youngest sister from Italy. In doing so I have filed affidavits with the American Consul at Naples, but he wants to recheck my business standing. I would, therefore, appreciate it greatly if you would write a letter of recommendation to the American Consul in Italy and mail it to me in order that I may send it along with the other letters that I will get here in Seattle.

Thanking you in advance and trusting that I will receive an early air mail reply, I am,

Very sincerely yours,

Ralph Capeluto

SEATTLE CURTAIN MANUFACTURING COMPANY

RC

UNITED FACTORS CORPORATION

1412 Broadway, New York

Maurice E. Bretzfield

Vice-President

January 23rd, 1939

<u>TO WHOM IT MAY CONCERN</u>:

Mr. Ralph Capeluto is a member of the firm of Seattle Curtain Manufacturing Co.

Seattle Curtain Manufacturing Co. has been a customer of our company and of affiliated companies for a number of years. We have extended liberal credit to Mr. Capeluto, and all of his obligations have been met in a manner that has been entirely satisfactory to us.

The writer has met him personally and feels that in view of our business experience, he is entitled to full consideration at all times and that he would not willingly enter into any obligation that he could not see his way clear to fulfill.

Yours very truly,

UNITED FACTORS CORPORATION

[signed]

Vice-President

meb:rs

M. Lowenstein & Sons, Inc.

Converters and Manufacturers of

COTTON GOODS

37-45 Leonard Street

New York

Jan. 25, 1939

TO WHOM IT MAY CONCERN:

We have been doing business with Mr. Ralph Capeluto as partner in Seattle Curtain Mfg. Co., Seattle, Wash., and are pleased to mention that our relations have been very satisfactory and are of a most friendly nature.

To my best knowledge, the character and reputation of this man are beyond reproach, and any statement made by him can be relied upon.

He is industrious and a hard worker, and has been successful in his business.

Yours truly,

M. LOWENSTEIN & SONS, INC.

[signed]

Credit Manager

SJB:HS

Mention upon answering

File No. 811.11 Barchi Abramo

FWJ: RC

THE FOREIGN SERVICE

OF THE

UNITED STATES OF AMERICA

AMERICAN CONSULATE GENERAL

Consolato Generale Americano

Naples, January 28, 1939

Mister Abramo Barchi

c/o Salomon Alhadeff and Sons

Post Office Box 193

Rhodes, Aegean

     In answer to your esteemed letter dated January 10, 1939, I hereby inform you that you must address yourself to the American Consulate of Athens.

     Yours truly,

For the American Consul General

Thomas D. Bowman

Signed, F. W. Jandrey

American Vice-Consul

P.S.

     If you will be unable to obtain a permit to enter Greece, you can again address yourself to this Consulate General.

FEDERATED JEWISH FUND

INCORPORATED

803 Fifteenth Avenue No.

Telephone Prospect 4324

Seattle

January 31, 1939

To Whom It May Concern:

This is to certify that Mr. Raphael Capeluto has been a subscriber to our fund for several years. He is a respected member of our community, is the proprietor of a well-established curtain manufacturing business, and has always maintained a high standard of conduct in all of his business and personal relationships.

We understand that he is desirous of bringing to this country two of his brothers-in-law, and from all of the facts at our disposal we feel confident that he is capable of providing a suitable home for them and that they will not be permitted to become a public charge upon this community or the government of the United States.

Any assistance which can be given in expediting the granting of visas will be very much appreciated by this organization and the writer.

Very truly yours,

FEDERATED JEWISH FUND

BY   [signed]
                 President

SE:FL

Phone Main 8785

Seattle Curtain Mfg. Co.

Manufacturers of

Novelty Curtains and Panels

Oil Silk Curtains and Shower Curtains

304 Prefontaine Building

Third and Yesler Way

Seattle, Washington

January 31, 1939

American Consul

Naples, Italy

Honorable Sir:

Enclosed you will find Affidavits in behalf of my two brothers-in-law, Abraam Barchi and Nessim Levy, together with supporting documents to substantiate my willingness to maintain them upon their arrival in this country so that they will not become a public charge.

It is my sincere desire to provide a proper home for them and from the enclosed documents it will be apparent to you that I am capable of so doing. I know that my two brothers-in-law, if permitted to immigrate, will become law-abiding and respectful citizens of this country, and any assistance which you can give me in the obtaining of the visas for them will be very much appreciated.

Respectfully yours,

[signed]

Raphael Capeluto

RC:FL

United States of America

State of ___Washington___

City of ___Kixgx Seattle___

County of ___King___

I, ___Raphael RaighxCapeluto___

age ___38___ being duly sworn, deposes and says:

I reside at ___807 30th Avenue So., Seattle, King Co., Wash.___

I am a Native American or Naturalized Citizen of the United States as evidenced by
(indicate which)
my certificate Naturalization Certificate No. 2303226 issued on Feb.21,1927
York
by Southern District of New Court at New York, New York

I am married and dependent on me for support are **wife and three children**
(married or single)

I am partner (one-half owner) Seattle Curtain Manufacturing Co.
(State fully business or occupation, location, earnings)
Address: 304 Prefontaine Bldg., Seattle, King Co., Washington
My income from this business is in excess of $3000.00 per year.

In addition, I have assets consisting of **residence, cost $5500.00 subject to**
(State investments, savings, life insurance, real property, etc.)
mortgage, $3024.00--my equity $2476.00. My one-half interest in Seattle
Curtain Manufacturing Company is conservatively worth $9,500.00.
I value this interest at $15,000.00.

I am the **brother-in-law** of Heccim Levy age 45
" **brother** relationship) Gioia Capeluto and Levy of persons abroad 35
" uncle Esther Levy 7
" uncle Mardecheo Levy 5
" uncle Mussani Levy 4
" uncle Rosa Levy 3

now residing at ___Island of Rhodes, Italy___

who desire to come to the United States to join me and others of the family, and whom I am most anxious to bring over.

I do hereby promise and guarantee that I will receive and take care of my **relatives**
who are applying for an immigration visa, and will at no time allow them to become public charges to any community or municipality. I do further promise and agree that those of my relatives covered by this affidavit within school age will attend public school, and will not be permitted to work until they are of age.

I make this affidavit for the purpose of inducing the United States Consular authorities to grant the visa to my said relative s, and herewith submit coroborative proof as to my personal standing.

I, ___Christine Weiss___, a Notary Public, duly commissioned, do hereby certify that this affidavit was sworn to before me this 31st day of January 193 9, and that affiant herein mentioned has exhibited to me the naturalization certificate above mentioned.

Christine Weiss
(SEAL) Notary Public

Raphael Capeluto

Form from January 31, 1939. Form from Ralph Capeluto promising that he has the means and ability to guarantee that he will take care of his immigrant family in the United States so that they will not become "public charges." Ralph filed four separate forms – one for his sister Gioia Levy's family (who eventually went to Palestine (Israel)), one for his sister Matilda Barkey and her six children (see page 80), one for his brother-in-law Abraham Barkey, and one for his sister Esther Capeluto.

United States of America

State of Washington)

City of Seattle) ss.

County of King)

I, RAPHAEL CAPELUTO, age 38, being duly sworn, depose and say:

I reside at 807—30th Avenue South, Seattle, King, Washington.

I am a Native-American or Naturalized Citizen of the United States as evidenced by my certificate, Naturalization Certificate No. 2393226 issued on February 21, 1927 by Southern District of New York Court at New York, New York.

I am married and dependent on me for support are wife and three children.

I am a partner (one-half owner) Seattle Curtain Manufacturing Co., address: 304 Prefontaine Bldg., Seattle, King County, Washington. My income from this business is in excess of $3000.00 per year.

In addition, I have assets consisting of residence, cost $5,500.00, subject to mortgage $3,024.00—my equity $2,476.00. My one-half interest in Seattle Curtain Manufacturing Company is conservatively worth $9,500.00. I value this interest at $15,000.00.

I am the brother-in law of Abram Barchi, age 47; brother of Mazaltov Capeluto Barchi, age 43; uncle of Clara Barchi, age 17; uncle of Rachel Barchi, age 15; uncle of twins Haim and Moshe Barchi, age 13; uncle of Jacques Barchi, age 10; and uncle of Regina Barchi, age 6, now residing at Island of Rhodes, Italy, who desire to come to the United States to join me and others of the family, and whom I am most anxious to bring over.

I do hereby promise and guarantee that I will receive and take care of my relatives who are applying for an immigration visa, and will at no time allow them to become public charges to any community or municipality. I do further promise and agree that those of my relatives covered by this affidavit within school age will attend public school, and will not be permitted to work until they are of age.

I make this affidavit for the purpose of inducing the United States Consular authorities to grant the visa to my said relative, and herewith submit corroborative proof as to my personal standing.

I, Christine Weiss, a Notary Public, duly commissioned, do hereby certify that this affidavit was sworn to before me this 31st day of January 1939, and that affiant herein mentioned has exhibited to me the naturalization certificate above-mentioned.

Christine Weiss, Notary Public
[signed]

Raphael Capeluto
[signed]

TRANSLATION

Letter dated February 3, 1939

Dear Uncle Raphael and Aunt Rachel,

You cannot imagine our worry of not receiving your news until now or an answer to so many of my letters. We don't know what to think, especially in these grave moments in which we find ourselves. We also are surprised of not yet receiving the papers for Aunt Esther that I requested. As far as ours is concerned, we see that in spite of your efforts we will not succeed. We have only one month left, and there is nothing new. Only this week we received from the Milan Committee a letter addressed to the Community of Rhodes asking the number of our passports. We already sent them and are awaiting an answer from them. But I don't believe we will get an answer to this letter as so much time it takes for you to answer. Perhaps in 15 or 20 days we will sail away from Rhodes and be in the high seas.

Today is the eve of Tu Bishvat, and Uncle Nissim received a letter from his sisters stating that he has not received a letter from you for a month. This worried us a lot to the point of sending perhaps a telegram, but we thought that it was just your habit.

I don't find anything else to say other than to say that we find ourselves in a tight spot.

Regards from Papa, Mama, Aunt Esther. Give our regards to Aunt Jamila and Uncle Shelomo.

Kisses and hugs from your niece.

Claire

P.S. Please send your letters to the following address:

Via G.M. Heredia No. 4, Rhodes

because I am home as my boss, also affected, has sailed this week.

TRANSLATION

ROYAL PROSECUTOR OF RHODES

Gov't of Rhodes &

Subordinate islands

CERTIFICATE

Register No. 174

The undersigned Secretary certifies that at this Royal Prosecutor's office that

NO

Penal proceeding is pending regarding the name of Barchi, Abramo, son of the late Haim and the late Lea Clara Alagem, born on February 2, 1891, at Aidin (Turkey).

This certificate is issued at the request of the person concerned.

Rhodes, Feb. 8, 1939 (XVII)

THE SECRETARY

[signed by Mr. Atanasio Caralambus]

The signature of Mr. Atanasio Caralambus, Secretary of the Royal Prosecutor of Rhodes, is hereby authenticated.

Rhodes, Feb. 8, 1939 XVII

The Royal Prosecutor

(G. Calzetti)

[signed]

TRANSLATION

GOVERNMENT OF THE ITALIAN ISLANDS OF THE AEGEAN

Register No. 181-12

BIRTH CERTIFICATE

From the existing registers at this office, it follows that

Barchi, Moshe

of Abraham [Barchi] and Matilde Capeluto (of the Jewish race) was born at Rhodes (Aegean) the 27th day of the month of March of the year one thousand nine hundred twenty-five.

Issued for personal use.

Rhodes, Feb. 10, 1939 XVII[27]

The chief of the Central Register Office.

[signed]

Maselli

---

[27] The number XVII after the date means 17 years after the march on Rome by Mussolini.

TRANSLATION

GOVERNMENT OF THE ITALIAN ISLANDS OF THE AEGEAN

Registration No. 584-N

BIRTH CERTIFICATE

From the existing records of this office it follows that:

BARCHI CLARA

of Abraham and of Capelluto Matilde (of the Hebrew race) was born at Rhodes (Aegean) the fourteenth day of the month of March of the year one thousand nine hundred twenty-one.

Issued for personal use

Rhodes, February 10, 1939 XVII

> The Chief of the Central
>
> Register Office
>
> [signed]
>
> A. Maselli

Civil and Penal Court

(Rhodes, Aegean)

... for the legalization of the signature of Mr. Cav. Antonio Maselli[28]

Rhodes, February 11, 1939 year XVII

> The President
>
> [signed]

---

[28] CAV after "Mr." is an abbreviation of Cavaliere title granted to an individual for having served the government. They were a dime a dozen.

TRANSLATION

CIVIL & PENAL COURT

(Rhodes (Aegean))

For the authentication of the signature of Mr. G. Calzetti

Rhodes, Feb. 11, 1939 XVII

The President

[signed]

GOVERNMENT OF THE ITALIAN ISLANDS OF THE AEGEAN

Visa for the authentication of the signature of Cav. Dott. Giuseppe Scrozelli, President of the Civil, Penal Court of Rhodes.

Rhodes, Feb. 13, 1939

The deputy for the authentication

ANTONIO AMZELLI

[signed]

TRANSLATION

GOVERNMENT OF THE ITALIAN ISLANDS OF THE AEGEAN

Register No. 583-

C A P E L U T O Matilde

From the existing registers at this office, it follows that

C A P E L U T O Matilde

of the late Mussani and the late Rachele Capeluto (of Jewish race) was born at Rhodes (Aegean) the fifth day of the month of March of the year one thousand eight hundred ninety-five.

Issued for personal use:

Rhodes, February 10, 1939 XVII

The chief of the Central Register
Office
[signed] Maselli

Civil and Penal Court

(Rhodes (Aegean))

(For the authentication of the signature of Mr. Antonio Maselli

Rhodes, February 11, 1939 Year XVII

The President
[signed]

GOVERNMENT OF THE ITALIAN ISLANDS OF THE AEGEAN

Visa for the authentication of the signature of Cav. Dott. Giuseppe Scorzelli, President of the Penal and Civil Court of Rhodes.

Rhodes, February 13, 1939

The deputy for the authentication

Antonio Maselli

[signed]

TRANSLATION

GOVERNMENT OF THE ITALIAN ISLANDS OF THE AEGEAN

Group CCRR Special Central Office

CERTIFICATE OF GOOD CONDUCT

We certify that the named

BARCHI, ABRAMO

OF THE LATE Haim (Barchi) and the late Lea Clara Alagem, born at Aidin (Turkey) on the 20th of February 1891, resident of Rhodes private employee, is of a good moral and political conduct. He has no previous penal record, nor pending, at the Local Judiciary Authority.

This document is issued at the request of the concerned for emigration purposes.

Date: Rhodes, Feb. 15, 1939, XVII

> The Commander of the Group CCR
>
> Chief of the Special Central Office
>
> [signed]
>
> Major F. Mittino

TRANSLATION

Rhodes, February 20, 1939

[Written by Marie Levy, wife of Sadik, sister of Mazaltov]

To my dear and esteemed brother Raphael,

With great joy I start to write this short letter to give you good news. My dear Leon who did not send a letter for four months, and God forbid, we did not know if he was dead, has, thank God, finally written, advising us of his return home and that this week he will be at our side.

You will excuse me for not having written for a long time. The reason is the poverty we endured while bringing up Leon and just when he started to help the family, he left for the Army and subsequently they sent him to war. No use telling us, dear Raphael, the life we led in the last two years, for this reason I did not have the inclination to write a few lines. What could I have said except sad tales. And these days, to have our sisters undertake few days to bid goodbye and do not know the destination, and they all have large families.

Upon Leon's arrival I will notify you. I sent a letter to Africa to dear Bohor Capeluto, asking him to send a [work] contract to bring him over, and if there is hope, see if you can bring him over to you. From now on we will write each other. We want to send him away from Rhodes to prevent them [the Italian government] from sending him to war again.

I want to close this letter by giving regards from all the sisters and brother-in-law. Regards from Sadik. Hugs and kisses to dear Rachel and the kids. Regards to dear Jamila and Shelomo, similarly to your mother-in-law Mazaltov [Alhadeff] and her family.

Bye, your dear sister,

Marie of Sadik Levy[29]

---

[29] In Rhodes married women wrote their husband's first name right after their own first name.

Leon Levy went to Tangier about the same time as the Barkey family. He later tried to cross the International line to go to French Morocco through Spanish Morocco, but was caught by the Spanish authorities, and after a short period, was returned to Tangier. (He planned to join the French Army of Liberation.) He then emigrated to Israel where he married and lived on a kibbutz.

TRANSLATION

Rhodes, February 25, 1939

Dear Uncle Raphael and Aunt Rachel,

We received two of your letters among which were the papers and we thank you a lot. What a pity that all the steps we are taking end up unsuccessfully, but what can we do? It comes from above and who knows, perhaps that by taking all the papers to the country we are destined to go, we will be able to succeed in going to Seattle. We finally realized that the Naples Consul is immovable. We did not take the trouble of sending the last papers that we received because we find it useless and we lack time. Papa wanted to go this week to Naples to have them sign the papers only for Mama and the kids because for him it is no use having been born in Turkey. But we dissuaded him as we saw that all those who went to try it proved fruitless, and for each one there was a pretext for refusal.

We hear now that the immigration to the U.S. is going to be opened to Jewish refugees who have guarantee papers, and after this the doors will be closed except for a deposit of millions. But who knows if this is true as we also hear other rumors every day. We have moved heaven and earth without budging from this spot. We would hear a door being opened, but then nothing.

One of them was Palestine to which will be our destiny to go according to the Community of Rhodes,[30] but we know that Palestine does not belong to us entirely and we are "tied" to the Arabs. We will not enter the harbor, but will land near a mountain far from the harbor at one hour distant and wade a river. If all of us were men, we could stand this, but old women being in our midst, pregnant and those having recently given birth, and more and more little kids, it would be impossible.

An application has been made to the Government asking for a delay, and we were given until April 15, 1939 to leave Rhodes; that is, until the time of the possible opening of the Palestine emigration, and will be able to enter through the harbor without much trouble. Another advantage is that contrary to the way of the mountain where everyone would be able to carry only whatever load he could personally, now one could take a trunk and bundle of bedding and a few suitcases. We could have reached our own destination by now, but we have preferred the delay they offered us.

The trip ticket is 1,000 lire for adults and 500 for those aged 12 and under.

I am writing all this to bring you up to date about what is happening in Rhodes, and God willing, when we reach destination, we will inform you of what has happened (hopefully all good news) to set you free from worry as you must be very preoccupied. I am writing this letter hurriedly because today is the

---

[30] This refers to the Jewish community of Rhodes.

Meldado[31] of the late Grandpa Mussani, and we have things to do in the house. Let us hope we do it always with joy and at an advanced age.

Now, I must give some news. The son of Aunt Marie, Leon, who was in the Spanish [Civil] War sent a telegram stating that he was in Naples and will leave for Rhodes tomorrow and will arrive here on Wednesday. We cannot imagine the joy we will feel of seeing him after not having his news for four months. May we also find joy after so much distress.

Nothing else to add. Regards from Papa, Mama, Aunt Esther.

Special kisses and hugs to the kids. Hugs from your niece,

Clara

---

[31] A Meldado is a religious service to celebrate the anniversary of a death, a yahrzeit.

TRANSLATION

Rhodes, April 14, 1939

Dear Uncle Raphael,

I don't know what to write because I have not received a letter from you. We all enjoy good health, and we hope all of you are well. You will be surprised to see that this letter is dated April 14, when we were supposed to leave Rhodes on the 15th, but they extended the date one month so that we have until the 15th of May. But we think that by the end of the current month we will be in Palestine. The immigration to that place has been opened, but we are awaiting the entry permits. We thought we would spend Passover in Palestine, but we did it here. You can imagine how upset we were because all the household effects were sold. Anyway, this has passed, but the worst is that they took away the ambulant [carts] permits which affected Uncle Nissim who found himself penniless, and to prepare for Passover was with great anguish. We pray that next year will be better and we will praise God.

Nothing else to add. Aunt Esther wants to write but you can imagine how upset she is only at the prospect of the three sisters separating from each other and especially from us where she has been like a daughter.

Please note that the name of the streets have changed. Write us at the address below:

Esther Capeluto

Via Heredia, No. 4

Rhodes (Aegean)

I think that the next letter will be from Palestine. Regards from everyone from Rhodes. Please kiss Aunt Rachel and the kids from me.

Bye, your dear niece,

Clara

TRANSLATION OF TELEGRAM DATED MAY 2, 1939

(Italian)

TO: RAPHAEL CAPELUTO

04 PREFONTAINE BLDG

SEATTLE, WASHINGTON

We must absolutely leave on the 14th. Wire to our account to Tangier, Morocco, one thousand dollars to enable us to disembark through Tangier Bank. Inform them that it is to be credited to Barchi, Rhodes. Send cable otherwise serious consequences.

Mathilda—Abraham Barchi

Telegram from May 2, 1939. Urgent telegram from Matilda and Abraham Barkey to Ralph Capeluto asking that he wire $1,000 (US) to a bank in Tangier otherwise they would face "serious consequences."

TRANSLATION

Rhodes, May 2, 1939

[Written by Claire for her father.]

Dear Uncle Raphael,

It has been two months without your news, and we are worried. We send you a letter from Rhodes almost every week, and they remained unanswered. Perhaps you are very busy and find no time to write.

Now, the most urgent reason for writing is to confirm the telegram I sent you today and to explain it in detail. We find ourselves, dear Raphael, in a most unpleasant situation. They had given us eight months, and we now have 13 days left and we until have not found a place to which to go. These are the facts: after six months had elapsed and not finding a place of refuge, they gave us another month. Just before the additional month, we took steps to be able to embark on a Greek ship going to Palestine, and to disembark in a clandestine manner without the knowledge of the Arab Government. But, when the ship was three hours away from Rhodes, three men of the Jewish Community of Palestine came to Rhodes to ask for one more month in order to be able to get the permits to enter Palestine legally. That meant that the immigration was to open on April 5. The signed permits were to arrive at Rhodes on April 30, all in order. But because of an illegal ship full of Jews, our permits were given to them, leaving us out in the cold. All the leaders of the Community of Rhodes have left, some for the Congo [Belgian], some for France, and the poor remained here. We are going crazy, like a regiment without a general. The 15th of this month we must leave Rhodes for sure. And if we don't, they will take us to the Rhodes concentration camp which is like a prison. Only one way exists for our salvation, and that will depend on you, dear Raphael. And as we wired you, it is Tangier, Morocco. To enter that place we must have a guarantee of foreign money, not from Rhodes, which we figure would amount to $1,000. The telegram reads as follows: "We must absolutely leave on the 14th. Remit payable to our order 1,000 dollars to be able to disembark. Wire urgently to the Bank of Tangier, advising them to credit Barchi, Rhodes. Wire urgent; otherwise serious consequences."

The telegram was in Italian as we could not use another language. The $1,000 that you will wire to the Bank of Tangier will be used as deposit and you will instruct the Bank to acknowledge receipt to us at our address in Rhodes. And this will allow us to obtain a visa and be able to embark at Rhodes.

As you see, dear Raphael, we are at a loss. And therefore, I beg you to come to our aid to save us from the fire that awaits us. I wait for your telegram and the Bank's to get ready and on time by the 15th of the month.

I believe that when you receive this letter you will do what is necessary. I thank you in advance and hope to repay you. Cordial regards from your dear brother-in-law.

Avraham Barchi[32]

---

[32] Although Avraham could write in Ladino with both Latin and Rashi characters, he relied heavily on Claire for his correspondence.

LEAVING RHODES

On Sept. 1, 1938, Italian dictator Benito Mussolini decreed that all foreign Jews who came to Rhodes from Turkey in March, 1919, were to be expelled, and so Abraham Barkey found himself forced to leave.

As the Barkey family figured out what to do, the children would go to the waterfront every other week and wave goodbye to their friends and the other families that had chosen to leave the island. The Jews of Rhodes spread throughout the world—to Palestine, the Belgian Congo, and Rhodesia.

Life on the island was becoming more difficult for the Jews. Jewish children, some of whom were attending Jesuit schools, were no longer allowed to attend school. The school had received orders from Rome not to let any Jews return.

The Italian government issued new anti-Jewish rules, making it nearly impossible to remain Jewishly observant. The rulings prohibited circumcision of babies, slaughtering for kosher meat, and outlawed synagogues.

Although everyone in the Barkey family—except Abraham—could have stayed, they listened to Mathilda's sister's husband, Chelibon Maish. A master boot maker, Maish had friends within the Italian guards (Carabinieri) who came to him to make and repair their boots. The guards had inside information about possible harm aimed at the Jews and warned Maish that he and his family should leave Rhodes.

However, the family didn't know where they could go. Just as they thought they would head for the United States or Palestine, doors closed on them.

"I knew we were going away, but we really didn't know until almost the last minute that we were going to leave," Jack Barkey said. "We could have gone to Palestine, to the Belgian Congo, but we had hopes we'd come to the U.S."

The only jurisdiction that would take the family was Tangier, an international zone at the northern tip of Morocco that was neutral during World War II. Two or three other Jewish families from Rhodes had already fled to Tangier.

For weeks, Abraham and Jack prepared for the journey by building two large trunks that would carry the possessions of the nine family members. Working at night, they built them out of wood, bending the tops until they were round. Tin corners reinforced these sturdy pieces of luggage that would carry the family's possessions. They lined the inside with beige and blue patterned velour.

"You could sit on it, slam it," Jack said.

The family packed mainly clothes, mattresses, blankets, and photographs into those two trunks—the only possessions they took with them from their life on Rhodes. The photographs included a portrait of proud Mathilda and Abraham Barkey with their six children and another photo of Claire and a boy with whom she had appeared in an elementary school play.

They took a few utility items—a heavy brass mortar and pestle, a Turkish coffee grinder, and a Chinese clock. They left the rest of their possessions behind, even dumping their furniture in a well next to the house.

Finally, on May 30, 1939, the Barkey family went to the same dock where they had bid goodbye to their friends. They waved goodbye to their aunts and cousins, not realizing it would be the last time they would ever see some of them.

They boarded the Mar Egeo, a cargo and passenger ship, and sat under a tarp on the deck, battered by rain and wind. "I remember it being windy and cold and there was no room down below," Regina Barkey said, so they slept on top of the wooden hatches.

First they stopped in Piraeus, Greece. From there they traveled through the Straight of Matapan, then for three or four days through the Corinth Canal to Naples.

During a long layover in Genoa, Italy, they stayed at a hotel for several days until the ship to Tangier arrived. Mathilda and Abraham visited friends in Milan while the Barkey children—who had never before been away from Rhodes—visited some of the Italian sites they had studied in school.

They boarded another ship to Tangier and traveled for a few days, stopping at ports in Barcelona, Malaga, Palma de Mallorca and Ceuta at the tip of Morocco before arriving in Tangier.

This time they had a cabin on the ship. But they had to go through the engine room to get there and the smell of the diesel made some of the children sick to their stomach.

They arrived in Tangier on July 2, 1939, with no place to stay. Funds from the Joint Distribution Committee allowed them to stay at the Hotel Saporta for a few days until they found an apartment. - CFH

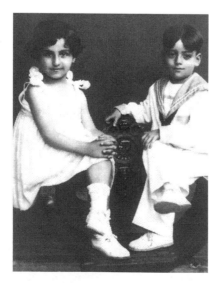

Claire Barkey with a boy in their elementary school play. Taken in Rhodes. Circa late 1920s.

GOVERNMENT OF THE ITALIAN ISLANDS OF THE AEGEAN

Register No. 130

BIRTH CERTIFICATE

From the existing registers at this office, it follows that

C A P E L U T O Esther

of the late Mussani and the late Capeluto Rachele (of the Jewish race) was born at Rhodes in the year one thousand nine hundred nine.

Issued for personal use.

Rhodes, May 11, 1939 XVII

> The Chief of the Central Register
> Office
> [signed] Maselli

CIVIL AND PENAL COURT

Rhodes (Aegean)

For the authentication of the signature of Mr. Cav. Antonio Maselli.

Rhodes, May 11, 1939 XVII

> The President
> [signed]

GOVERNMENT OF THE ITALIAN ISLANDS OF THE AEGEAN

Visa for the authentication of the signature of Cav. Dott. Giuseppe Scorzelli, President of the Penal and Civil Court of Rhodes

Rhodes, May 12, 1939 Year XVII

> The Deputy for the authentication
> Antonio Maselli

GOVERNMENT OF THE ITALIAN ISLANDS OF THE AEGEAN

Register No. 132

<u>CERTIFICATE OF SINGLE</u>

From the existing registers at this office, it follows that:

<u>C A P E L U T O</u> Esther

of the late Mussani and the late Capeluto Rachele (of the Jewish race) was born at Rhodes in the year one thousand nine hundred nine, is not tied by any matrimonial bond.

Issued for personal use.

Rhodes, May 11, 1939 XVII

> The Chief of the Central Register
> Office
> [signed] Maselli

CIVIL AND PENAL COURT

Rhodes (Aegean)

For the authentication of the signature of Mr. Cav. Antonio Maselli.

Rhodes, May 11, 1939 XVII

> The President
> [signed]

GOVERNMENT OF THE ITALIAN ISLANDS OF THE AEGEAN

Visa for the authentication of the signature of Cav. Dott. Giuseppe Scorzelli, President of the Penal and Civil Court of Rhodes

Rhodes, May 12, 1939 Year XVII

> The Deputy for the authentication
> [signed]
> Antonio Maselli

OFFICE OF THE ROYAL PROSECUTOR OF RHODES (AEGEAN)

Certificate Number 520 protocol

The undersigned Secretary certifies that at this Royal Attorney NO criminal proceedings is pending to the name of Capelluto Ester of Mussani and Capelluto Rachele born in 1909 in Rhodes.

This certificate is issued on request of the person concerned.

Rhodes May 12, 1939 XVII

The Secretary

(signature)

Seen to legalize the signature of Mr. Atanasio Caralambus Secretary of the Prosecutor of the King of Rhodes

Rhodes May 12, 1939 XVII

The Crown Prosecutor

G. Calzetti

R. District Court of Rhodes (Aegean)

Visa for the legalization of the signature of Mr. Cav. Dr. Calzetti

Rhodes, 15 May 1939 XVII

The President

(signature)

Government of the Italian Islands of the Aegean

Visa for the legalization of the signature of Cav. Dr. Giuseppe Scorzelli President of the District Court of Rhodes

Rhodes, 15 May 1939 XVII

Delegate to the legalization

(Anotonio Maselli)

OFFICE OF THE ROYAL PROSECUTOR OF RHODES (AEGEAN)

JUDICIAL FILES

Certificate No. 603

We certify that in our judicial files that on the name of Capeluto Esther of the late Mussani and the last Rachele Capeluto, born in 1909 at Rhodes (Aegean)

IT SHOWS N O T H I N G

Rhodes (Aegean) May 13, 1939 Year XVII

THE SECRETARY

[signed]

A. Corraiambus

Visa authenticating the signature of Mr. Atanasio Corraiambus

Secretary of the Royal Prosecutor of Rhodes (Aegean)

Rhodes (Aegean) May 13, 1939 Year XVII

THE ROYAL PROSECUTOR

ROYAL CIVIL AND PENAL COURT

Visa for the authentication of the signature of Mr. Cav. Dott. Giolabretti

Rhodes, May 15, 1939 Year XVII

The President

GOVERNMENT OF THE ITALIAN ISLANDS OF THE AEGEAN

Visa for the authentication of the signature of Cav. Dr. Giuseppe Scorzelli, President of the Civil and Penal Court of Rhodes

Rhodes, May 15, 1939

The Deputy for the authentications

[signed]

Antonio Maselli

GOVERNMENT OF THE ITALIAN ISLANDS OF THE AEGEAN

CENTRAL REGISTRY OFFICE

CERTIFICATE OF FAMILY SITUATION

(In other words, composition of the family)

(On Page 2)

From the register of the population of this Royal Office No. 662 of the Department of Rhodes (Aegean), it follows that the family of the named Esther Capeluto, daughter of the late Mussani and the late Rachele Capeluto, born at Rhodes (Aegean) in the year 1909 is composed as follows:

LAST NAME AND FIRST NAME	Father	Mother	Place and Date of birth
Capeluto, Ester	Mussani	Rachele	Rhodes, 1909

Place of residence

Rhodes (Aegean)

GOVERNMENT OF THE ITALIAN ISLANDS OF THE AEGEAN

Visa for the authentication of the signature of Cav. Dott. Giuseppe Scorzelli, President of the Civil and Penal Court of Rhodes (Aegean)

Rhodes, May 12, 1939, Year XVII

The Deputy for the authentication

[signed]

Antonio Maselli

Cable transfer of money from Ralph Capeluto to Abraham Barkey to bank in Tangier, Morocco.

JUDICIAL CERTIFICATE

Model Number 15
Number 202 of order
Number 664 Chronological
Day 3 May 1939 XVII
Issued 2 copies to ???
Specifics
Sheets 2 Lire 16.00
Writing Lire 4.80
Total Lire 20.80
The Chancellor

In the year nineteen hundred thirty-eight on the twenty-eighth of the month of December, at Rhodes, and in one of the offices of the District Court, at eleven o'clock -

Before Cav. Dott. Mario Franco Police Magistrate of Rhodes assisted by the undersigned Chancellor and Interpreter for the purpose of causing, by judicial act, the truth to emerge under the circumstances indicated below at the instance of Mr. Barchi, Abramo of the late Haim, aged 47, resident of Rhodes, personally appeared the gentlemen:

1) Buenavida Heskia of the late Mosé born at Magnesia, resident of Rhodes, aged 50;

2) Levi Nissim of the late Behor, born at Smryne, resident of Rhodes, aged 45;

3) Cadranel Behor of the late Benson, aged 68, born at Milas, resident of Rhodes;

4) Coen Aronne of the late Salamone, aged 60, born at Magnesia, resident of Rhodes.

witnesses all unbiased toward the Petitioner.

The police magistrate admonishes the above on the moral importance of the oath, on the religious bond that the believers contract with it before God, and the punishments sanctioned by the laws against the false and reticent witnesses.

Then he invites them to swear, one after the other, and they swear and pronounce the wording: "I swear to tell the truth and nothing but the truth."

Afterwards, separately as well as jointly, they have declared and attested to the following:

"We, aforementioned and below undersigned witnesses, under the bond of the oath given with the knowledge that we have of everything below, the plain truth and being besides a public and well-known matter, we attest that the named

BARCHI, ABRAMO, of the late Haim and the late Lea Clara Alagem, was born at Aidin, the 20th of February 1891. It was read, confirmed and signed except for the Cadranel and Coen who have declared themselves illiterate.

Signed   Buenavida Heskia

"   Levi Nissim

"   The Chancellor V. Cardone

"   The Police Magistrate M. Franco

This is a certified copy of the original issued at the request of the concerned.

Rhodes, May 31, 1939—XVII

THE CHANCELLOR

(signature)

ROYAL CIVIL AND PENAL COURT

(Rhodes (Aegean))

Visa for the authentication of the signature of Mr. _____ Elia

Rhodes, May 31, 1939 Year XVII

THE PRESIDENT

(signature)

GOVERNMENT OF THE ITALIAN ISLANDS OF THE AEGEAN

Visa for the authentication of the signature of Cav. Cott. Giuseppe Scorzelli, President of the Civil and Penal Court of Rhodes (Aegean)

Rhodes, June 1, 1939

The Deputy for the authentication

Antonio Maselli

[signed]

TOWN HALL OF RHODES (AEGEAN)

CERTIFICATE OF TRANSFER OF RESIDENCE

The undersigned Mayor certifies:

that BARCHI, ABRAMO, of the late Haim and the late Lea Clara, born at Aiden (Turkey) in 1891, merchant by trade, of the Jewish race, transfers his residence from this City to Tangier (French Morocco)[33], taking with him nine packages of used utensils and personal articles of clothing.

This certificate is issued at the request of the concerned to use at the custom house.

Rhodes, June 9, 1939 XVII

FOR THE MAYOR

By His order

THE CHIEF CLERK

[signed]

---

[33] Tangier was not French, but international.

TRANSLATION

Tangier, July 3, 1939

[Written by Claire for her parents.]

Dear brother Raphael and sister-in-law Rachel Capeluto:

After a great kiss from the bottom of our hearts, we hereby inform you how on the 2nd of this month (Sunday) we arrived here; we, and Sarina's family all, thank God, in good health. Dear brother and sister-in-law, our duty was to wire you, but as you know, here you have to watch your pocketbook and the telegram being somewhat expensive, we decided to send this letter via Air Mail. Since we left Rhodes, it has cost us a pretty penny, you can imagine, from June 11th to the 2nd of July, date of arrival. During this interval we stayed ten days in Genoa and we had to spend quite a bit. And now that we have arrived safe and sound, we pray that good jobs are available.

Dear Raphael, regarding business, we can't write anything yet since we have been here two days and were just looking for a house as we can't stay in the hotel any longer. We will bring you up to date in the future. Chelibon went to seek help from the [Jewish] Community because he came at the [Rhodes'] Community's expense, and they took care of finding him a house and giving him food until he found a job. But, due to the merit of his children, Chelibon's business prospect appears to be good.

For the moment we can't give you any more news. Now that we have more time at our disposal we will write each other a lot.

Dear Esther sends you kisses and hugs. Sarina, Chelibon and family sends you regards. Regards to dear Jamila and Shelomo. Kisses and hugs from your sister and brother-in-law.

Mazaltov and Avraham Barchi

[Same letter, but from Claire.]

Dear Uncle Raphael and Aunt Rachel,

I am adding a couple of words to Mama and Papa's letter to tell you that we are all feeling fine.

Dear Uncle Raphael, we rented a house[34] because it is impossible to stay more than one night in the hotel and we are very preoccupied [with financial problems].

At first sight it appears to be difficult for us, especially as far as finding a job. For this reason, we beg you, do not stop trying to bring us to America, and we here will leave no stone unturned.

Kisses,

Claire

---

[34] It was actually an apartment.

Tangier, July 26, 1939

To: Ralph and Rachel Capeluto

From: Nissim & Gioia Levy[35]

Translation by Jack Maimon at his home on December 6, 1992

We feel all right. Gioia arrived in Tangier and got sick a little. Since I am sick I am laying down with a new baby. Nissim suffers from stomach trouble. It was necessary for him to have an operation, and he was to go to Athens. But he heard of a doctor from Rhodes, and he gave him an injection and he became cured.

Gioia wants Ralph and Rachel to know that Abraham Barkey moved to Tangier. Nissim knew the difference between the two places and tried to discourage him from leaving Rhodes. It would be hard for him with six children as it would be a new beginning. Gioia did not like the welcome from her two sisters who were there. Gioia did not like the idea of the sisters asking for help from Uncle Ralph.

Everything is settled and we are all fine. Say hello to everyone and with much good health always.[36]

---

[35] This is written by one of Mathilda and Ralph's sisters and her husband.

[36] Notes from Esther Huniu: In Rhodes Nissim sold fabric and material (cloth) in the villages.
In Tangier Gioia made candies and Nissim sold them in the marketplace.
They had eight children: Stella, Morris, Shoshana, Rivka, Shelomo, Salvo, Rachel, and Marcel. All of them are in Israel today.
Nissim was always taking medicine (baking soda) for his stomach problems.
Nissim was very jealous of Mathilda.
Uncle Ralph and Rachel did not have very much at that time.

TRANSLATION

Tangier, August 5, 1939

[From Esther to Aunt Rachel in Esther's writing.]

Dear and esteemed sister-in-law Rachel Capeluto,

I did not write to you for such a long time because we had to contend with a period of unsettledness and did not know what to do. It has been 11 months of unrest for us and for you. May God reward you.

Nissim Israel was in Rhodes when we left. When we arrived at Tangier, we found out that he had left for Seattle. It is easier to bring parents over. We did not have that chance. He will relate to you what had happened to us. I offered to give him some things for you and for dear Jamila, but they refused. But it irritated me because you deserved to receive some good things. Later, when they thought it over and changed their minds, we already had taken our luggage to Customs. Perhaps it would be better for us to bring them to you when we leave. May God facilitate things for us as this is not the place to live.

Kiss the kids for me. Regards to your parents. Hugs and kisses to you.

Esther

ARRIVING IN TANGIER

Although the family had no one to greet them in Tangier, they did arrive to a Jewish community populated in part by other Italian Jews and Jews from Rhodes. Two of Mazaltov Barkey's sisters, Sarina and Gioia, and their families, also joined the Barkeys in the dusty Arab city.

They rented a three-room apartment in a three-story building that had four units on each floor. Part of a residential neighborhood, 77 Paseo Cenarro (Azancot Building) was the address engraved in the Barkey children's minds.

One room was the kitchen, the other the bathroom, and the third the living quarters. Having very little money, the Barkeys rented part of the living area to a childless couple from Turkey, who befriended Regina. The couple eventually moved to an apartment across the hall.

The war made it difficult to get enough food. Esther would stand in line at the bakery for a couple of hours every morning to get bread. Some of their clothes came from the Hebrew Sheltering and Immigrant Aid Society (HIAS).

Regina and Rachel were enrolled in a nearby French school for girls, *L'ecole Francaise de Jeune Filles,* while the boys went to *l'Ecole de l'Alliance Universelle.* Claire eventually found a job as a bookkeeper for an import-export company owned by Jews.

Rachel earned money by darning silk stockings with crochet needles. Jack and Esther would pick up and deliver the repaired stockings to their owners, mainly local Jews.

After school each day Morris and Victor would sew sandals for Maurice Hasson, a man from Rhodes.

Victor also sold homemade coconut candy at the Capitol Cinema, a movie theater. He and Morris, whom everyone knew because they were twins, used to sneak each other into the movies.

Abraham Barkey and Chelibon set up a shoe repair business, but the partnership was dissolved following an argument. Chelibon took over the business. Meanwhile, Abraham found other work and at one point partnered with another man to open a bar. That business eventually failed.

Mazaltov would make almond toffee that Jack would sell on the streets. One time, when he and Morris were selling candy, they found the equivalent of a $10 bill. Not wanting to explain to their mother where the extra money came from (for fear that they would have to return it), they ate leftover candies for several days to make it look like they had sold it all. Then they gave their mother the extra money.

Jack would also sell shoes with rubber soles made from tires, going into the stores, taking orders, picking them up at the warehouse and delivering them.

"We all worked for a common goal—to survive," Jack said. "We all worked to support the family. We're all self-educated. We were all striving for a better way of life."

During their seven years in Tangier all the children except Claire attended school, some learning how to type, to keep books, and take stenography.

Meanwhile, Mazaltov stretched the money by buying the least expensive food she could find. She would buy beef pancreas and boil and boil it. Once in a while the family would get a fish.

Jack would serve meals at the Jewish school. Always hungry, he would eat before the meal was served, and then again afterwards if there was anything left.

The family never had enough money, and the fact that their father was not working for long periods of time took a toll on the family. - CFH

TRANSLATION

Tangier, August 5, 1939

[From Esther, in her writing.]

Dear and esteemed brother Raphael Capeluto,

    I write this letter to let you know that, thank God, we are in good health and that we hope to hear good news from you. Dear brother, it has been four months since we last received a letter from you. We are worried, especially since we were aware that dear Rachel is about to give birth. We have sent you two letters from Tangier and have received no answer. We hope Rachel has an easy childbirth for she has a great merit for what she is doing for all the sisters.

    You can't imagine our great anguish to see dear Avraham without work. May God give all of you a long life for what you are doing for us. Don't ever think, dear brother, that Avraham wanted to cause you any pain. Nissim has such a bad character that since the day he found out that you sent some money to Avraham, he has given us no rest, cursing us directly or behind our backs. After so many years of marriage, he until asks us for dowry. After all that Avraham did for them, especially after each childbirth when we all would go to look after her [Gioia] and would spend a lot of money to cover up for Nissim. And now he [Avraham] has given them more than 1,000 francs because he took pity on Gioia. And when we embarked, he gave him 600 francs [actually lire, which were commonly called francos in Rhodes], and when we reached Genoa, he [Nissim] asked for more and he arrived at Tangier three weeks after us. We went to meet him, and dear Mazaltov found a house for them and paid one month in advance. But he did not even thank her.

    Dear brother, these letters that he sent to you, unbeknown to us, is to flatter you but he would make life miserable for us after so many acts of kindness from our part. Dear brother, don't think that I am ashamed to stand up to him.

    Dear brother Avraham showed up at the Bank but did not withdraw the money. He is waiting to open up a little store. May God show him the Gates of Pity for the merit he gained for what he did for our dear father [Grandpa Mussani] and for me as an orphan who is worried about all the sisters. He really treats me as if he were my brother. From the day we arrived he is sick, but walking around thinking about how the end will unfold. He wants to be like a bird and fly to your side.

    Clara is trying to get a job at a bank and says that we will get ahead each month a little at a time. And when there is a cruise, she will go to see you. This is not a place to live and difficult for men to find work because there are many Moors who work for nothing. No store can be found [to rent]. Chelibon is in Tangier and thank God has a trade which is in demand. He has found temporarily a little shop and has started to work after nine months of idleness for they had taken his license [in Rhodes] away from him, and Sarina suffered a lot. I do not have the inclination to write because of that, and Nissim makes me ill. But because of what people may say, we keep our mouth shut. Please, do me a favor and tell me how much you sent him because he says that it comes from his sister [from New York]. He wanted us to leave Rhodes and to find himself unhindered in order to ask for money.

Dear brother, the reason I came here is because they said that it is easier to go to America from here, and I have the papers in Naples. I sent them my address, and when they are signed, they will send them to me.

Dear brother, I beg you, if there is a way, to bring dear Avraham and his family because this is not a place to live. He has been unhappy and ill the last two weeks. Don't feel bad about what I wrote about Nissim. They pass by our house and do not speak to us. We do not attach any importance to it because he is a little empty-headed.

Dear brother, you can imagine how we separated from the dear sisters and brother-in-law. May God always keep us together. When we left Rhodes, dear Bohora [Capeluto, also by marriage] received a letter from dear brother Abraham [from Argentina] stating that his daughter has heart trouble and this adds to our sorrow. She has to be taken care of well so that she can recover her health.

Dear Bohora, David, and daughters and Sadik and his family send you regards. Dear Leon [Sadik's son] who is here with us has not found work yet. He came here to avoid being drafted again.

Dear Avraham sends you regards and sends excuses for not writing separately. Whenever Clara writes, it is on behalf of everyone. Dear Mazaltov and her sons send regards, and her sons wonder when they will meet Uncle Raphael.

Chelibon, Sarina and family, Nissim, Gioia and family send regards. Please let us know how is Aunt Rachel because we are worried. Kiss your son for me. Regards to all the relatives. These are all the news from me. I greet you.

Your dear sister,

E. Capeluto

TRANSLATION

Tangier, August 10, 1939

Dear Uncle Raphael,

I wrote to you more than a month ago and have not received an answer. You cannot imagine our worry, especially since Aunt Rachel is expecting. We pray God that you are all well.

Now, dear Uncle Raphael, please know that it has been five weeks since our arrival at Tangier, and we have not found work unfortunately. Dear Papa is going crazy and especially since he came to look for a future. But what can we do? Patience, may God have pity on us and show us a good way.

Now, dear Uncle Raphael, as I wrote to you on my previous letter, here you cannot do much if you don't have a trade and a great capital. It is true that Papa is very handy, but not enough to set up shop. Therefore, we are looking for a small store for items to be sold retail. But we must think before we go into business and not do things in a haphazard manner and eat up the money we brought with us. Stores like that cannot easily be found as they ask too much for the goodwill. And if we are to pay three or four thousand francs for the goodwill, we will have nothing left as capital.

For this reason we have found nothing. Besides, in Tangier, you find no wholesale merchandise that can later be sold retail at some profit. Even if you bought a great deal of merchandise, they ask for retail prices. For this reason, Papa decided to go to Casablanca which is two hours away from Tangier and where you can find some merchandise to buy and bring it for resale. But, since we have an Italian passport marked "Refugees," we cannot leave Tangier, especially for a French city. We have applied with the Consul and have not received an answer as yet. Others have tried but the response was negative.

Uncle Chelibon found a shop and started to make shoes for some local people, and they are so pleased that they are recommending him to many customers. We pray God to give him patience and not be weary of working, because you can imagine, dear Uncle Raphael, that after one year of idleness, it is difficult to reorganize anew. Papa does not budge from the shop to keep him inside. He [Chelibon] has a good trade and you cannot find good trade workmen here.

We have near us Uncle Nissim who is Gioia's husband, who from the day of his marriage has given us such a bad time. I would not know where to begin to tell you, but I limit myself to the last events just to give you an idea. I thought him to be naive as he may have given you the impression on his letters. What is he capable of doing! As soon as he learned that you placed $500 of guarantee for us, he would stay the whole day in the marketplace and would curse at Papa with so many bad words, saying that he also is a brother-in-law and has as much right to the money and all the more since we owed him 2,000 lire of the dowry as promised to him. He complained of being penniless and that they had taken away his work permit. But a lot of people lost the permit and did not need anyone because they had more brains than him, were thinking of tomorrow, and did not squander their money.

But don't think that he was making little money, just the opposite for he knew how to make it. Everything would eventually go to gambling, which left him without a cent. If you could only see how Aunt Gioia looks, and it is all the fault of this husband who never gave her a day of joy. I wonder what is marriage for if people do not respect others, especially their wives. Gioia never goes out. She is kept in the house as in Rhodes. This woman does not know the meaning of going to the movies. After raising a child who could barely walk, she would be pregnant again and this "refrain" keeps repeating itself.

Coming back to the case of the husband. After giving us a bad time during some period at Rhodes and not letting Gioia get near Mama, and you know how much the sisters love each other, he came the last night to our house and brought another man to make peace between them [Avraham and Nissim]. Papa, in order not to remain at odds with him, told him, "I do not wish to be angry at you." The latter remained astonished and could find nothing to say. He asked Papa for money and was given 500 lire besides the 500 Papa had given him the previous week. That is besides what Aunt Esther gave Aunt Gioia in order to buy a pair of shoes she did not have for the trip. Also, while in Genoa, where we met Uncle Chelibon on the way to downtown, he sent us word through a man that if we had Italian money left over, to send it back to him. He thought we took along Alhadeff's wealth.

I swear to you, Uncle Ralph, that only God knows how we spent days from the time we left Rhodes until now, always thinking of the prospect of remaining penniless. We are not like Uncle Nissim[37] who is spending like mad other people's money. He is a dupe to his friends. The last name is "Levy," and as you may recall while in Rhodes, the saying "Empty-headed Levy" and the last name fits him well.   From the first day of his arrival he has not talked to us. After having helped him and having found a place for him to stay after his voyage, he quarreled with Aunt Esther. He left us in the lurch, taking care of Aunt Gioia who was sick, in order to entertain himself with some friends from Rhodes who only wanted to profit from him. He is gullible when dealing with these friends. Money goes through him like water. We are very glad that we did not go together to America because you would be vexed getting to know him.

In reference to the papers, we appeared before the local American Consul and he told us that it is very difficult for us, but he wrote us down, advising us that the Turkish quota had been filled long ago and that it is more difficult than for the rest of us.

It is not our fate to be near you, it appears. It would be our great wish to see such a good uncle like you. Patience! Perhaps some day.

Nothing else to add. Please write to me, Uncle Raphael, letting me know if Aunt Rachel has given birth to a boy or a girl. Regards to Aunt Jamila, Uncle Shelomo, especially from Mama.

---

[37] Uncle Nissim emigrated to Israel and later committed suicide by drowning.

Uncle Chelibon, Aunt Sarina send you regards. Mama, Papa, Rachel, Victor, Moshe, Giaco, and Regina send you kisses. Similarly Aunt Esther. Kisses to Aunt Rachel with all my heart. To dear Maurice, Betty, Marlene kisses. And you receive tireless kisses from your grateful niece.

My address is: c/o Mr. Abraham Barchi, Rue Dtr. Cenarro No. 77, Immeuble Azancot, 2e etage, Maroc

[Claire]

TRANSLATION

Tangier, August 10, 1939

[Written by Claire for her mother.]

Dear brother Raphael,

I send you kisses from afar and thank you for all that you are struggling to do for us. This increases the love in our hearts. You know how we were, you and I, as children, more than with all the sisters. For this reason dear Abraham does not consider you only a brother-in-law, but more than a brother, and he mentions is that he does not know how to pay you for what you are doing for us. He feels that you have a great feeling for us. Someday we will meet in good health.

Please answer dear Esther for only your letters console her.

I send you kisses.

Your sister,

Mazaltov

TRANSLATION

Tangier, October 9, 1939

Dear Uncle Raphael,

You can't imagine how surprised I am for not having received any answer to all the letters I have addressed to you since our arrival at Tangier, especially since Aunt Rachel was expecting. I pray God that you are in good health. I can't understand your long silence. I can't believe that of all the letters I have written, none has reached you. Otherwise, they would have returned them. Of all the people who came with us, no one has missed receiving an answer to letters sent to America. Oh, well! Everything is possible, and for the reason that perhaps only our letters have gone astray, I am sending a certified letter with the acknowledgement of receipt to make sure it reaches you. Please answer me without fail as we are worried. There is not a day without hope of receiving your news.

Dear Uncle Raphael, dear Papa this week went into partnership with Uncle Chelibon. They rented a small store where Uncle Chelibon will make shoes and Papa will display on the showcase some items for sale.

What can we do? We must get along, and we happen to be in a place where we must work hard to earn a living. I, who came here with great hope of finding employment, nothing has materialized. We have come at a bad time, when even the employees of longstanding run the risk of being terminated due to the interruption of [business] relationships.

Do not leave us without news. It is your letters that bring us relief. This is not like Rhodes where we would see the relatives ten or 15 times a day. Here we live at a distance from each other. We are like "strangers." It is not easy to become separated.

Aunt Esther sends you kisses and hugs. Regards from Aunt Sarina and Aunt Gioia and their families. Mama, Papa, and the kids send regards. To dear Jamila with Uncle Shelomo we send kisses. Likewise to Aunt Rachel and the kids. A big hug from the bottom of my heart.

Claire

P.S. Dear Uncle, please send us as soon as possible the latest catalog of men's and women's shoes as we are in great need of them.

TRANSLATION

Tangier, November 10, 1939

Dear Uncle Raphael and Aunt Rachel,

I just received your esteemed letter dated October 24, and we are happy to know you are in perfect health.

Dear Uncle and Aunt, I know you are very busy, and that is the reason you have not written until now. But I believe you should put everything aside and write a couple of lines to inform those who worry about you that you are in good health. You do not need to write a lot, just a few words, because we find consolation from your letters.

We know that the majority of the family is here, but it is not like Rhodes where we would see each other frequently. Now, I have no doubt that you are going to write more often. We should be at your side to help you in your work and hold your kids as we do here with our neighbors. Alas, it was not our chance to realize our wish. But we do not lose hope that with the help of God we will see each other.

Dear Uncle Raphael, I thank you very much for the catalogs you sent us, but we have not received them yet. We hope they will be of use. Papa also thanks you.

Dear Aunt Rachel, you did not need to mention; we know all the sacrifices you made out of pity for us. Until now we had no need of pestering you, but now we are forced to annoy you persistently. We only wish to repay everything because neither Papa nor all of us do not like to feel obligated to anyone. We will never forget the dear ones who rescued us from the terrible times. We do not even know how to thank Aunt Jamila. May God reward her for her good heart and for what she has done for us.

Please accept, Uncle Raphael, from all of us the most sincere congratulations for the newborn girl. May she bring you luck and, with her birth, peace to the whole world.

We are all well. We keep regularly in touch by mail with those who remained in Rhodes.

Nothing else to add other than to send hugs and kisses to Aunt Jamila and Uncle Shelomo. Regards to brother Nissim Israel and family. Sarina, Gioia and Aunt Esther send regards. Papa, Mama and the kids embrace you. Please give tender kisses to Moshe, Betty, Marlene, and Amelia (Mimi). I wait for pictures of them. A big hug from your dear niece who wishes you well.

Claire

P.S. We have just received the catalogs. We thank you and we liked it a lot. We were pleased about what concerns your business. May you prosper more and more.

TRANSLATION

Tangier, March 18, 1940

Dear Uncle Raphael,

We have just received a letter from Aunt Behora [Capeluto] from Rhodes, stating that they appeared before the representative of the American Consul of Naples who is in Rhodes to inquire about Esther's papers and were told that they [the papers] are until in Rhodes and they need more guarantee. I can't understand how difficult it is becoming only for Esther because in each letter that we receive from Rhodes, they write that two or three families are leaving every so often. When we stopped at Naples on the way to Tangier, we gave our address to the Consul and he promised us that he would write when the moment came. But they did differently; they wrote to their Rhodes' representative who happens to be a "Mazalbashu,"[38] and if they [our relatives] had not appeared in front of him, he would have forgotten for years.

I see more and more that the easier way would be to direct yourselves to the Government and through them prepare the papers anew for the local American Consul, stating that this sister is all by herself and has no one and that you are responsible for her sustenance. It is the only way, and from here it is easier. I believe you will concern yourself immediately and do everything as should be in order not to waste time.

I don't know what else to add. Nothing else new from here. Regards to all the relatives. Kiss Aunt Rachel and the kids for us. Kisses from Mama, Papa, Esther and the kids. A strong hug from your niece.

Claire

Mr. Abraham Barchi
Paseo Cenarro No. 77
Tangier, Maroc

P.S. Regards to Aunt Jamila and Uncle Shelomo, and tell her that next week we will write at length to her and to you as well.

---

[38] A bad sort.

TRANSLATION

Tangier, April 17, 1940

[Letter from Mazaltov, which seems to be in Rachel's writing, although Morris is credited.]

Dear and esteemed brother Raphael Capeluto:

The purpose of this letter is to let you know that we are all in good health, and we hope to hear likewise from you. I hope this letter finds you in good health.

Dear brother, last week we received a letter from dear Rachel and were very glad to hear from you. May God reward her for being a good sister-in-law and caring for dear Esther who was very nervous awaiting your letter. At the moment she received the letter, she started to cry from joy. Dear Rachel tells us to try to send Esther. The papers that you sent us are no longer valid. Now, dear brother, prepare new ones with much more guarantee and send them directly to the American Consulate of Tangier. On the papers you write that you are like a father to her, that she is an orphan and has no one here.

Dear Raphael, Claire has sent you two letters that have been unanswered. Dear brother, please do it for Esther as soon as possible. And after you are successful with her, we will try for the rest of us, one by one, because this is not a livable town and we want to get them out of here so that they won't keep company with the Arabs.

We are grateful people. You know, dear brother, that when you were a child I was not like the other sisters toward you. We loved each other, and may God keep us together. My sons vie with each other to be at your side. My third son is named after dear Yacob and is 12 years old. He always says, "I am going to America and will stay with Aunt Jamila like a son." May God give her the satisfaction of having her own sons. I have him in school and [he] is always the first in his class. Please take a picture with dear Jamila and Shelomo and your sons as we want to see you together. At least it will appease us and we will get to see the newborn girl.

Give regards to dear Rachel and tell her that until now I loved her like a sister-in-law, but kind-hearted as she is with Esther and the rest of us, I consider her like a sister. *Que no manque para sus hermanos.*[39]

Dear Raphael, give regards to dear Shelomo together with dear Jamila and let me know how is her health.

Regards from Avraham. The reason he has not written is that he has little desire to stay in this place and because the climate does not agree with him. Please write to him and console him. You know, he con-

---

[39] This expression is difficult to translate, literally it is, "May she not be missed by her brothers." In other words, "May the relationship for whatever reason remain the same."

siders you like a brother. I swear to you, dear Raphael, there is no better son-in-law than him, having taken care of the departed Papa and Mama so well, not to brag about it. When dear Esther will hopefully leave, she will tell you everything.

Claire sends you regards. She did not write because she found as good a job as she had in Rhodes and the employers are very satisfied with her.

Dear brother, I beg you to answer all my requests and read the letter with great care, especially on account of dear Esther. That is all for now.

Hug the kids for me and give regards to your in-laws. Regards from Esther, Chelibon, Sarina and the kids, Nissim and Gioia and the kids. Your sister who has a desire to see you. When will the day of our reunion arrive?

Mazaltov Barchi

P.S. Two more days until Pesach. This letter was written by Moshe.[40]

---

[40] You will note the emphasis placed on regarding Esther as an orphan. Jewish tradition emphasizes the importance of caring for widows and orphans as a mitzvah (good deed). The letter also mentions Mazaltov's brother Yacob. He died very young as a result of being hit on the head with a ruler by a teacher. Discipline was strict in the classroom and the teacher was all-powerful.

TRANSLATION

Tangier, May 7, 1940

Dear Uncle Raphael and Aunt Rachel:

I confirm my two letters from some time ago that remained unanswered by you. I write this one to only let you know that we are in good health and in order not to leave you without news from us.

Dear Uncle Raphael and Aunt Rachel, I must inform you that after so many tries, I finally found a very good job in a business representative office where I am satisfied in every aspect. Dear Uncle, reiterating what they informed me from Rhodes, the Consul of Naples called Aunt Esther telling her that the papers are outdated and that it would be necessary to renew them. But since Aunt Esther is here, please address them to the American Consulate of Tangier rather than the one in Naples as before. I beg you, dear Uncle, to do the necessary without wasting time; that is, new documents with more guarantee, stating that you are like a father to her, that she has no one but you to take care of her.

I don't know what else to write, not having received news from you. Everyone sends regards from here. Please kiss Aunt Jamila and Uncle Shelomo. Kisses to the kids from the bottom of my heart.

Awaiting your answer to all my previous letters. Hugs and kisses from,

Claire

R. Consolato Generale d'Italia

n° 771/iv

FOGLIO DI VIA PROVVISORIO
PER UN SOLO VIAGGIO
----

che si rilascia a BARCHI Abramo fu Haim e fu Alagem
Lea Clara, nato ad Aidin (Turchia) il 20 Febbraio
1891, residente a Tangeri,-----------------------------
        Valido per recarsi a Tetuan e ritorno a Tange-
ri.--
        Tageri, lì 20 Novembre 1940/XIX
            p/ IL R.CONSOLE GENERALE

CONNOTATI

Statura m. 1,70
Capelli: brizzolati
Occhi: castani
Fronte: regolare
Corporatura: normale
Barba: rasa
Baffi: a punta
Colorito: pallido.

Firma del titolare
Barchi Abramo

n° 32101

Visto en este Consulado General de España
Bueno para su viaje
a Tetuan
Tanger 21 de Nobre de 1940
EL CONSUL ENCARGADO
DE LA CANCILLERIA

Provisional passport from November 20, 1940. One-time only passport allowing Abraham
Barkey to travel from Tangier to Tetuan, Morocco.

Royal Italian General Consulate

PROVISIONAL PASS FOR

ONLY ONE TRIP

Issued to Barchi, Abramo, of the late Haim and the late Lea Clara Alagem, born at Aidin (Turkey) the 20th of February 1891, resident of Tangier.

Valid to go to Tetuan[41] and return to Tangier.

Tangier, November 20, 1940 XIX

For the Royal General Consul

(signature)

Description:

Height:	M 1.70
Hair:	Grizzled
Eyes:	Brown
Forehead:	Regular
Build:	Normal
Beard:	Shaven
Moustache:	Pointed
Complexion:	Pale

Visa from the General Consulate
of Spain

Good: for his trip to Tetuan

Tangier, November 21, 1940

THE CONSUL IN CHARGE OF THE CHANCELLERY

(signature)

Signature of the holder

[signed] Barchi, Abramo

---

[41] Tetuan was at that time a town in Spanish Morocco. Now it is part of independent Morocco.

TRANSLATION

Tangier, March 3, 1941

Mlle Claire Barki

Paseo Cenarro No. 77

Tangier (Maroc)

Dear Uncle Raphael and Aunt Rachel:

After waiting so much time without receiving any letters from you, I have decided to address you this letter, hoping that you will not fail to answer it. The truth is that it is no trouble for me to write more often, but I don't do it to avoid bothering you. But I see now that you are lax and we cannot wait any longer without your news. We hope everything is all right.

Thank God we are all in good health, but leading a not too pleasant life due to the facts that I will later relate. Besides the fact that life is very different from before for everyone in general because of the current events, for us it is more so having been unfortunately disappointed in everything. To mention only one, Papa has been idle for six months. This only gives you an idea of the rest. This was due thanks to Uncle Chelibon, who, as Uncle Raphael knows, from the time he came to our doors was a jinx.

These are the facts: As you well know, you were kind enough to help us to come here as well as Uncle Nissim. For Uncle Chelibon it was not the same because truly he did not deserve it. While in Rhodes, contrary to the jealousy displayed by Uncle Nissim, Uncle Chelibon showed good demeanor and said nothing. But he is very cunning, and it followed that when we arrived at Tangier, it got into his head to become a partner with Papa, as I wrote to you. His reasoning was that since you did not send him any money, he tried to profit from ours. And he, being penniless, had us put all the money in the partnership, and he supplied the work. We tried our best to advise Papa against the partnership because we knew what would happen, but Papa, being coaxed, felt sorry and also thought that Uncle Chelibon could do nothing without money.

As newcomers, no one wanted to give credit and everything was paid cash, and that was the only way to do business. Of course, I did not stop writing letters upon letters to make him receive the leather[42], but everything was for naught. Soon he forgot everything, even what Aunt Esther and Mama did for his family. And in short, he made life impossible for Papa, and there was nothing left but to dissolve the partnership. Everything went to his profit. He was left with the shop, the money, and all the assets. We did not want to pursue it further because the only way to discuss would have been a fight and be exposed to shame in a strange country.

---

[42] This refers to shoe leather, from Abraham and Chelibon's business.

He was now well settled, and Papa is walking the streets without being able to do anything because now it is not the same as when we arrived. Then everything was cheap and stores were plentiful. But now, with the refugees coming from everywhere, there is nothing to do. You can imagine in what situation we find ourselves. We hope everything will be for the best.

How are you over there? Are the children all right? And Aunt Jamila and Uncle Shelomo?

Give them regards from us. We would be delighted to receive photos of all of you. I believe you will not fail to answer us. Papa, Mama, and the children send regards. Kisses from Aunt Esther.

It does not matter that she does not write; I also write for her. You know she is a little lazy. I beg you to write to her before me as she has more of a right than I. And if I receive a letter rather than her, she is vexed. I don't know anything else to write. I reiterate my love for all of you.

Kisses from the heart to all of you in general. Your niece who loves you very much.

Claire

TRANSLATION

Tangier, March 18, 1942

Dear Uncle and Aunt:

After waiting so long and seeing that if I do not write, there is no way of receiving news from you, I address you this short letter, hoping it will have a better chance than the others and that you deign answering me.

No matter how busy you say you are and do not have time, I do not believe that in two years you did not find a free moment to write two words. The truth is that I do not understand the cause of your silence. Is there something that has happened between us? It is an enigma. In Rhodes at least we would receive a letter from you once in a while, but now here in Tangier it seems that you forgot you have people. Not so much us, but you must remember you have a spinster sister here who has no more hope than with you. The truth is that we console her and we treat her not as an aunt, but as an older sister. But she knows after all that she has a brother, and if she were to receive a few comforting words from you, it would be a big thing to her. It is very painful to end up like she did, an orphan at any early age without the joy of being comforted by a mother and without seeing any joy. You, too, dear Uncle Raphael, will say that you left as a stranger and had bad times. But for a man it is different. Now, thank God, you have created a home with your family. May they always be protected by God. And I believe you should think from time to time about your poor sister who, I repeat, has only you as a recourse.

Even just two words, but comforting, will bring some joy in her poor heart. This Aunt Rachel will understand as a woman, and I, as a woman, say that to us, neither money nor riches interest us, but a little affection and friendly words. With these things, a woman would consider herself the most fortunate in the world. And in the case of Aunt Esther, it would be receiving such an affection from you, a brother, since she cannot receive either paternal or maternal affection.

I hope you're all well over there. Here we are experiencing penury in that we do not find things [food] and everything is expensive as Papa is idle after what occurred with Uncle Chelibon. And it is thanks to Rachel and me who are working that we are able to live.

Give kisses to the dear children from me. I believe that they all have grown, and I have a great desire to see them. Let us if you send us their photos. Kisses to Aunt Jamila and Uncle Shelomo. Regards from Papa, Mama, Aunt Esther, Rachel, Haim [Vic], Moshe [Morris], Giaco [Jack] and Regina.

Receive a strong hug from your niece.

Claire

P.S. I am including two photos, one for you and one for Aunt Jamila. They are of Haim and Moshe who by chance had them taken this week.

TRANSLATION

Tangier, July 12, 1942

Dear Uncle Raphael,

No matter how much I search for the reason, I cannot explain your silence. This is too much, and we are very worried. We pray God that you are well.

Dear Uncle Raphael, it is strange coming from you because according to what Mama tells me as I did not have the pleasure of meeting you, you would write a lot and would even send stamps. And is it because you do not have time? But I believe that in two years you must have had a free moment to write a few words just to reassure us. But I believe that you will write us and I hope soon.

Dear Uncle Raphael, you cannot imagine how difficult life is in Tangier. Everything is so expensive, and there is little of everything; especially clothing is out of reach. When we wear out some clothing, we think that we cannot afford replacement. Dear Uncle, food is so expensive that what Rachel and I earn, as Papa is idle, is hardly enough for food. Life is impossible now.

How are you over there? Aunt Rachel and the children, how are they? We are anxious to see them. Perhaps you can send some photos. How are Aunt Jamila and Uncle Shelomo? How happy we would be if we were all together. But unfortunately, this was not possible, and now we realize it more and more. Business is dead here. In Rhodes, we had at least sustenance because Papa worked, but here what Rachel and I earn does not suffice us. And now, *mashala*, we have all grown and it is when we need more resources that the situation is critical. Haim [Vic] and Moshe [Morris] are very tall but very thin for they are at the age that requires good nourishment. And Mama is worried that she cannot do what is needed because, dear Uncle, people are like houses. The stronger the foundation, the longer they last. And thus, if the children are well fed, they will have the strength to bear life's hardships. Things have happened and [we] have no choice but to tolerate them and may God speedily improve them.

Nothing else to add. I hope and I beg you, dear Uncle Raphael, you answer without fail as we worry.

Papa, Mama, Aunt Esther, Rachel, Haim, Moshe, Giaco, and Regina send you kisses. Kisses to Uncle Shelomo and Aunt Jamila. Please Aunt Rachel write also a line. Kisses to the kids. A strong hug from your niece.

Claire

TRANSLATION

Tangier, May 22, 1943

[Letter written by Vic for his mother.]

Dear and esteemed brother Raphael and sister-in-law Rachel Capeluto:

We have received your letter and were very glad to hear that you are in good health; similarly we hope you all are.

Dear ones, it had been almost three years without news, not having received any letters from you. We did not fail to write to you, and it seems that you did not receive them. We sent you photos of the children. We received your photos and were very glad to see you. May you see the kids at their wedding. May God give us the *zehu* to meet you all in good health.

You are inquiring about the whereabouts of the sisters. Dear Behora [Capeluto, both maiden and married name] and family and Mary [Marie Levy] and family are in Rhodes. Gioia [Levy] and Sarina [Maish] are here in Tangier. They all send you regards.

Now, dear ones, we beg you not to let us without news and write once in a while to dear Esther to console her as she lives sorrowfully. With regards to the photos you requested, we will send them shortly because Regina and a twin had typhoid fever and had their hair completely cut.

No more to add. Give regards to dear Jamila and tell her that we were saddened upon learning of the unfortunate death of dear Shelomo. May God give her patience and no more misfortune. Thank God you are all together and she will be somewhat relieved. Kisses to the kids. Regards to your father-in-law Rahamin and family and to the brothers of dear Shelomo.

Dear Avraham sends you regards and not being in the mood, has not written separately. The children send you regards. To you, dear brother and sister-in-law, hugs from your dear

Mazaltov Barchi[43]

---

[43] It's uncertain if Regina and Vic had typhus or typhoid fever. Possibly the family did not know the difference, however, a letter from Claire dated the same day mentions typhus. It is more likely the latter.

Regarding Uncle Shelomo's death, Uncle Ralph was driving Uncle Shelomo somewhere and they were hit by an Army truck. Uncle Shelomo was thrown from the car quite a few yards away and died either at the scene or on the way to the hospital. Uncle Raphael was injured, but obviously recovered.

TRANSLATION

Tangier, May 22, 1943

[Letter from Esther—Part I—to Uncle Ralph]

Dear brother Raphael and sister-in-law Rachel Capeluto:

I write this letter to let you know that we are all very well. We hope you give us good news also, amen.

Dear ones, we have received your esteemed letter and were very glad as we did not have your news and were worried, especially upon receiving the telegram stating that dear Jamila was living with you, making us understand that dear Shelomo died.

Now, we pray God that you have long lives and you see no more sadness.

Dear brother, we can imagine the bad times you had having a kind heart at these dark hours on account of the ill-fated death of dear Shelomo. What can we do? It was the will of Heaven.

Dear brother and dear sister-in-law Rachel, I sincerely hope you console her because being a widow she will bewail a lot the unfortunate death. We pray God you will not be affected that way.[44] Thank God dear Raphael came out without any harm.

Getting away from the subject, we have received the photos of the dear children and were overjoyed to see the beautiful family. My desire is to see you. Dear brother, from the day you promised to bring me to your side I became agitated, but I see it is hopeless. Many times I lose patience so much that I become ill from thinking so much and wonder why I had the bad luck not to be able to leave. But I have the hope that some day we will meet.

I am unable to continue. I beg you to take care of the children. Give regards to your mother-in-law and family. Kisses to dear Rachel and the kids. Dear Avraham (Barkey) and family send you regards.

Bye, your dear younger sister who always thinks of you.

Esther Capeluto

---

[44] Sephardic way of wishing someone well.

TRANSLATION

Tangier, May 22, 1943

[Letter from Esther—Part II—to Jamila]

To my dear sister Jamila Almeleh:

Dear Jamila, I write this short letter to let you know that we are, thank God, in perfect health and hope it finds you well and healthy, amen.

Dear Jamila, we received the bad news about dear Shelomo. It was on a Saturday, and you do not know what an uproar. Everyone crying and above all, crying because he did not see any joy and that his was a violent death.

Dear Jamila, we had great hope that someday we were to meet and remember his jokes and his goodness. What can we do? So willed Heaven. May God give you patience and thank God you are with a good brother and sister-in-law who is like a sister. I can imagine how you are with the dear children. Take care of your health because health is better than anything else.

Dear Jamila, this week we received a letter from dear Behora and they always ask us about all of you and send you regards. We had a twin, Haim, and Regina with typhoid fever at a hospital for three months. That gives you an idea of the little rest we had. Avraham has been for the last three years idle on account of the wicked Chelibon, and life is expensive.

Dear Avraham, Mazaltov, and the children send you regards. Your very dear sister,

Esther Capeluto

TRANSLATION

Tangier, May 22, 1943

Dear Aunt Jamila,

I am sorry that the first letter I write deals with such painful happening. I would have liked to greet you when everything goes well and not be presenting condolences as it behooves me with the present writing. But everything is written and is the will of God. Our destiny is inscribed and we have no choice but to submit to it. We have to take everything with patience and resign ourselves when things happen all of a sudden. Naturally, [word missing] impedes you from crying over him and speak of him for it was unfortunately a death you would not wish to the worst enemy. Had he been sick and bedridden, sinking slowly day by day, one could prepare for the worst. But sending him off healthy into the street and receive him in such a condition is very sad. And even though you may not write anything about it, we can imagine how you were. What can be done? We pray God not to bring us more harm, and may his soul rest in peace and may he pray for us and world peace.

Dear Aunt Jamila, even though I don't know you, from what I hear from Mama you are very dear to me and I would like to be at your side in order to share your sorrow. But our apprehension is diminished at the thought that, thank God, you are not alone. And at Uncle Raphael's house you will be at home for they are very kind and with the children's affection, you will not feel lonely. This is a consolation. May God not forsake anyone.

Dear Aunt Jamila, here we do not have an easy life. It is not easy to make a living, but we hope for better days and we will relate this when the situation is better. As far as food is concerned, we are on a diet without necessity, and we put clothes on in order not to be naked. Last February we had Haim and Regina in the hospital with typhus and had to spend without limit and sell things to save them. And, thank God, they recovered and now we can talk about it. The only thing that worries me is that following this illness good nutrition is needed and this is difficult today be it for lack of things [to sell] and money. We hope that the little they eat will sustain them and replace eggs, milk, meat, et cetera, which would do them so much good.

Dear Aunt Jamila, I would like to prolong my letter, but it is one o'clock at night. I am sleepy and very tired. I will write you more next time. Please remind Uncle Raphael to write to us once in a while, especially to Aunt Esther who worries so much about you.

Papa, Mama, Aunt Esther, the children send you kisses from afar. A big hug from your niece.

Claire

TRANSLATION

Tangier, May 23, 1943

Dear Uncle Raphael and Aunt Rachel,

I could not describe the joy we felt upon receiving your letter. If it had not related the sad news, we would have celebrated. Unfortunately, happiness is never complete, and there is always a cloud; that is, the unfortunate death of Uncle Shelomo which caused us sadness. Had his death been natural, that would have been his destiny as all of us sooner or later have to surrender our souls. But this violent death is very sad and afflicting, and although we have few details, we are aware of the mishap, can imagine the sad picture and understand very well that you cannot erase it from your mind, especially dear Uncle Raphael who was part of it. In what state did he find himself in this horrendous scene? If one feels sorry for a stranger, what would be toward a brother-in-law? No wonder you delayed in writing, and going crazy, we had to send you a telegram. Although your answer was clear, we could not help but suspect something upon learning that Aunt Jamila was living with you. Nor can I explain why we looked at each other as we all had the same idea instinctively. But I abstain from saying anything and Mama the same, but Aunt Esther could not contain herself and said, "It cannot be anything else but something has happened to dear Shelomo." I, to put her mind at ease, told her many things, like the cost of living being high, you were trying to economize, and Aunt Jamila and Uncle Shelomo, being all by themselves, wanted to keep company to the children, et cetera. But upon receiving your letter, our doubt dissipated and saw our suspicions turn into reality, sad reality that one prefers to ignore. Unfortunately, everything is predestined, and we cannot escape from it so that we must resign ourselves and pray God his soul rest in peace and that he pray for the good of his dear ones and the whole world and that everything be normal in order to enable us to lead our lives without fear and in abundance.

Because, dear ones, we have suffered enough until now, with the present scarcity and high cost of everything. Just to mention one thing, we are eating bread of chocolate color and full of dirt. You cannot imagine how difficult it is to get nourishment today, especially in our condition. Papa being idle, no matter how much Rachel and I earn, it is barely enough to feed nine people. As far as clothing is concerned, no use mentioning it; it is out of reach. And Mama is very economical, but we are a large family. We pray God to bring us success and not be in need for here in Tangier people are different, selfish, and distrustful. We hope God will bring all this to a happy end.

Dear ones, inside the letter a little beautiful family came to visit us, and we would not stop looking at it. I don't know who is the most beautiful. They are all a delight. *Mashala*.

Dear Morris is a strapping youth. Betty, Marlene, Mimi are truly little Americans. We also would like to send some pictures, but to take them ourselves we find no film, and at the photographer's it is too expensive and it takes a long time. But we will not delay in sending them anyway. I believe you must have received the photo of Haim and Moshe. As it takes a long time to arrive, perhaps you will receive them after we received your letter dated 19 of November 1942. To show you how it delays, we received it on May 15, 1943.

Willy-nilly, please write more often to give us your news. I do not have time as I am busy at the office until six o'clock in the evening and attend a class of English nursing. And it takes a lot of my time, having to take a test every three months, and I study a lot. Dear Uncle, last year I started to take English lessons and the same instructor advised me to take the class in order to get some practice. I assented fully aware that I could practice the language and learn something useful. Besides, we must be grateful because they are fighting for the good of ours [brethren], and I would have the pleasure of being useful the day they would need me. I have been successful in three tests and have been awarded a certificate for each. I don't speak English fluently, but I understand it very well. And we must admit that it is a difficult language, and I did not know a word of it. The telegram I sent was probably not well written, and you may have made fun of me, but I like to tackle everything with good or bad results, so that I said to myself, "I'll do it and I want no help. They will understand it even though incorrect." And I believe it was so as you understood what I wanted to say. I hope we will not have to use the same means because it is expensive and you will write often.

I believe my letter tired you, but in my case, I would wish to receive a letter from 10 to 20 pages long because the letter you sent us was like a "puff" and contained only two lines. Write a longer one to give us more news.

Mama, Papa, Aunt Esther, and the children send you kisses. An affectionate hug from your niece.

Claire

JULY 9, 1943

———

ALLIED FORCES LANDED IN SICILY TO TAKE ITALY.

JULY 9, 1943

———

MUSSOLINI RESIGNS AS PRIME MINISTER AND IS IMPRISONED.

TRANSLATION

Tangier, August 12, 1943

Dear Uncle Raphael and Aunt Rachel,

Without having the pleasure of answering any letter from you, although it seems to me that it is time to receive one, I hereby expound for you something that I believe you will take care of right away, that is if you have not changed your mind.

It's about looking for a solution in Tangier to send to America, a few at a time, the refugees who are here. This is being dealt with by a Refugee Committee, that is [located] in America, and having representation in Lisbon (Portugal). Being close to here, a Delegate pays us a visit from time to time and the situation improves for those that he deems are having a hard time.

In the past, they made us register the young ones under 18 years of age and we registered everyone starting with me to Regina, but nothing positive came of it. We registered just in case there was no harm to it and always it is better to register in case something happens and to remind them of us.

Now I believe things are different and there is talk of something more serious and what they ask us to submit a letter from a relative who could receive us as immigrants and this is to be done as soon as possible. I believe you will not delay in sending it to us. The mail takes so long to arrive, but it is better if you take care of sending this letter as soon as possible to avoid wasting time. The letter should state that you could assume the charge of those you sponsor and that they will not be a "public charge," as you call it. The sponsorship should be made in three letters:

1. For Haim (Victor), Moshe (Morris) and Jacob (Jack) Barki

2. For Esther Capelouto

3. For Abraham, Matilda, Clara, Rachel, Haim (Victor), Moshe (Morris), Jacob (Jack) and Regina BARKI

The first one for the boys, who are not older than 17 years, would perhaps be admitted first. Besides, they are young men and we do not want them to remain in Tangier because here there is too much perdition [moral decay].

The second one is for Aunt Esther. Since she's not part of the same family, it should be separate.

And the third one for the whole family in case it becomes necessary when needed, we will have the letter ready.

I think that I have given you all the details and you will have no problem in sending us the letters as soon as possible. You must know that the expenses of the journey will be incurred by the above mentioned committee.

Dear aunt and uncle, there is no need to repeat that the good results of this action will be owed to you and we will not fail to repay you properly. Our happiness will be to be able to show you our gratitude.

Everyone is well. We hope to hear the same from you. Heartfelt kisses from the children to Aunt Jamila.

Papa, mama, aunt Esther, the boys and girls send you kisses. You will excuse me if I'm not writing at length as it is getting late to send this letter and I'm afraid that it may miss the plane. Kissing you with all my heart,

Your niece who hopes to see you soon.

Claire

SEPTEMBER 3, 1943

———

ITALY SIGNS ON WITH THE ALLIES. IT SETS THE STAGE FOR HITLER TO INVADE ITALY.

SEPTEMBER 12, 1943

———

BRITISH INVADE THE DODECANESE ISLANDS. THEN THE GERMANS INVADE IN OCTOBER AND NOVEMBER.

JUNE 4, 1944

———

ROME IS LIBERATED.

TRANSLATION

Tangier, June 22, 1944

Dear Uncle Raphael and Aunt Rachel:

I have just received your esteemed letter of May 31, 1944, and as you see it did not delay reaching us, which is strange due to the present situation.

I cannot describe the joy we felt, no matter how much I write, by reading your letter and especially with so much hope. We pray God to smooth the way, fulfilling thus our wish.

Dear ones, I thank you very much for busying yourselves with this matter that concerns us, and I already wrote to you the local Committee is ready to help us. To be exact, I must tell you that among the refugees who came to Tangier, the majority are registered for Palestine and they await the boat anytime. Perhaps when you receive the present writing, they would have left. Another group, that is most of them Polish, German, Hungarian, in short Ashkenazi, are on the list for Canada, and to these also the hour is approaching because this week a delegation with a doctor arrived and they are going through the medical examinations. Very few ill remain here; that is, those on the list for the U.S. and the too old who are not allowed to go to Palestine. Aunt Sarina and Gioia and their families are registered for Palestine.

We, dear ones, besides our desire to be at your side, are also interested in the boys' future. As far as the girls are concerned, it is something else, but the boys must forge their future so that tomorrow they will be able to fend for themselves and not rely on anyone. Palestine did not appeal to me since the beginning because, first of all, we do not want again to be among Moors [Arabs], and it is also difficult to make a living with all the people who found refuge there. Do not think that those destined for Palestine will be in the big cities, but out in the countryside, in bungalows [cabins] because they want to extend the limits. As you see, it is very hard to start earning a livelihood anew, and this type of work is not for our brothers. A family who left two months ago wrote that you cannot find housing and life is difficult over there. You will thus understand that the place is not for us. Besides this, dear Uncle Raphael, we are tired of moving. We had enough suffering in Tangier.

Life has not been easy for us, and all of us work without hardly being able to earn for food, each one in his own way. I am in the office until the evening, and then I must help Rachel to darn silk stockings together with Aunt Esther. It is a type of work that brings in some income, but tires you enormously. Everything is done by hand and not by machine; that is why we have a lot of customers. But you must hold the needle steady and pick up stitch by stitch. This affects everything. Because of our being busy, Mama must do all the housework without our help. Anyway, we hope to see the end of this and to forget the past.

Papa, it would seem strange, as I noted on the enclosed papers, tired of being idle, had no choice but to learn something, and as he learns everything quickly, is now making shoes, not for other people as unfortunately he would need a capital to buy material and the capital ended up in somebody else's hands, and a shop and in Tangier you do not find an empty hole as there are many war refugees. For us his trade is good because he always finds something to make and we don't worry in this respect.

Dear ones, as soon as I received your letter, I went to the Committee which takes care of us and asked for the same papers as previously filled in. An employee gave them to me. I would have preferred talking to the Delegate who handed them to us last time, but he is not in Tangier. Enclosed I am sending these forms which are similar to those sent to America, and I made a copy which I will send by mail separately next week with a copy of my letter just in case this mail is lost. I believe you will need more details than appear here, and we hope to be lucky this time with God's help. I beg you not to be negligent and do the necessary and as quickly as possible because this is the opportune moment. As you stated, "Hot pitas have a different taste." From here the Committee has already sent the papers, and we hope they arrive in good time.

It is impossible to describe the joy to know that perhaps we will meet soon. We are building up hopes and castles in the air. Mama thinks it is a dream with only thinking that soon she will meet dear Uncle Raphael for you loved each other so much. And as far as my feelings are concerned, I can't begin to explain. I feel that I am floating in the air and hope that everything will not be in vain as it will bring a great disillusionment.

Dear Aunt Esther does not consider us anymore as nephews [and nieces]. She only says, "When I join my brother, you will not see my 'mug.'" Tell Morris, Betty, Marlene, and Mimi that if they are glad to see us, we are doubly happy and wishing it every day. They will see that when we get there, they will be our brothers and friends, and you too. Anyway, everything is destiny and hope ours is favorable.

Regarding Aunt Jamila, although it did not cause a surprise, we were glad because we understand that over there it is different from these parts, and she did very well. We wish her much happiness and may they live to a ripe old age. I suppose she is also very glad to know that there is some hope of seeing us. Please give her a kiss and tell her I especially wish her much happiness.

Dear Uncle and Aunt, in reference to what you wrote regarding Aunt Behora and Marie, I must inform you that we have not received any news in the last eight or nine months. It is even more difficult to receive news from Rhodes than from Italy, it being an island and in German hands. I twice sent letters through the International Red Cross, but I have yet to receive an answer. Undoubtedly they must suffer, but we pray they are alive and healthy and that all this ends as soon as possible. We have not received any news for some time from the daughters of Aunt Behora, residing in Egypt.[45] I sent them a telegram this week but have received no answer. Even the telegrams take a long time. I hope they have received the telegram because

---

[45] The Capeluto cousins from Cairo (Vida and Rosa's sister) were named Rachel Israel and Matilde Cherez. It is believed that Rachel's daughter married a son of Gioia in Israel.

the address I had was old. Perhaps they have moved, but I sent it taking a chance.

From Haim Capeluto, Aunt Behora's son who is in the Belgian Congo, we received through the Belgian Consulate during Passover 10 pounds sterling without a letter. As I did not know his address, I sent a letter through an acquaintance of Papa who resides in the Congo. The latter handed it to him, and last week we received another 10 pounds sterling for us and 10 for Esther, but this time at our address, which proves that he received our letter, but without a word from him. I don't know why there are lazy people who do not like to write to those who worry about them. We would have preferred receiving his news rather than money. I am awaiting an answer to the telegram I sent to Cairo in order to write to him and give news of his sisters and family who are in Rhodes; that is, if Matilde and Rachel give us news. This situation, besides having hurt us, disturbed us even more because we are without news of the dear ones, those who fight for a just and noble cause, and free the world of the tyranny and save the Jews who unfortunately are the people who most suffer.

I believe I have written enough or you will call me a pest. But, when I start typing, no one can stop me, and I keep on writing and don't realize that I have filled pages and that the letter will weigh a lot. I can't help it. The solution will come when I will be with you. I will not write, but will relate it all, as I have many things to relate, things about all my life.

That's all for now, and I hope this letter does not cost me more than double postage.

Kisses to Morris, Marlene, Amelia from all of us. Regards to Aunt Jamila with her husband[46] and all our acquaintances. All the relatives send regards. Papa, Mama, Aunt Esther, Rachel, Haim, Moshe, Jacques, and Regina send you kisses.

Many hugs and kisses from your dear niece who wishes to see you soon.

Claire

JULY 7, 1944

ALL THE JEWS OF RHODES ARE INTERNED BY TRUCK BY THE GERMANS AS POLITICAL PRISONERS AND EVENTUALLY TAKEN TO AUSCHWITZ.

---

[46] Aunt Jamila remarried Abraham Huniu from Portland, Ore.

Seattle-First National Bank

Seattle, Washington

August 11, 1944

American Consul or American Authorities

Gentlemen:

Mr. Ralph Capeluto, who has been a valued customer of ours for a number of years, informs us that he is negotiating to bring in to this country a number of his relatives who are now residing at Tangier, Morocco.

At his request we are pleased to inform you that Mr. Capeluto is carrying a good personal account with us. He is one of the partners of the Seattle Curtain Manufacturing Company, which firm has also been a client of ours ever since it commenced business in 1930. They are carrying a very desirable account with us, and in the past we have granted the company credit accommodation in connection with its business up to $40,000, most of which has been upon an unsecured basis. And in addition to this, we have also made them substantial loans for the purpose of purchasing United States Government bonds. The financial statement of the Seattle Curtain Manufacturing Company as of December 31, 1943 indicates a net worth in excess of $90,000 with an excellent position of affairs reflected. Mr. Capeluto owns one-half of this business, and we understand that he also has other assets, which, in our opinion, would bring his personal net worth over $50,000. We regard him as being a man of excellent character and reliability and believe that he is in a position to fully protect his reasonable commitments.

Very truly yours,

[Frank Jerome][47]

Vice President

FEJ:KB

---

[47] All letters from the bank over initials "FEJ" are from Frank Jerome.

Seattle-First National Bank

Seattle, Washington

August 12, 1944

Mr. Ralph Capeluto

Seattle Curtain Manufacturing Company

Prefontaine Building

Seattle, Washington

Dear Ralph:

I am pleased to enclose an original and three copies of a letter addressed to the American Consul or American Authorities regarding the subject about which we talked yesterday.

I trust that this is the type of letter required.

With kindest regards,

Very truly yours,

Vice President

FEJ:MB Encls.

TO WHOM IT MAY CONCERN:

This is to certify that Charles B. Alhadeff, partner in the Whiz Fish Products Company and the Palace Fish and Oyster Company, 1525 Alaskan Way, Seattle, Washington, in my opinion, is financially able to guarantee that any person sponsored by him for immigration into the United States will not become a public charge.

Certified Public Accountant

5505 White Building

Seattle, Washington

September 11, 1944

Seattle-First National Bank

Seattle, Washington

September 12, 1944

Mr. Ralph Capeluto

Seattle Curtain Manufacturing Company

Prefontaine Building

Seattle 4, Washington

Dear Ralph:

At the request of Mr. Charles Alhadeff, I am enclosing a letter in quadruplicate, which I hope will serve your purpose.

With kindest regards,

Very truly yours,

Vice President

FEJ:MB Encls.

Seattle-First National Bank

Seattle, Washington

September 12, 1944

TO WHOM IT MAY CONCERN:

We understand that Mr. Charles D. Alhadeff has issued his guaranty in connection with the support of aliens which are being brought into this country, and we have been requested by Mr. Alhadeff to write this letter to vouch for his ability to carry out the requirements of the aforementioned guaranty.

Mr. Alhadeff has been known to us for many years, and we consider him to be a man of excellent character and reliability. He is one of the partners of the Whiz Fish Products Company and the Palace Fish and Oyster Company. And in connection with the business operations of these firms, we have granted them a substantial line of unsecured credit which has always been handled in a most satisfactory manner. We are sufficiently familiar with Mr. Alhadeff's affairs to know that he is well qualified to execute the guaranty under discussion, and we consider him abundantly responsible for such obligations as he may incur there under.

Very truly yours,

Vice President

FEJ:MB

TRANSLATION

Tangier, September 29, 1944

Dear Uncle and Aunt:

I hereby am confirming my letter of June 26, 1944, and I am enclosing a copy thereof, although I do not deem it necessary because of the two copies I sent. One must surely have reached you, but I am doing it to be more sure and because it contains information that you may need.

Dear ones, as you will observe, my last letter is dated three months ago and it is strange not to have received an answer from you as here people have been continually receiving mail from the United States within short periods of time. We would like to receive more often news from you as we have the good fortune of exchanging letters. Unfortunately, we cannot do this with all the relatives, and it is a pity to waste time and not even write a couple of lines.

Dear ones, as I wrote to you in a previous letter, I sent a telegram on June 19 to Cairo inquiring about the daughters of Aunt Behora. Upon seeing that there was no answer, I wrote a letter. You see that I am not lazy, and it is I who has to write to all the relatives in order to receive news from them; otherwise, there is no way to find out anything. Anyway, this does not bother me, and it all depends on my time. And to satisfy Mama who worried about everybody, I do it with pleasure.

This is what prompted me to decide to write for the confirmation of my telegram. This week I received a letter from one of them in which they acknowledge receipt of the same. It is strange that I did not receive theirs because in my office we receive regularly telegrams from Egypt. But since this is a telegram from a private person and not commercial, perhaps the censor did not allow it. In the present situation, you cannot trace anything, but the main thing is that we received their news.

As far as our relatives from Rhodes are concerned, they find themselves in the same situation, without news for more than one year. It is very sad, and I hope all of this will be over in favor of those who defend a just and noble cause.

Dear ones, in the matter that concerns us, that is, our entry into the U.S. there is something I want to make clear. After having received your letter wherein you told us that you need all the exact dates of birth, etc., the Committee received many letters from the Immigration Department of Washington informing them that in what concerns the relative guarantors for the refugees residing in Tangier, they are taking the necessary steps to bring them over. This is because of the documents we filed here. The delegate who handed us the papers sent them to Washington after being filed. All the guarantors were called in and helped by the American Jewish Joint Distribution Committee in doing the necessary. Of all those destined for America, we are the only ones not called in by the local Committee. That is strange because we really thought we were supposed to be among the first for you had given us so much hope in your letter. Please write to us more often to avoid despair. For you it is easier since you are in Washington[48] while many people have relatives in Atlanta, New York, and other far away places. And even so, they have received the notification. Again, I beg you not to neglect things and to get busy as soon as possible. I could write every day to remind you, but I would not want to bother you any more than necessary. But if you really have the intention of bringing us over, take care of things as soon as you can before it is too late. You yourselves said that this is the opportunity and it is a shame to lose it.

Other people who had less guarantee than us have already been advised that they endeavoring over there, and with a little goodwill, everything will come to a good end. Excuse me if I am annoying, but I already told you that besides my wish to know you closely, there is the question of my brothers' future, and I do not want to miss the opportunity.

I can't find anything else to add. Everyone here is well. We hope all of you are the same. On the occasion of the holidays, I wish you and your family much happiness and a long life, and may we have the *zehut* to spend future festivities together.

Papa, Mama, Aunt Esther, Rachel, Haim, Moshe, Giaco, and Regina send you big hugs and kisses.

Regards to Aunt Jamila, her husband. Regards from Aunt Sarina and Aunt Gioia and their respective families.

Kisses to the children from me. And to you, dear Uncle and Aunt, with all my affection I close this letter hoping to have the pleasure of reading your letters. Kisses from your niece who wishes to be at your side very soon.

Claire

---

[48] Claire thought perhaps that Washington state was the capitol or the central bureau as many people were unaware at that period that Washington state was not Washington, D.C.

October 7, 1944

Visa Division of the State Dept.

Dear Sirs:

Since it is not possible for me to personally appear at one of your IVRC hearings, I thru this letter ask and plead that advisory approval be given my sisters, brother-in-law, nieces and nephews for eventual admission into the country. To further assist you in reaching a favorable decision in this case I herewith will give you, to the best of my knowledge, a biographical statement concerning the members of the family group in question.

Mr. Abraham Barki, was a resident of the city of Aidin in Turkey. In 1918 during the Turko-Greek conflict this city was destroyed and burned by the advancing Greek hordes, who had landed at Smyrna. He fled the city losing all worldly possessions and entered the Island of Rhodes, in the Aegean Group which at that time had been under Italian military occupation since the Italo-Turkish war of 1912.

Here he began life anew by becoming an ambulant merchant, a way of securing a livelihood followed by many in that part of the world.

After three years in this occupation he found a job in a department store as a salesman and remained there until 1939. Meantime in 1924 the Dodecanese group by consent of the Allied Powers became an Italian possession and all residents therein were granted Italian citizenship. In that

In that year 1938, when Germany and Italy or rather their Fuehrers officially joined hands, the Nuremberg Laws long in effect in Germany, and intended for the ultimate destruction of all men, women and children of the Hebrew faith were promulgated in Italy. He was one of the first victims of this decree of expulsion which gave those residents in the Island of Rhodes of foreign birth six months in which to leave. Meantime shortly after his settling in Rhodes, Mr. Barki married Matilda Capeluto, sister of the undersigned and have had six children by their marriage.

Letter dated October 7, 1944. Copy of letter from Ralph Capeluto to the U.S. State Department Visa Division outlining the Barkey family's plight and asking the committee to approve the family's visa request.

-2-

Visa Division of the State Dept.

In 1939 he was forced to leave Rhodes with his entire family of
six, taking also with them Esther Capeluto, a younger sister of
Mrs. Barki, as well as a sister of the petitioner. The only place
that offered refuge at that time for the evacuees was the International zone of Tangier, Morocco. There the family moved and Mr.
Barki learned the shoe repairing trade as it was not possible to
find employment in the positions which he previously had filled
elsewhere.

He has been in Tangier ever since struggling to eke a mere existence for his family. In this task he has been assisted by two of
his daughters, one being an accomplished bookkeeper with shorthand
and typing at her command, and the other being a specialist at sock
darning. Claire, the bookkeeper, has also been active in British
Red Cross work and is the proud possessor of certificates covering
the fields of Home Nursing, First Aid and Hygiene and Sanitation.
Mrs. Barki has always been a housewife and can read and write her
mother tongue of Ladino Spanish. Among the members of the family
the following languages are spoken: Spanish, French, Italian, Greek,
Turkish and one member only, namely Claire having some knowledge
of the English language. All the children have had at least elementary education and the older ones were a little more fortunate to
obtain the equivalent of our highschool training.

The family has always carried on with dignity and always inspired
the respect of all of those with who they came in contact. They
have always been affiliated with the Orthodox branch of the Hebrew
Faith and are God fearing and law abiding citizens in whichever
country they may have lived.

Thru conditions imposed upon them by tyrannical governments and the
vicissitudes of war they have been uprooted from their homes and
forced to leave behind their small worldly belongings.

In view of their present suffering and the extreme likelihood that
the future does not hold much promise for him and his growing children, I pledge myself to support them upon their admittance into the
country, and thru affidavits properly drawn and executed which have
already been forwarded to the proper authorities, I further show
my willingness and financial ability to support these distressed
members of my family.

-3-

Visa Division of the State Dept.

I therefore pray that a favorable verdict might be reached as regard my petition.

                          Sincerely,

RC/ml

October 7, 1944

[To the] Visa Division of the State Department

Dear Sirs:

Since it is not possible for me to personally appear at one of your IVRC [Interdepartmental Visa Review Committee] hearings, I, through this letter, ask and plead that advisory approval be given my sisters, brother-in-law, nieces, and nephews for eventual admission into the country. To further assist you in reaching a favorable decision in this case I herewith will give you, to the best of my knowledge, a biographical statement concerning the members of the family group in question.

Mr. Abraham Barki was a resident of the city of Aidin in Turkey. In 1918 during the Turko-Greek conflict this city was destroyed and burned by the advancing Greek hordes that had landed at Smyrna. He fled the city, losing all worldly possessions and entered the Island of Rhodes in the Aegean Group, which at that time had been under Italian military occupation since the Italo-Turkish war of 1912.

Here he began life anew by becoming an ambulant merchant, a way of securing a livelihood followed by many in that part of the world.

After three years in this occupation he found a job in a department store as a salesman and remained there until 1939. Meantime, in 1924 the Dodecanese group by consent of the allied [word unclear] became an Italian possession and all residents therein were granted Italian citizenship.

In 1938, when Germany and Italy or rather their Fuehrers officially joined hands, the Nuremberg Laws long in effect in Germany and intended for the ultimate destruction of all men, women, and children of the Hebrew faith were promulgated in Italy. He was one of the first victims of this decree of expulsion which gave those residents in the Island of Rhodes of foreign birth six months in which to leave. Meantime, shortly after his settling in Rhodes, Mr. Barki married Mathilda Capeluto, sister of the undersigned and has had six children by their marriage.

In 1939 he was forced to leave Rhodes with his entire family of six, taking also with them Esther Capeluto, a younger sister of Mrs. Barki, as well as a sister of the petitioner. The only place that offered refuge at that time for the evacuees was the International zone of Tangier, Morocco. There the family moved, and Mr. Barki learned the shoe repairing trade as it was not possible to find employment in the positions which he previously had filled elsewhere.

He has been in Tangier ever since, struggling to eke a mere existence for this family. In this task he has been assisted by two of his daughters, one being an accomplished bookkeeper with shorthand and typing at her command, and the other being a specialist at sock darning. Claire, the bookkeeper, has also been active in British Red Cross work and is the proud possessor of certificates covering the fields of Home Nursing, First Aid, and Hygiene and Sanitation. Mrs. Barki has always been a housewife and can read and write her mother tongue of Ladino Spanish. Among the members of the family the following languages are spoken: Spanish, French, Italian, Greek, Turkish, and one member only, namely Claire, having some knowledge of the English language. All the children have had at least elementary education, and the older ones were a little more fortunate to obtain the equivalent of our high school training.

The family has always carried on with dignity and always inspired the respect of all of those with whom they came in contact. They have always been affiliated with the Orthodox branch of the Hebrew Faith and are God-fearing and law-abiding citizens in whichever country they may have lived.

Through conditions imposed upon them by tyrannical governments and the vicissitudes of war they have been uprooted from their homes and forced to leave behind their small worldly belongings.

In view of their present suffering and the extreme likelihood that the future does not hold much promise for him and his growing children, I pledge myself to support them upon their admittance into the country. And through affidavits properly drawn and executed which have already been forwarded to the proper authorities, I further show my willingness and financial ability to support these distressed members of my family.

I therefore pray that a favorable verdict might be reached as regard my petition.

Sincerely,

RC/mi[49]

---

[49] This letter is not signed, but it has Ralph Capeluto's initials on it. All further letters initialed in this way are from Ralph Capeluto.

Wire—October 11, 1944

We left today for Malaga-Spain. Probably will arrive in New York June 6, 1944.

Please notify Larry Huggs [sic], Mama, Rachel, Regina, and Claire.[50]

---

[50] Although this telegram was in Claire's papers, it was either misdated or contains an erroneous date in the body of the message. Either way, it's clear the family did not leave at this time.

TRANSLATION

Wire dated October 11, 1944

I CONFIRM MY LETTER OF 6/22 FAMILIES REGISTERED FOR AMERICA RECEIVING NOTIFICATION VIA COMMITTEE. PLEASE WRITE RESULTS OUR PAPERS.

ABRAHAM BARKI

TRANSLATION

Postcard dated October 25, 1944

Dear Uncle Raphael:

We have received the wire of October 18 and, as you will notice, it was received after six days when we were starting to despair, thinking you had not received ours. I thank you very much for having at least let us know that you had not forgotten us. I think this is the fastest means and thinking perhaps that you need this urgently, I am hereby sending you the addresses you requested on the aforementioned wire.

Albert Cherez

167 Rue Kobessi

1, Rue Amin El Dawla

Le Claire, Egypte

Haim D. Capeluto

Mueka (Congo Belge)

Also, if it may concern you somewhat regarding the papers, here is the address of the son of Aunt Rizula

Salvator Levy

c/o Levy Freres

Bakua Kenge (Congo Belge)

with whom I exchange letters very often and who is very well. I hope to receive the letter from mentioned in the wire. With all the affection from all the family to all of you, I send you kisses.

Claire[51]

---

[51] Haim D. Capeluto was the son of Aunt Behora Capeluto. The "D" stands for David. It was the custom to add the father's initial after the first name, similar to the custom in parts of the U.S. of having two first names, or when Catholics add the name of their saint.

Salvator Levy is the brother of Rahamin Levy of Toronto. He and Claire were very good friends, besides being cousins. Family members suspected that he had romantic feelings for Claire, but she did not return them.

TRANSLATION

Tangier, November 15, 1944

Dear Uncle and Aunt:

I have received your long awaited letter of the 18th of October, and naturally I am answering it immediately. I can't describe the joy we felt upon reading it, especially in its affectionate manner. We hope as you do that God will make everything easy and will grant us our mutual wish.

Dear ones, you do not know how much consolation your letters bring us, and it is true that everyone is busy with his own affairs, but even a couple of lines once in a while would not be too much and with a little effort and goodwill you will let the pen slide swiftly over the paper [letter]. This means a lot to us for, as you know, we are depending on your proceedings and results.

Dear ones, in reference to the papers, I believe you have taken a step forward, but what I wish to know is if there is some hope over there. We are nine, and you're right if you find it difficult. God be with us and perhaps a miracle will occur to make us lucky to leave. We have seen many little miracles, especially in this war. Perhaps the Lord will remember us and cause them to have goodwill over there.

Dear ones, as I said in my previous letter, here all the families are registered for the Americas, and each one is receiving in turn through the Refugee Committee of Tangier notifications that the Society in America is contacting the relatives in order for them to do what is needed. It seems strange that this very Society, having our papers brought by the Delegate who was in Tangier, has not written to you about the matter. I must add that at the end of the month a family will leave, but I believe this is a special case and it concerns a son who is in America and who brings his mother and his brother. This is easier. This is a matter that cannot be repeated because the voyage expenses are small and everything was paid for. Even the boat captains were reserved, and they did not have to spend anything. It will be the same in our case. The main thing is for people over there to accept. May God instill in them goodwill.

Dear Uncle and dear Aunt, to be truthful we had already started to despair and to lose hope. Everything was working against us, the matter of the son of Aunt Rachel's uncle, your being busy, etc. But, thank God, everything fell into place, and God did not want that my father become embittered like many others who unfortunately fell victims to the tyrants. We hope and wish to see everything end with the victory of the Allies and that our fears end and that we receive good news from our dear ones. This worries us so much. It is so sad to be without news from Rhodes. We do not know what to think or what means to use to hear from them. Let it be until God wills and we hope our fears will dissipate.

Dear Uncle and dear Aunt, we must inform you that last week dear Aunt Sarina, her husband, and family departed for Palestine. They left in a Portuguese boat which arrived with more refugees from Lisbon and Spain. Very few left Tangier because there was no room. Leon Levy, the son of Aunt Marie, also left. Aunt Gioia and family will leave with the next boat, and we believe in a few weeks. Thus, we are being separated and remain all by ourselves until the day when our wish to join you is fulfilled.

Dear ones, I entreat you to write more often, even a few lines, bringing us up to date concerning the papers and the results from the N.Y. Refugee Committee as we cannot let things lay dormant in their hands. And it is necessary to remind them periodically. Thanks for all you have done and for what you will do for us; someday we will repay you.

Dear ones, as far as the addresses of Cairo and Belgian Congo are concerned, upon receiving your wire I sent them by postcard. In case you do not receive it, here they are again:

Monsieur Albert Cherez

107 Rue Kobessi

or 1 Rue Amn El Dawla

Le Caire (Egypte)

Monsiur Hiam D. Capeluto

Commercant (Merchant)

Mweka (Congo Belge)

Also I add the address of

Monsieur Salvator D. Levy

Commercant (Merchant)

Bakia Renge (Congo Belge)

He is the son of Aunt Rizula[52] with whom we exchange letters frequently and who is well off. I add this in case it may be useful for the papers.

Nothing else to add except to repeat my plea to you not to leave us without a letter. Just pretend you are answering a business letter which is not too long and would satisfy me even though short. Not a bad idea!

Dear ones, in reference to the money you sent to Aunt Esther, we received in the month of March through the British Bank of Tangier by instructions from the Standard Bank of South Africa Ltd. of N.Y. the sum of $98.50, which with the transfer fees, etc., would amount to $100. After that we received nothing until now. I say it if by chance you have sent anything additional. I thank you for your concern as well as Aunt Jamila's. Please tell her it is a well appreciated gesture.

---

[52] Married to David Levy.

Regards to all the relatives. Kisses to Aunt Jamila and her husband. To my dear little cousins, Morris, Betty, Marlene, and Amelia affectionate kisses. From here, Mama, Papa, Aunt Esther, Rachel, Hiam, Moshe, Giaco, and Regina send you kisses.

Many, many hugs and kisses from your niece who greatly desires to see you.

Claire

TRANSLATION

Tangier, December 20, 1944

Dear Uncle and Aunt:

I am hereby confirming my letter dated November 15, old by now, and without being able to write to you as the end of the year approaches and you're well aware of the work that exists in all the offices. I am writing today, though a few lines, in order not to let you without news and to inform you of the following:

The 15th of this month we received from the Banco Espanol del Credito of Tangier a letter inviting Aunt Esther to withdraw the sum of 1,090 Spanish pesetas, equivalent to $100, at the rate of exchange of 10.9 to the dollar. The sum was remitted as per instructions from the Madrid branch which had received the money from the Public National Bank & Trust Co., of New York.

Dear ones, Aunt Esther could certainly make good use of it. As you will wonder, she was obliged to send it back for the following reason: You must know that in Tangier there is free money market and it varies every day or twice or three times a day as it is an international zone. The dollar is worth 17 to 18 Spanish pesetas. Going through Spain this varies and as you have seen, the dollars are valued at 10.9 pesetas. It is almost a loss of 75 percent of its value. Aunt Esther and I went to the Bank when we found out they would not exchange it at 17 or 18 pesetas. We asked them to give us a check for $100 and as an excuse we told them that Aunt Esther did not need the pesetas as she was leaving for America. They told us at the Bank that since it went through Madrid, they could not give us a check. The only solution, not to arouse suspicion that our intention was to exchange it at a higher rate, was to tell them that Aunt Esther was leaving very soon and having done all her shopping, it would be better to send back the money and that her brother would give it to her in America. We had to write a letter to that effect, so do not be surprised if they return the check, and you will understand that we acted wisely. Why should they earn 700 pesetas if Aunt Esther needs it more? Upon receiving it, it is better to send it through Standard Bank of South Africa Ltd. of N.Y. as you did last time. We will thus be able to exchange it at a higher rate in the Market.

It seems that we are unwillingly dealing in business in this letter. Just to keep you up to date with the Tangier "black market."

Now, to what concerns us; that is, our leaving for America. Last week a family of refugees left for California. That is really luck. Being our neighbor, we noticed that the expenses that the Committee incurred were not few. It is an opportunity that could hardly repeat itself. It is a pity that we cannot profit by it. As long as you do not write, we do not know what to think, whether you have done anything or not. Do not neglect the matter and write often to the National Refugee Service of New York, asking for news about results of our papers. You have to inconvenience these people once in a while, even though they may not like it;

otherwise, they do not remember us. I would like to be able to do something, but I do not see any solution. As you are the ones who wrote to them, you can write again.

Dear Uncle Raphael, it seems I am taking advantage of your kindness and have bothered you enough, but everything is justified by our wish to leave Tangier and for the good of my brothers. It seems a pity for them to waste time when at their age they should be working for their future. All of this would end at the destined hour and I wish it to be soon.

Dear ones, be as it may, do not leave us without a letter. I will do likewise. Please write if you have news from the Refugee Committee of New York, where you sent the papers. I believe in your next letter we will receive some well-founded hope.

Dear ones, you will excuse if this letter is badly written and is not long. It is 8:00 a.m., and the office does not open until nine. I came in early to write to you, and I am almost sleepy. It is early and somewhat dark, being wintertime. But, I do not worry; it is for my uncle and aunt, and they will not judge me badly. They know me well enough even though through exchange of letters. I wish we would know each other from near. May this wish be fulfilled, amen!

Dear ones, my brothers asked me to include with this letter some snapshots they took while on an excursion this week with some friends. They took them with the intention of sending them to you, even though they did not include their friends. They are only of the three of them alone. They told me it is for you to start to get to know them and they wished to receive also some photos from you. I believe you will send them with your next letter, even if they are small.

We are all in good health, thank God. We hope you are too. Affectionate regards to Aunt Jamila and her husband. Kisses to Morris, Becky (Betty), Marlene, Amelia (Mimi). Regards to all the acquaintances. Regards from Aunt Gioia and her family.

Papa, Mama, Aunt Esther, Rachel, Moshe, Haim, Jacques, and Regina send you kisses. Kisses from the depth of my soul.

Your niece who wishes to see you soon.

Claire

TRANSLATION

Tangier, January 24, 1945

Dear Uncle and Aunt:

Without having the pleasure of answering any of your letters, I confirm my last letter of December 20th, 1944, copy attached. It seems strange not to have received your news, which worries us a lot. Mama and Aunt Esther do not stop asking me to wire you, but I deceive them by telling them to wait a little week longer and perhaps we will receive with the next arrival of mail. Weeks go by without your letters. This is deplorable as we are here pending with the expectation of some news, thus spending the time and living with hope.

Now, dear ones, please write to us about the papers. That concerns us greatly and we would like to know the results.

Dear ones, we received today a letter from the Banco Espanol de Credito, inviting us to withdraw the sum of 1,090 pesetas, the equivalent of $100. Also the same thing occurred as in the previous one for Aunt Esther. The loss is greater this time as the market rose to 22 pesetas and the bank, as you see, wanted to pay us at 10.9 pesetas. Again, we addressed a letter to the bank, asking them to return the check to you. You will receive it, and it would be best to send it through the Standard Bank of South Africa Ltd. of New York. We would be thankful and grateful.

What concerns us, dear ones, is not any money or a lottery win, but to be at your side. Please do not neglect this matter and as I told you, it is a great opportunity and it is a pity we cannot take advantage of it. Please write again repeatedly to the Committee of New York where you sent the papers to make them move and remember us.

All of us are well. Papa, Mama, Aunt Esther, Rachel, Haim, Moshe, Jacques, and Regina send you hugs.

Receive a strong and affectionate hug from your niece who wishes to see you very soon.

Claire

RALPH AND RACHEL CAPELUTO IN AMERICA

A lthough it seemed to Claire that sometimes her letters would go unread or unanswered in Seattle, that was far from the truth. Most likely some letters got lost in transit, suggests Ralph and Rachel's son Morris.

When the letters arrived, the Capeluto family would sit around the dinner table and Rachel would read them to Ralph. Every night the family would gather at 6 p.m. to listen to Gabriel Heater's news broadcast. The family would sit quietly and listen to updates from the war overseas, knowing that their relatives were over there and in some way were involved.

After the news Rachel would read the latest letter from Claire and she and Ralph would discuss what their next step would be to help bring the family to the United States. Ralph would then dictate a response to Rachel, who would write the letter.

He was the type of man who helped anyone who sought his assistance. Unlike many other immigrants, he did not seek assistance from others when he entered the United States, but that didn't stop him from giving to those in need. It is with those values that he vowed to help bring his sister Mazaltov and her family to the United States, and he did it quietly, preferring to work in the background instead of boasting about his deeds.

Coming from abroad, Ralph was uncomfortable with his foreign accent and lack of higher education. He let his wife act as the main spokesperson and communicator for the family. Although his name was on many of the official documents needed to bring his relatives to the United States, the couple worked in tandem.

Rachel, who entered the United States as a toddler, not only graduated from high school, but unlike many Sephardic girls, went on to business school. She was a woman who participated in every activity she could—from sports to music—and always took on leadership roles.

During the war, even as she helped bring the Barkey family to the United States, she worked on other war efforts, selling government bonds in Seattle's Victory Square, and gathering together a group of Sephardic women to sew blankets. She was the type of person who would do anything for anybody.

ADDRESS OFFICIAL COMMUNICATIONS TO
THE SECRETARY OF STATE
WASHINGTON, D. C. **25**

Visa Form IVRC—2

DEPARTMENT OF STATE
WASHINGTON

In reply refer to visa case
VD 811.111 Barki, Abraham

February 2, 1945.

Mr. Ralph Capeluto,
807 Thirtieth Avenue South,
Seattle, Washington.

Sir:

An examination of this case under the regulations
covering the control of persons entering the United
States indicates that a favorable recommendation to
the American consular officer concerned is not warranted at the present time. However, the case will be
considered by the Interdepartmental Visa Review Committee at Washington and an opportunity will be given
to interested individuals to appear in person or
through an attorney or other intermediary before the
Committee to make additional statements and answer
possible questions. A form of Application for Appearance is attached.

To persons filing Applications for Appearance,
notice of hearing will be sent at least ten days in
advance of the date set for the hearing. If, on the
other hand, it is desired that the case be considered
without a hearing, it is requested that the Department
be so advised.

Very truly yours,

Howard K. Travers
Chief, Visa Division

Enclosure:

Form IVRC-1.

Letter dated February 2, 1945. Letter from Visa Division of the U.S. State Department to Ralph
Capeluto denying approval of visa recommendation but opening the door to testify before the
Interdepartmental Visa Review Committee.

Visa Form IVRC-2

In Reply refer to visa case

VD 811.111 Barki, Abraham

February 2, 1945

Mr. Ralph Capeluto

807 Thirtieth Avenue South

Seattle, Washington

Sir:

An examination of this case under the regulations covering the control of persons entering the United States indicates that a favorable recommendation to the American consular officer concerned is not warranted at the present time. However, the case will be considered by the Interdepartmental Visa Review Committee at Washington and an opportunity will be given to interested individuals to appear in person or through an attorney or other intermediary before the Committee to make additional statements and answer possible questions. A form of Application for Appearance is attached.

To persons filing Applications for Appearance, notice of hearing will be sent at least ten days in advance of the date set for the hearing. If, on the other hand, it is desired that the case be considered without a hearing, it is requested that the Department be so advised.

Very truly yours,

Howard K. Travers

Chief, Visa Division

Enclosure: Form IVRC-1

PHONE MAIN 8785

Seattle Curtain Mfg. Co.

MANUFACTURERS OF

NOVELTY CURTAINS AND DRAPERIES
OIL SILK CURTAINS AND SHOWER CURTAINS
PREFONTAINE BUILDING
THIRD AND YESLER WAY
SEATTLE, WN. (4)

Feb. 14, 1945

Dear Dave:

I suppose you will be surprised to receive this letter from me but it seems that you are just the friend I am looking for at this time. I hope it will not be imposing too much upon you as I am about to ask you a personal favor for which I will always be grateful and indebted to you. It is a subject which you must acquaint yourself with so I will start from the beginning.

In 1939 when Germany and Italy joined bands the Nuremburg Laws long in effect in Germany and intended for the ultimate destruction of all men, women and children of the Jewish faith were promulgated in Italy. My three brothers-in-law and their families were among the first victims of this decree of expulsion which gave those residents in the Island of Rhodes of foreign birth six months in which to leave. The only place that offered refuge at the time was the International settlement of Tangiers, Morocco. They have been living there for the last five years under very unsatisfactory conditions. The cost of living is extremely high, and the place is very corrupt and unsuitable for raising a family.

One of my sisters, Sarina and her husband and children have left for Palestine and another sister, Joya is also completing arrangements for her family to leave for Palestine. My sister Mazaltov and her family have had their hearts set on coming here to the United States and they have been writing us letter after letter begging us to see what could be done.

In 1939 we tried to bring them here, but for some reason or another and then the war broke out, things had died down. Recently we received a letter from my neice, Claire Barki, who by the way does all the corresponding saying that several families were leaving for the United States with the aid of the Refugee Committee of New York and begged us to see what we could do about bringing them to this country. We immediately took steps and with the aid of the Hebrew Immigrant Aid Society we filled out Visas for my brother-in-law, Abraham Barki, my sister Matilde Barki, a son Jacque, a daughter Regina, a daughter Claire, another Rachel and twin sons Haim and Moise, and with the family has been living my youngest sister still single, Esther Capeluto. Also guaranting their support in the United States is my cousin, Charles Alhadeff, son of Nessim Alhadeff.

Letter dated February 14, 1945. Letter from Ralph Capeluto on his company letterhead asking Washington, D.C. lawyer and friend Dave Amato to see if he could help get the Barkey visa application through the governmental process.

PHONE MAIN 8785

Seattle Curtain Mfg. Co.

MANUFACTURERS OF

NOVELTY CURTAINS AND DRAPERIES
OIL SILK CURTAINS AND SHOWER CURTAINS
PREFONTAINE BUILDING
THIRD AND YESLER WAY
SEATTLE, WN. (4)

-2-

We are now in receipt of a letter from the Department of State requesting that I go to Washington to appear personally at a hearing for the case. Due to the difficulty in traveling and hotel accomodations and due to the shortage of help it seems almost impossible that I could go to appear in person. The State Department further notified me that if I could not go myself I could give someone the power of attorney to act for me, and that is the favor I am asking of you Dave, to see what you can do. They are really desperate and I feel with my assistance they will find a haven here with me.

Abraham is capable of working and he has three or four grown children that can work almost immediately. I am sending you all the informationwe have filed and if you will note my neice is very active. She has an office position and is already learning English. She is also very active in the British Red Cross, and Home Nursing, etc. The other children are also educated in their language.

I am enclosing copies of the Visas, letters of recommendation from the bank, etc., so that you may become familiar with the case.

I feel confident in your ability and a man of your position you no doubt know how to go about handling the situation. I believe I have sent you all the information, but if there is any doubt about anything I will be glad to furnish further detail.

I want to assure you any effort on your part will be greatly appreciated and I want to thank you in advance as I feel sure you will do me this great favor.

My wife, Rachel and the children send kindest regards to you and your family. Sincerest regards from my father and mother-in-law and Emma. Believe me, I am sincere when I tell you we think of you often and the pleasant day we spent in our back yard during your stay in Seattle. I was glad to know you suffered no ill effects from the cherries you ate.

If for any reason you feel that you cannot do this for me, I would greatly appreciate it if you would recommend some good lawyer I could contact.

Thanking you again, with kindest regards to all of you, I remain,

Very sincerely yours.

P.S. I am also enclosing a letter received by Charles Alhadeff from the Department of State and he begs that/represent him also.
you

RC/mi

Seattle Curtain Manufacturing Company

Manufacturers of

Novelty Curtains and Draperies

Oil Silk Curtains and Shower Curtains

Prefontaine Building

Third and Yesler Way

Seattle, Washington

February 14, 1945

Dear Dave[53]:

I suppose you will be surprised to receive this letter from me but it seems that you are just the friend I am looking for at this time. I hope it will not be imposing too much upon you as I am about to ask you a personal favor for which I will always be grateful and indebted to you. It is a subject which you must acquaint yourself with so I will start from the beginning.

In 1939 when Germany and Italy joined hands the Nuremburg Laws long in effect in Germany and intended for the ultimate destruction of all men, women, and children of the Jewish faith were promulgated in Italy. My three brothers-in-law and their families were among the first victims of this decree of expulsion which gave those residents in the Island of Rhodes of foreign birth six months in which to leave. The only place that offered refuge at the time was the International settlement of Tangiers, Morocco. They have been living there for the last five years under very unsatisfactory conditions. The cost of living is extremely high, and the place is very corrupt and unsuitable for raising a family.

One of my sisters, Sarina, and her husband and children have left for Palestine and another sister, Gioia, is also completing arrangements for her family to leave for Palestine. My sister, Mazaltov, and her family have had their hearts set on coming here to the United States, and they have been writing us letter after letter begging us to see what could be done.

In 1939 we tried to bring them here, but for some reason or another and then the war broke out, things had died down. Recently we received a letter from my niece, Claire Barki, who by the way does all the corresponding, saying that several families were leaving for the United States with the aid of the Refugee Committee of New York and begged us to see what we could do about bringing them to this country. We immediately took steps and with the aid of the Hebrew Immigrant Aid Society we filled out Visas for my brother-in-law Abraham Barki, my sister Matilde Barki, a son Jacque, a daughter Regina, a daughter Claire, another Rachel, and twin sons Haim and Moise, and with the family has been living my youngest sister single, Esther Capeluto. Also guaranteeing their support in the United States is my cousin, Charles Alhadeff, son of Nessim Alhadeff.

---

[53] Dave Amato was a lawyer and friend of Ralph Capeluto's in Washington, D.C.

You are now in receipt of a letter from the Department of State requesting that I go to Washington to appear personally at a hearing for the case. Due to the difficulty in traveling and hotel accommodations and due to the shortage of help, it seems almost impossible that I could go to appear in person. The State Department further notified me that if I could not go myself, I could give someone the power of attorney to act for me, and that is the favor I am asking of you, Dave, to see what you can do. They are really desperate, and I feel with my assistance they will find a haven here with me.

Abraham is capable of working, and he has three or four grown children that can work almost immediately. I am sending you all the information we have filed. And if you will note, my niece is very active. She has an office position and is already learning English. She is also very active in the British Red Cross and Home Nursing, etc. The other children are also educated in their language.

I am enclosing copies of the Visas, letters of recommendation from the bank, etc., so that you may become familiar with the case.

I feel confident in your ability and a man of your position you no doubt know how to go about handling the situation. I believe I have sent you all the information. But if there is any doubt about anything, I will be glad to furnish further detail.

I want to assure you any effort on your part will be greatly appreciated, and I want to thank you in advance as I feel sure you will do me this great favor.

My wife, Rachel, and the children send kindest regards to you and your family. Sincerest regards from my father and mother-in-law and Emma. Believe me, I am sincere when I tell you we think of you often and the pleasant day we spent in our backyard during your stay in Seattle. I was glad to know you suffered no ill effects from the cherries you ate.

If for any reason you feel that you cannot do this for me, I would greatly appreciate it if you would recommend some good lawyer I could contact.

Thanking you again with kindest regards to all of you, I remain,

Very sincerely yours,

[Ralph]

P.S. I am also enclosing a letter received by Charles Alhadeff from the Department of State and he begs that you represent him also.

February 14, 1945

Secretary of State

Department of State

Washington 25, D.C.

In reply to Visa Case: VD 811.11 Barki, Abraham

Dear Sir:

In reply to your letter of February 2nd, since it is not possible for me to personally appear at one of your IVRC hearings, I have asked my friend, Mr. David Amato of 6309 Third Street NW, Washington, DC, to appear for me.

Hoping you will give the matter your favorable consideration, I am,

Very sincerely yours,

RC/mi

Federal Security Agency

Office of Vocational Rehabilitation

Washington 25, D.C.

D.C. REHABILITATION SERVICE

402 Sixth Street, N. W.

February 17, 1945

Mr. Ralph Capeluto

c/o Seattle Curtain Manufacturing Company

Prefontaine Building

3rd and Yesler

Seattle 4, Washington

Dear Ralph:

Upon the receipt of your letter, I contacted HIAS. As you know, they have a wealth of knowledge and experience in dealing with the State Department here and would be glad to give us any guidance. Accordingly, I have made an appointment for Monday, February 19, to speak with their attorneys. I shall keep you posted on any developments that will result from Monday's meeting.

Feel assured that I will do everything I can.

Sincerely yours,

David Amato

Federal Security Agency

Office of Vocational Rehabilitation

Washington 25, D.C.

D.C. REHABILITATION SERVICE

February 19, 1945

Mr. Ralph Capeluto

c/o Seattle Curtain Manufacturing Company

Prefontaine Building

3rd and Yesler

Seattle 4, Washington

Dear Ralph:

I met today with HIAS and they strongly advised that, if at all possible, you come to Washington. They have had daily experiences in presenting such cases, and their experiences have proven that the State Department is much more impressed by a personal presentation than by a presentation which I would make or HIAS would make. The State Department feels that persons in this country who are interested in bringing relatives here should be interested enough to present a personal plea in their behalf.

In view of these facts, I felt impelled to write you before doing anything further. I didn't want to do anything to weaken your case or the chances of the State Department giving favorable consideration. I am, therefore, suggesting that you consider these recommendations. If you feel that you want me to follow through, I shall be glad to do what I can. I think, however, that, if at all possible, you should come here yourself. HIAS will be glad to go over to the hearing with you, and they shall so arrange it if you want to.

Kindly let me know of your wishes in this matter.

With warmest personal regards, I remain

Sincerely yours,

David Amato

February 27, 1945

Dear David,

As per our telephone conversation I will wait for the papers that I am to fill out to appear in person for the hearing. The reason I called was because I thought I had to leave immediately. I am very happy that it will not be for a while because this way it will give us a little time to arrange things so I can take my wife with me.

I had contemplated this trip for some time as I wanted to take Rachel for our wedding anniversary this June. I enjoyed very much talking with your father. I am really looking forward to a pleasant visit with you folks. Little did I dream this summer when you were here that we would see each other so soon.

Yours very truly,[54]

---

[54] This letter is not signed, but it appears to be from Ralph Capeluto.

Federal Security Agency

Office of Vocational Rehabilitation

Washington 25, D.C.

402 Sixth Street, N. W.

March 2, 1945

Mr. Ralph Capeluto

c/o Seattle Curtain Manufacturing Company

Prefontaine Building

3rd and Yesler

Seattle 4, Washington

Dear Ralph:

Following your telephone call the other night, which made us very happy, I contacted HIAS to determine the next step. They suggested you do two things immediately.

First, file with the State Department the enclosed application forms. Secondly, write a letter to HIAS, 1317 F Street, N. W., to the effect that you are authorizing them to attend the proposed hearing, listing the names of the immigrants involved, and they will file an application of the same type as yours. The State Department will notify you and HIAS, after their usual investigation, to appear. As I told you the other night, you are to wait until the State Department advises you of the date of the hearing before you come to Washington.

With kindest regards, I remain

Sincerely,

David Amato

Enclosures

March 5, 1945

Secretary of State

Department of State

Washington 25, D.C.

In Reply to Visa Case: VD 811.11 Barki, Abraham

Dear Sirs:

You will please find enclosed application for appearance.

I will wait for your reply as to the date of the hearing and will make a personal appearance in behalf of the above.

Yours very truly,

RC/mi

March 6, 1945

Hebrew Immigrant Aid Society
1317-F Street N. W.
Washington, D. C.

Dear Sirs:

I wish to inform you that I have filed visa applications for my
sister and her family and also for a single sister. I am listing their
names and places and dates of birth below for your information:

Name	Date and Place of birth		Present Address	Relation to Sponsor
Esther Capeluto	Mar.10, 1909	Isle of Rhodes	Paseo Cen- arro No.77 Tangier, Morrocco	Sister
Abraham Barki	Feb.20, 1891	Aidin, Turkey	"	Brother-in-law
Matilda Barki	Mar.5, 1895	Isle of Rhodes	"	Sister
Claire Barki	Mar.14, 1921	" " "	"	Niece
Rachel Barki	Mar.5, 1923	" " "	"	Niece
Haim Barki	Mar.27, 1925	" " "	"	Nephew
Moise Barki	Mar.27, 1925	" " "	"	Nephew
Jacques Barki	Mar.5, 1928	" " "	"	Nephew
Regina Barki	Jan.9, 1932	" " "	"	Niece

I wish to authorize you to appear with me at a hearing for the above,
and I wish to thank you for any cooperation you will extend me.

Yours very truly,

RC/mi

Letter dated March 6, 1945. Letter from Ralph Capeluto to the Hebrew Sheltering and Immigrant Aid
Society in Washington, D.C., asking for accompaniment to the Barkey visa hearing.

March 6, 1945

Hebrew Immigrant Aid Society

1317-F Street N. W.

Washington, D.C.

Dear Sirs:

I wish to inform you that I have filed visa applications for my sister and her family, and also for a single sister. I am listing their names and places and dates of birth below for your information:

Name	Date and Place of Birth	Present Address	Relation to Sponsor
Esther Capeluto	March 10, 1909	Pasea Cenarro Isle of Rhodes Tangier, Morocco	Sister No. 77
Abraham Barki	Feb. 20, 1891 Aidan, Turkey	"	Brother-in-law
Mathilda Barki	March 5, 1895 Isle of Rhodes	"	Sister
Claire Barki	March 14, 1921 Isle of Rhodes	"	Niece
Rachel Barki	March 5, 1923 Isle of Rhodes	"	Niece
Haim Barki	March 27, 1925 Isle of Rhodes	"	Nephew
Moise Barki	March 27, 1925 Isle of Rhodes	"	Nephew
Jacques Barki	March 3, 1928 Isle of Rhodes	"	Nephew
Regina Barki	January 9, 1932 Isle of Rhodes	"	Niece

I wish to authorize you to appear with me at a hearing for the above, and I wish to thank you for any cooperation you will extend me.

Yours very truly,

RC/mi

BIOGRAPHICAL DATA
CONCERNING VISA APPLICANTS

Filed with .... at .... on ....
    (name of agency)   (name of city)   (date)

NOTE: Use separate form for each person over 16 years of age, other than accompanying spouse. It is essential that the information be accurate and complete since persons signing the visa applications do so under oath.

1. Name of applicant and of accompanying relatives:

| | Rela-tionship to (1) | Marital status* | Marriage | | Religious Affilia-tion | Present address |
			Date	Place		
(1) Claire Barki	Daughter	Single	–	–		77.Paseo Canarro
(2) Rachel	"	"	–	–		Tangier
(3) Haim	Son	"	–	–		Morocco
(4) Mose	"	"	–	–		

*S.(single); M (married); W (widowed); D (divorced).
    Additional data on those listed above. Be careful to give information on line with same number as precedes name of person to whom it refers.

Date of birth	Place of birth	Citizenship (If stateless give last citizenship)	How acquired*	Date	Country (if not by birth)
(1) 14/3/1921	Rhodes -Italy	Italian	By birth		
(2) 5/3/1923	"	"	"		
(3) 2/3/1925	"	"	"		
(4) 2/3/1926	"	"	"		

*State whether nationality was acquired by birth, marriage, naturalization, or derivative (through parent's naturalization).

2. If purpose in entering U. S. A. is other than for permanent residence, state what and explain fully on attached sheet.

3. (a) Consulate at which application is to be made: ....
    (b) Has (have) visa applicant (s) to your knowledge previously obtained United States visa?   Yes ☐   No ☐
    If answer is "yes" give following information:

Name	Date obtained	Where obtained	Kind of visa (Refer to listing under 3)	Date and place of entry to U.S.
–	–	–	–	

4. Is Passage Money available? .... What amount? ....
    From whom: (Give name and address) ....
    Where deposited: ....

5. Close relatives in the United States, including spouse, parents, children, brothers, sisters. If deceased so indicate in column for address. (If there are no close relatives, so indicate).

| | | | Fill in, if known | | |
Names	Relation-ship	Last known address	Citizenship (If stateless give last citizenship)	Length of residence in U.S.	Whether citizen (c) or first papers (FP)
Raphael Capeluto	Uncle	807 30th Ave. So Seattle-Wash.			
Djamila Capeluto	Aunt				
Relatives of spouse: (Whether or not spouse is accompanying.)					

6. Have any above named promised, or prepared, affidavits of support? If so, when? On January 31st, 1939

7. Close relatives in countries other than the United States, including spouse, parents, children, brothers, sisters. If deceased so indicate in column for address. (If there are no close relatives, so indicate.)

Names	Relation-ship	City and country in which residing	Nationality
Abraham Capeluto	Uncle	Buenos-Aires	
Haim Capeluto	Cousin	Lweka - Congo-Belge.	
Relatives of spouse: (Whether or not spouse is accompanying.)			

8. Educational background. (List schools and universities attended, degrees taken, and general field of studies)

Visa applicant   Spouse
                                        (Whether or not spouse is accompanying)

Visa application document.

9 Occupational experience: (List names and addresses of employers and positions held, with dates, commencing not later than 1930 and bringing up to the present time.)

Visa applicant	Spouse (Whether or not spouse is accompanying)
Book - Keepers	
Shorthand - writers	
Typewriters	

10. Activities and affiliations: Give names of organizations, political parties, groups, and societies of which visa applicant(s) is (are), or ever has (have) been, affiliated anywhere in any way. Give dates and state whether applicant was an officer, and if so whether or not paid. Detailed information concerning each affiliation should be furnished on separate sheets. If no affiliations, state NONE.

Visa applicant	Spouse (Whether or not spouse is accompanying)

The 1st one is a member of the British Red Cross Society and possesses 4 Certificates - One of Home Nursing - Two First-Aid and One Hygiene and Sanitation.

11. Has/Have visa applicant(s) membership in the following political organizations? (Answer YES or NO.)
   (a) Communist No. b) Anarchist No. (c) Any group advocating violent overthrow of government No.

If answer is affirmative, explain fully:

Visa applicant	Spouse (Whether or not spouse is accompanying)
-	--

12. Has/Have visa applicant(s) ever been convicted of any offense, political or otherwise? Yes   No
   (If answer is "yes," give date, place, and nature of offense and sentence)

Visa applicant	Spouse (Whether or not spouse is accompanying)
--	

13. Military training and experience of visa applicant. State countries with which visa applicant has served in military or naval forces, and give rank. If visa applicant has not served, answer NONE. None.

14. Previous marriage of visa applicant or/and spouse. If no previous marriage state NONE.

Name of former spouse	If living, city and country of residence	How terminated (Whether by death or divorce)	Date	Country
Of visa applicant: ---	---	---		
Of spouse: (Whether or not spouse is accompanying)				

15. Places of previous residence (city and country), giving approximate dates, since age of 14 yrs. (If visa applicant or accompanying spouse has at any time been interned in any foreign country, give place and dates of internment).

City	Country	For U.S. addresses Number	For U.S. addresses Street	Dates
Of visa applicant: Rhodes	Italy			From birth/1939
Tangier	Morocco			1939
Of spouse: (Whether or not spouse is accompanying)				

16. What professional or vocational field of activity does (do) the alien(s) plan to follow if admitted into the United States?

Visa applicant	Spouse

17. Where does (do) the applicant (s) plan to reside if admitted into the United States? Seattle - Wash.

NOTE: Supplementary information provided by the interviewer to U.S.A. Agencies, which points up any positive qualities of applicant's personality, attitudes, humor, physical vigor, language facilities and special skills and capacities may prove enormously helpful in obtaining a favorable decision.

Languages spoken : Spanish - French - Italian - English and a little

BIOGRAPHICAL DATA
CONCERNING VISA APPLICANTS

Filed with _____ at _____ on _____
(name of agency)   (name of city)   (date)

NOTE: Use separate form for each person over 18 years of age, other than accompanying spouse. It is essential that the information be accurate and complete since persons signing the visa applications do so under oath.

1. Name of applicant and of accompanying relatives:

| | Relationship to (1) | Marital status* | Marriage | | Religious Affiliation | Present address |
			Date	Place		
(1) Abraham Barki	x x x	Married	1920	Rhodes	Jujah	77, Paseo Cenarro
(2) Matilde "	Wife				"	Tanger
(3) Jacques "	Son	Single			"	Morocco
(4) Regina "	Daughter				"	

*S (single); M (married); W (widowed); D (divorced).

Additional data on those listed above. Be careful to give information on line with same number as precedes name of person to whom it refers.

| Date of birth | Place of birth | Citizenship (If stateless give last citizenship) | How acquired* | Date | Country |
					(if not by birth)
(1) 20/2/1891	Aidin - Turkey	Italian	Naturalization	1924	Rhodes
(2) 5/3/1695	Rhodes - Italy	"	by birth		
(3) 9/ /192	"	"	"		
(4) 9/1/193	"	"	"		

*State whether nationality was acquired by birth, marriage, naturalization, or derivative (through parent's naturalization).

2. If purpose in entering U. S. A. is other than for permanent residence, state what and explain fully on attached sheet.

3. (a) Consulate at which application is to be made:
   (b) Has (have) visa applicant(s) to your knowledge previously obtained United States visa?   Yes ☐   No ☐
   If answer is "yes" give following information:

Name	Date obtained	Where obtained	Kind of visa (Refer to listing under 3)	Date and place of entry to U.S.
-	-	-	-	-

4. Is Passage Money available? _____ What amount? _____
   From whom: (Give name and address) _____
   Where deposited: _____

5. Close relatives in the United States, including spouse, parents, children, brothers, sisters. If deceased so indicate in column for address. (If there are no close relatives, so indicate).

Names	Relationship	Last known address	Citizenship (If stateless give last citizenship)	Length of residence in U.S.	Whether citizen (c) or first papers (FP)
			Fill in, if known		
Raphael Capeluto					
Relatives of spouse: (Whether or not spouse is accompanying.)					
Raphael Capeluto	Brother	807 30th Ave. So Seattle-Wash.	Naturalized on Feb.21, 1927		
Djamila Almeleh	Sister				

6. Have any above named promised, or prepared, affidavits of support? If so, when?   On January 31st, 1939

7. Close relatives in countries other than the United States, including spouse, parents, children, brothers, sisters. If deceased so indicate in column for address. (If there are no close relatives, so indicate.)

Names	Relationship	City and country in which residing	Nationality
Relatives of spouse: (Whether or not spouse is accompanying.)			
Abraham Capeluto	Brother	Buenos - Aires -	
Haim Capeluto	Nephew	Lweka - Congo-Belge	

8. Educational background. (List schools and universities attended, degrees taken, and general field of studies)

Visa applicant   Spouse
                                  (Whether or not spouse is accompanying)

9   Occupational experience: (List names and addresses of employers and positions held, with dates, commencing not later than 1930 and bringing up to the present time.)

Visa applicant	Spouse (Whether or not spouse is accompanying)
Shoemaker	

10. Activities and affiliations: Give names of organizations, political parties, groups, and societies of which visa applicant(s) is (are), or ever has (have) been, affiliated anywhere in any way. Give dates and state whether applicant was an officer, and if so whether or not paid. Detailed information concerning each affiliation should be furnished on separate sheets. If no affiliations, state NONE.

Visa applicant	Spouse (Whether or not spouse is accompanying)
None.	None.

11. | Has | Have visa applicant(s) membership in the following political organizations? (Answer YES or NO.)
(a) Communist No   (b) Anarchist No   (c) Any group advocating violent overthrow of government No.
If answer is affirmative, explain fully:

Visa applicant	Spouse (Whether or not spouse is accompanying)
-	-

12. | Has | Have visa applicant(s) ever been convicted of any offense, political or otherwise? Yes   No
(If answer is "yes," give date, place, and nature of offense and sentence)

Visa applicant	Spouse (Whether or not spouse is accompanying)

13. Military training and experience of visa applicant. State countries with which visa applicant has served in military or naval forces, and give rank. If visa applicant has not served, answer NONE.

14. Previous marriage of visa applicant or/and spouse. If no previous marriage state NONE.

Name of former spouse	If living, city and country of residence	How terminated (Whether by death or divorce)	Date	Country
Of visa applicant: None.	None.	None.		
Of spouse: (Whether or not spouse is accompanying)				

15. Places of previous residence (city and country), giving approximate dates, since age of 14 yrs. (If visa applicant or accompanying spouse has at any time been interned in any foreign country, give place and dates of internment).

City	Country	For U.S. addresses Number	Street	Dates
Of visa applicant: Aidin	Turkey			From birth/1919
Rhodes	Italy			1919/1939
Tangier	Morocco			1939/1
Of spouse: (Whether or not spouse is accompanying)				
Rhodes	Italy			From birth/1939
Tangier	Morocco			1939

16. What professional or vocational field of activity does (do) the alien(s) plan to follow if admitted into the United States?

Visa applicant	Spouse

17. Where does (do) the applicant(s) plan to reside if admitted into the United States? Seattle - Wash.

NOTE: Supplementary information provided by the Interviewer to U.S.A. Agencies, which points up any positive qualities of applicant's personality, attitudes, humor, physical vigor, language facilities and special skills and capacities may prove enormously helpful in obtaining a favorable decision.

Languages spoken : Spanish, French, Italian, Turk and Greeck.

TRANSLATION

Tangier, March 10, 1945

Dear Uncle and Aunt:

Just as I was about to sit down to write this letter, they brought your much appreciated letter of the 7th of this month, which upset us more than ever.

Dear ones, with what joy would we have read its contents because not everyone welcomes this way his relatives, but with what sadness we read your good words thinking that the wish of reunion we both long for is not destined to be fulfilled yet.

As I mentioned in my previous letter, even though this does not worry me much, we have the matter of the quota to arrange. Unfortunately, this has been the only thing that has changed our plans lately. I told you that when we went to the American Consulate with the steamship company's letter, they agreed to ask for the numbers of the quota and notify us for the purpose of granting definitely the visas. On the 5th of March they called us and, to our dismay, told us that the Turkish quota was exhausted. This surprised us beyond measure and left us stunned. Upon recovering from this blow, Papa expressed the wish that all of us under the Italian quota should go and that he would remain until the Turkish quota would be opened. According to what they told him at the Consulate, it will be opened on July 1, 1945 when the 1945 quota ends on June 6, and as it is a matter of two months' delay, we all agreed with Papa. They told us to return after two days to give us an answer.

We appeared before the Vice Consul in charge of visas. The first thing he said was that it all depended on the age of the members of the family. Jacques, Regina, being minors of less than 21 years of age, pertain to the Turkish quota and we the Italian quota. In order not to miss the boat, which was the reason for the present delay, we suggested that he give us the visas for Mama, Esther, Rachel, Haim, Moshe, and me, and that Jacques and Regina would remain with Papa. Since he was finding obstacles on every proposal, the Vice Consul told us that the law was for the whole family together to leave for the United States. We had no other choice but to return home, deprived of strength. I returned to the office upset, and upon consulting with my boss, he asked me if I wanted him, as American protege, to go to talk to the Vice Consul. When he was about to leave, I stopped him and told him that the Vice Consul, being an intractable man, would only repeat what he had just told me. He told me I was right, and suggested for me to write to the Consul himself, without accusing anyone, only to present the facts as they are. I wrote this letter, copy of which I enclose, and after waiting five days, he answered, see copy attached.

It is deplorable what is happening. Really, this voyage will cost us, besides money, a lot of effort and work to overcome the many obstacles. Let's hope it brings results.

Now, please try to see if HIAS can intervene. Perhaps they can do something. It will be impossible for May 5, but for July when the quota is opened, perhaps they can succeed in time for us to board the boat at Bilbao on July 5, 1945. I would write likewise to that effect.

Dear ones, you can't imagine how desperate we are on account of the disappointment at the last hour.

We were planning everything, counting the days, and building castles in the air.

My dear little cousins so anxious to see us and we, who were together with so many cousins in Rhodes, have remained all alone. We can hardly wait, therefore, to join all of you. We pray that God smooth the way and approach the hour of our reunion.

I have delayed in informing you all of this because, truly, I was trying to do my best to find a way and was awaiting a favorable answer from the Consulate, even if it were for some of us. Everything went according to the will of God and will be for the best.

Please write if you succeed in anything.

Everyone sends you regards. Please give regards to Mlle. Taranto from me and my brothers.[55] The news greatly surprised me, but pleasantly so. The truth is that since we left her in Rhodes, we thought she had experienced the same fate as the rest. We are glad for her; similarly we hope to hear good news about other people.

Regards to all relatives, and to you, dear Uncle, Aunt, little cousins, an affectionate embrace from your niece.

Claire

P.S. From Rebecca, wife of Moshe Hasson, many regards to Mazaltov, wife of Jacob Pasha, also to Mlle. Taranto.

---

[55] Claire's French teacher from Rhodes.

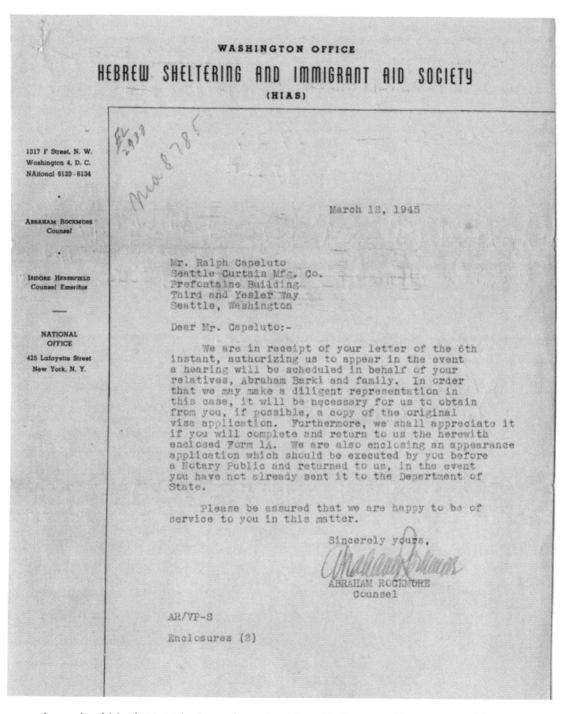

WASHINGTON OFFICE

HEBREW SHELTERING AND IMMIGRANT AID SOCIETY

(HIAS)

1317 F Street, N. W.
Washington 4, D. C.
NAtional 6120-6134

ABRAHAM ROCKMORE
Counsel

ISIDORE HERSHFIELD
Counsel Emeritus

NATIONAL
OFFICE

425 Lafayette Street
New York, N. Y.

March 12, 1945

Mr. Ralph Capeluto
Seattle Curtain Mfg. Co.
Prefontaine Building
Third and Yesler Way
Seattle, Washington

Dear Mr. Capeluto:-

We are in receipt of your letter of the 6th
instant, authorizing us to appear in the event
a hearing will be scheduled in behalf of your
relatives, Abraham Barki and family. In order
that we may make a diligent representation in
this case, it will be necessary for us to obtain
from you, if possible, a copy of the original
visa application. Furthermore, we shall appreciate it
if you will complete and return to us the herewith
enclosed Form 1A. We are also enclosing an appearance
application which should be executed by you before
a Notary Public and returned to us, in the event
you have not already sent it to the Department of
State.

Please be assured that we are happy to be of
service to you in this matter.

Sincerely yours,

ABRAHAM ROCKMORE
Counsel

AR/VP-S

Enclosures (2)

Letter dated March 12, 1945. Letter from the Hebrew Sheltering and Immigrant Aid Society
(HIAS) to Ralph Capeluto requesting a copy of Barkey family visa application form.

WASHINGTON OFFICE

HEBREW SHELTERING AND IMMIGRANT AID SOCIETY (HIAS)

March 12, 1945

Mr. Ralph Capeluto

Seattle Curtain Mfg. Co.

Prefontaine Building

Third and Yesler Way

Seattle, Washington

Dear Mr. Capeluto:

We are in receipt of your letter of the 6th instant, authorizing us to appear in the event a hearing will be scheduled in behalf of your relatives Abraham Barki and family. In order that we may make a diligent representation in this case, it will be necessary for us to obtain from you, if possible, a copy of the original visa application. Furthermore, we shall appreciate it if you will complete and return to us the herewith enclosed Form 1A. We are also enclosing an appearance application which should be executed by you before a Notary Public and returned to us in the event you have not already sent it to the Department of State.

Please be assured that we are happy to be of service to you in this matter.

Sincerely yours,

ABRAHAM ROCKMORE

Counsel

AR/VP-S

Enclosures (2)

Federal Security Agency

Office of Vocational Rehabilitation

Washington 25, D.C.

402 Sixth Street, N. W.

March 27, 1945

Mr. Ralph Capeluto

c/o Seattle Curtain Manufacturing Company

Prefontaine Building

3rd and Yesler

Seattle 4, Washington

Dear Ralph:

I just received an application from the State Department regarding my appearance at the proposed hearing.

The representative at the HIAS office advises me that my appearance will not be necessary, and I am therefore not filing the application. I am notifying the State Department accordingly.

Will you advise me when you get your notice to appear? We're looking forward anxiously to seeing you. With kindest personal regards, I remain

Sincerely yours,

David Amato

TRANSLATION

Tangier, April 2, 1945

Dear Uncle and Aunt:

With the greatest joy we received your letters dated February 15 and February 19, the contents of which were read attentively. And we were glad to know you are all well for this is our wish.

Dear ones, I do not know how to thank you for all you are doing for us. With the new steps you have taken we hope to attain something. We are awaiting your news about the result of the meeting that Mr. David Amato had with HIAS on February 19. Do not think that we are inactive here. Everything that is possible to do we will do, provided they give us instructions. I was with the Committee here and told them that in view that so many months have elapsed and nothing was accomplished, that it would be a good idea if the local Committee would write the National Refugee Service of New York, asking for news about our papers. But you know that people do not like to bother. They told me it was unnecessary. It seems to me that what we are doing is little. Their answer did not satisfy me, so I wrote directly to N.Y. on March 7 for the purpose indicated above. As you see, almost a month has gone by and I have not received any answer. I believe this agency has nothing to do with it as it seems that they have sent the papers to Washington. I tell you because of what happened this week, that is, the Committee called us to tell us that they were notified by Washington that the papers are there and are waiting for a meeting to decide. I told them that we already knew that from your letter. That is all. I believe we have taken a step forward and what remains to do is for God to instill in them goodwill and that the decision be favorable.

Now, dear ones, what I would like to know is what Mr. Amato has accomplished. Dear ones, I read your two letters and understood them perfectly well. Only you will excuse me if I do not answer in the same language, and as it happens with all (new) languages, one can understand them very well, but when it comes to speaking them, it is another matter. It is foolish to say that I cannot write in English, for whatever I may write, no matter how many mistakes, my uncle and my aunt will not make fun of me. As I do not have much practice, it would take me longer; that is why I am writing in Spanish and time is what is lacking.

These weeks, Passover weeks, end of the fiscal year at the office, an exam at the Red Cross to be taken, all arrived together and in order not to leave you without news, I am writing even though just a couple of lines, so please excuse me.

Dear Uncle, please also make excuses for me to our "*simpatica*"[56] Mary Israel[57] whom I deeply thank

---

[56] Pleasant, nice.

[57] Mary Israel was the daughter of Ralph's business partner. She worked in the curtain factory and became a pen-pal of Claire's.

for a friendly gesture. I am very glad to have made her acquaintance even though through letters, a friendship to be renewed in person. Tell her to excuse me as I was regretfully unable to answer promptly her first letter. But, God willing, I will write to her next week. Meanwhile, give her my affection and friendly feelings.

Dear ones, on Saturday, March 31, we were notified by the Bank about the $100 of Aunt Esther. We were unable to withdraw as yet because the bank was closed yesterday, today also, on account of a holiday. We hope to go tomorrow. We thank you very much for everything. May God give you health, a long life, and success in your business.

Dear ones, we are in the middle of Pesach and you can't imagine how sad this Passover has been, thinking of the dear ones about whom we have no news. Unfortunately, nothing can be done. Here, some people from the Rhodes contingent have received letters from their sons residing in the Belgian Congo, telling them that there are some Rodeslis[58] in Smyrna. They mentioned some names, but as we see these are people protected by Turkey or even their spouses. Only one person protected by Italy appears, and he is a banker who certainly must have fled as he did not take his wife along. These Turks were allowed to leave Rhodes for certain, before Turkey entered the war. At any rate, I will write this week to Behor Capeluto (Behora Capeluto's son) in Belgian Congo to ask him if he knows anything. I doubt whether Behor will answer me because I think he does not like to write. I have written to him four times, and he has not deigned to answer. I will also write to Salvator Levy [Rizula Capeluto's son]. He will answer me for sure.

We hope the news is good because you cannot imagine how worried we are about all of them. It is a worry that does not let us live. Of all the aunts, the most affectionate and attached to the family was Aunt Behora. Her daughters, besides being my cousins, were also my friends, and truly it hurts a lot to think that something bad has happened to them. I hope we awake from all of this with good news about all our relatives.

Dear ones, I would like to continue writing, but I have things to do. Mama, Papa, Aunt Esther, Rachel, Haim, Moise, Jacques, and Regina send you kisses. Give everyone regards from us. When you have an opportunity to see Aunt Jamila, kiss her for us and give regards to her husband. And to all of you and the children, receive a strong embrace from your niece who loves you very much.

Claire

P.S. Don't you think it has been a long time since your visit? You should come to see us, even through photos.

As I was closing this letter we received your letter of February 10, which should have been received before the above-mentioned letters of February 15 and February 19. Upon reading its contents we realize what is going on and why you had to address yourselves to Mr. Amato. We are waiting news about this gentleman's activities. Again, kisses from

Claire

---

[58] People from Rhodes.

COPY

NRS
NATIONAL REFUGEE SERVICE, INC.
139 Centre Street
New York 13, N.Y.

April 5, 1945

Airmail

Miss Marianne K. Weingarten
Washington Emigre Bureau, Inc.
320 Smith Tower Annex
Seattle 4, Washington

Dear Miss Weingarten:

      Re: BARKI, Abraham and Family
                Tangiers
                NRS Case #A-38812

Please refer to our letter of February 21st in which we advised you that we had learned that the Visa Division of the State Department had forwarded an invitation to Mr. Ralph Capeluto to come to Washington for a hearing on the above-named family. Since we did not hear from you, we wonder whether Mr. Capeluto had replied. He will be interested, of course, to learn that we have now received a very lengthy letter from Miss Claire Barki describing the family's situation and expressing great anxiety because she has not heard from the relative.

We are replying to Miss Barki, indicating that the documents have been filed and also informing her that we hope that the application will be acted upon promptly.

We have already notified the Joint Distribution Committee in Lisbon that the documents have been forwarded to the Visa Division. May we hear from you?

Assuring you of our interest and desire to be of service, I am,

                Sincerely yours,

                [signed] D. Spielberg
                Migration Department
                Ann S. Petluck, Director

Reply to:
Ann Rabinowitz for
Dorothy Spielberg
rw

NATIONAL REFUGEE SERVICE Inc.

139, Centre Street

N E W - Y O R K, 13, N.Y.

-COPIA

April 5, 1945.

Miss Claire Barki
Paseo Cenarro No.77
Tangiers, Morocco

Re: BARKI, Abraham and
Family
Tangiers
Case #A-38812

Dear Miss Barki:

We have your detailed letter describing your family's situation
in Tangiers.

We had assumed that the Joint Distribution Committee in Lisbon,
to whom we had written in February advising them that the affidavits for an American visa had been submitted by your relatives
to the State Department, had communicated with you. As yet no
action has been taken.

You must appreciate the fact that there are very many applications
pending with the State Department and for that reason it takes some
time before an application can be acted on. You can be sure that
your relatives are doing everything possible to help tou and your
family reach the United States. As soon as action is taken we will
notify the Joint Distribution Committee so that they can convey
this news to you. We have already notified your relatives that we
have received your letter.

Assuring you of our cooperation, we are,

Sincerely yours,

Ann S. Petluck, Director
Migration Department.

A.Rabinowits for
D. Spielberg
rw.

Letter dated April 5, 1945. Letter from National Refugee Service Inc., New York, to Claire Barkey with
update on immigration status.

NATIONAL REFUGEE SERVICE Inc.
139, Centre Street
NEW YORK 13, N.Y.
Copy

April 5, 1945

Miss Claire Barki
Paseo Cenarro No. 77
Tangiers, Morocco

      Re: BARKI, Abraham and Family

              Tangiers

              Case #A-38812

Dear Miss Barki:

We have your detailed letter describing your family's situation in Tangiers.

We had assumed that the Joint Distribution Committee in Lisbon, to whom we had written in February advising them that the affidavits for an American visa had been submitted by your relatives to the State Department, had communicated with you. As yet no action has been taken.

You must appreciate the fact that there are very many applications pending with the State Department, and for that reason it takes some time before an application can be acted on. You can be sure that your relatives are doing everything possible to help you and your family reach the United States. As soon as action is taken, we will notify the Joint Distribution Committee so that they can convey this news to you. We have already notified your relatives that we have received your letter.

      Assuring you of our cooperation, we are,

                        Sincerely yours,

                        Ann S. Petluck, Director

                        Migration Department

A. Rabinowitz for

D. Spielberg

rw

<u>Copy</u>

Air Mail

April 9, 1945

Miss Ann Rabinowitz
for Miss Dorothy Spielberg
Migration Department
National Refugee Service, Inc.
139 Centre Street
New York 13, N.Y.

Dear Miss Rabinowitz:

      RE: BARKI, Abraham and Family

                Tangiers

                NRS Case #A-38812

We wish to thank you for your letter of April 5th.

We have communicated with Mr. Ralph Capeluto and beg to advise you that he had heard from Washington but that a date for a hearing has not been set as yet. Mr. Capeluto is ready to attend the hearing if he will be given sufficient time to take the trip East.

As soon as we have further information, we shall advise you, and thanking you for your cooperation, we remain,

                         Yours very truly,

                         Frances Pick

                         Secretary

                         WASHINGTON EMIGRE BUREAU, INC.

April 10, 1945

Air Mail

Miss Ann Rabinowitz
for Miss Dorothy Spielberg
Migration Department
National Refugee Service, Inc.
139 Centre Street
New York 13, N.Y.

Dear Miss Rabinowitz:

      RE: BARKI, Abraham and Family

                 Tangiers

                 NRS Case #A-38812

We beg to refer to our letter of yesterday.

Mr. Ralph Capeluto has just advised us that he is ready to advance the money for the passage for his relatives to come to this country.

Please note, and oblige,

                              Yours very truly,

                              Frances Pick

                              Secretary

WASHINGTON EMIGRE BUREAU, INC.

cc: Mr. R. Capeluto

TRANSLATION

Tangier, April 19, 1945

Dear Uncle and Aunt:

I can find no words to express our gratitude and to thank you for all you are doing for us. You don't know how much we appreciate your gestures. All the people who keep track of our steps regarding our going to the U.S. are astonished that you are trying so hard and also spending in order to bring us to your side. They are even more surprised when they find out that we do not know each other personally, but they say that my uncles know what they are doing and that never will they be sorry to bring us over because, dear ones, as I have repeated thousands of times, our obligation and wish is to reimburse you for everything you are paying for us in anticipation, although we will remain eternally grateful for your efforts and work. We wish everything would go the way we wanted for we are tired of waiting and being so disappointed.

Had they told us from the first moment that we had to wait so long, it would have been all right. But we were sure of everything so many times, especially the last one, another complete disappointment happened.

How much work and displeasure this trip to America costs us. But, if it is for our own good, as we do not doubt, it does not matter if we wait a little longer. Be it until God wills.

Dear ones, first of all, I acknowledge receipt of your telegram and of your letter. Even though I wished the opposite, I did not get up hopes of your succeeding in anything over there. It appeared to me impossible for May 5, as I had tried everything and done my best here. I hope you inquire when they intend to issue numbers for the Turkish quota. Everything depends there because there are boats whenever we wish, not as before. Boats of Spanish lines leave every month. What seemed very distant today we would gladly leave in July. We are so desperate and agitated that we do not know what we are doing, nor do I feel like working here. I had taken leave for the end of March, but I still keep on working until I receive new orders. While we are here, we have no choice but to keep on living. But I assure you that I fulfill my obligations reluctantly, which is unusual for me as I like office work. It is not that I perform badly for it is not in my makeup, nor does my conscience allow it, but I assure you it requires a lot of effort on my part. Therefore, I ask you to please give us exact information as to the day of our departure. It is easier over there because the local consul does nothing. He only tells us that he would call at the opportune moment, but this can take months and years if they feel like it. What concerns us is to know when the numbers of the Turkish quota will be available.

Meanwhile we fear that the affidavits dated July 30, 1945, would be useless. Then that would create another mess.

Now, dear Uncle and Aunt, I will give you some news you didn't expect. When they called us to tell us that the Turkish quota was filled and that we could not avail ourselves of the Italian quota because we had to follow my father to leave together as a family, I propounded to the Consul that Esther had a last name different from ours and had nothing to do with us. The Consul did not offer much hope but promised to write to Washington. As we had been deceived so many times, I did not give it much thought. But what ensued is that on April 6, he called her to give her a visa, having received her number of the quota, and told her to get ready to leave on April 5, 1946 [sic]. You can imagine with how much haste and worry she is getting ready. Meanwhile, Passover is here, and God willing, she leaves Tangier on the 26th of April for Cadiz, and she departs on the 2nd or 5th of May for America. She does not know the itinerary as yet. When she finds out, I will write right away. Meanwhile, please advise Heskia Benatar to find out the date of arrival of the steamship "Marques de Comillas" at New York so that he may go to receive her. Esther is dejected to leave by herself, and is also thinking of our separation. You can imagine after so many years of being together, but we console her by telling her that it is for a short while. That is what we wish and hope. The truth is that I envy her, she was lucky. I envy her for good reason as we both were born in Italy but only she can leave. That is the limit! What can we do? We will wait a little longer.

Dear ones, now I will allow myself to suggest something. I know I am taking advantage of your kindness, but since you are on the "dance floor" and gave us a taste, please listen carefully. Agreeing with Papa, we thought that if the Turkish quota will not resume for a long while, it would be advantageous since the Italian quota is opened, to prepare separate affidavits for the six of us, namely, Rachel, Haim, Moshe, Jaques, Regina and I. Having everything ready, papers, renewed passports, and Italian quota being opened, I supposed that upon receiving the affidavits they will find no obstacle. But before undertaking anything, I would like you to inquire because I do not want you to spend money needlessly; you already have spent enough.

1) If the Turkish quota will take long to be opened.

2) If having the six of us together will be possible, easy, and bring results.

On your next letter, please give us the details.

Dear Uncle and dear Aunt, you know that one cannot repay, be it in good or bad. As we have seen in many cases, good or bad actions are given an immediate response by God. The Almighty will reward you for what you're doing for us with good health, which is the main thing, happiness, a long life, and well-being, amen.

My blessings are also addressed through me on behalf of my cousins, Vida and Rosa, Lea, and Rachel. Each letter they write adds more praise and blessings. Everything they receive from you is like manna from heaven. They are enduring poverty, especially Lea and Rachel, who have no income. Vida and Rosa at least receive something from their brother in Congo and are waiting from one moment to the next to join him. But Lea and Rachel are lacking help except when they receive yours. You can image with what joy they receive your assistance. We have Aunt Rachel in our hearts as she has us in hers, as we know that these[59] are women's work and she is the one who will take care of it.

Well, it is time to close. You have had enough of it! Everyone sends kisses. To you and my dear little cousins, kisses from

Claire

---

[59] Meaning, all this business of the trip.

TRANSLATION

Tangier, April 24, 1945

Dear Uncle and Aunt:

I hereby confirm my letter of the 2nd instant. I am enclosing a copy of the letter I received from the National Refugee Service of New York in answer to my letter of March 7, which I mentioned in my last letter. I hope we will soon receive favorable news.

I am still waiting for the results of the proceedings by Mr. Amato in Washington.

250 refugees left Tangier for Israel, among them Aunt Gioia and her family. They are going to Gibraltar where they will embark in another boat to be escorted by a convoy which navigates the Mediterranean. We pray they have a good voyage and good luck over there.

Only the people who have an opportunity to go to America remain here. We hope that when the people have left for Palestine, they will take care of us.

Hoping to have the pleasure of receiving your news soon, I send kisses to all.

Your niece,

Claire

WASHINGTON OFFICE

HEBREW SHELTERING AND IMMIGRANT AID SOCIETY

(HIAS)

April 30, 1945

Seattle

Abraham, Mathilda BARKI, et al

Immediately upon receipt of your letter of the 25th instant, we contacted an appropriate official in the Department of State in order to ascertain the exact status of the above-named's visa application. We have now been informed that the case is ready to be scheduled for hearing before an Interdepartmental Visa Review Committee.

Since you indicate in your letter that Mr. Capeluto is coming East in the end of June, we could arrange with the Department of State to have the hearing scheduled to his convenience. Will you please advise us immediately on which date Mr. Capeluto will be in Washington.

Sincerely yours,

ABRAHAM ROCKMORE

Counsel

AR/VP-S

cc: HIAS, Mr. Ralph Capeluto

RAPHAEL A.M. LAREDO

C P A

TANGIER

P. O. Box 87

Tel #2965

CERTIFICATE

I, the undersigned, Raphael A.M. Laredo, CPA for the Courts of Tangier, hereby certifies that I have had the opportunity to audit the accounting work presented by Miss Claire Barki of various commercial enterprises for which I have been the administrative and accounting examiner since the year 1940. She has also assisted in my own field of expertise.

Of great intelligence and of an unwearying devotion, Miss Barki has always performed her task to the satisfaction of all her employers. Called up for family reasons to leave Tangier to settle in America, she will be greatly missed by all of those who have used her services and with whom she leaves a souvenir of excellent collaboration, of real competence, and honesty. I am very pleased to recommend her and to express my best wishes of success.

In testimony whereof, I issue this certificate for whom it may concern.

Tangier, April 26, 1945

(signed by Raphael A.M. Laredo)

MAY 7, 1945

———

ALLIED FORCES REACH

NORTHERN ITALY, ENDING WAR

IN ITALY.

WASHINGTON OFFICE

HEBREW SHELTERING AND IMMIGRANT AID SOCIETY

(HIAS)

May 8, 1945

Seattle

Abraham, Matilde BARKI, et al

Immediately upon receipt of your letter of the 4th instant, we contacted an appropriate official in the Department of State in order to have a hearing set in the case of the above-named.

We have just been informed that a hearing before an Interdepartmental Visa Review Committee has been scheduled for June 7, 1945 at 1:30 p.m.

We shall, therefore, appreciate it if Mr. Capeluto will contact our office by 12:00 noon on June 7th.

We shall keep you advised of further developments.

Sincerely yours,

ABRAHAM ROCKMORE

Counsel

AR/VP-C

cc: Mr. Capeluto

Visa Form IVRC-4

DEPARTMENT OF STATE

WASHINGTON

May 8, 1945

In reply refer to

VD 811.111 BARKI, Abraham

IVRC Docket No. 23,053

Mr. Ralph Capeluto

807 Thirtieth Avenue South

Seattle 44, Washington

NOTICE OF HEARING

Case: BARKI, Abraham and Family

Take notice that this case is assigned to hearing before an Interdepartmental Visa Review Committee at 261 Constitution Avenue NW, Washington, D.C. The calendar will be called promptly at 1:30 p.m. on June 7, 1945, and you will be expected to answer the call at that time and be prepared to make any statement you may deem appropriate in connection with this case.

If because of compelling reasons you are unable to appear on the above date, you should inform the Review committee by registered letter, telegraph, or telephone at least three days prior to the hearing date, giving the reasons for such inability to appear in order that appropriate consideration may be given thereto.

Only persons who have submitted B or C and IVRC-1 forms and the attorneys of such persons, if any, are entitled to appear at the hearing. (See reverse side.)

Secretary of Interdepartmental

Visa Review Committee

The purpose of these hearings is to provide the Review Committee with the fullest and most accurate information possible regarding visa applications. <u>Attendance is not compulsory but in the interest of applicants, it is desirable, particularly in the case of a person now in this country who is himself seeking a permit for permanent residence.</u>

If because of distance from Washington or other controlling reasons the recipient of the accompanying notice finds it impracticable to be present, he is requested to notify the Visa Division without delay. He may at the same time, if he desires, submit a statement in the form of an affidavit which will convey to the Review Committee such information as he is in a position to furnish (not duplicating the details in the documents already in the hands of the Committee), so that it may proceed with the case.

A sponsor or other supporter of an application should be pre-prepared to make clear his own qualifications to furnish useful and reliable information. He should be prepared further to answer such questions, both as to the application and as to his own relation to it, as the members of the Review Committee may wish to ask, and to aid in clearing up any ambiguities or apparent inconsistencies in the material already before them.

The specific matters upon which the Committee desires the fullest information available regarding such applications include the following:

The applicant's understanding of the ideals and principles of our form of Government, his sympathy and accord therewith, and should the visa be granted, his complete loyalty thereto.

Such information as to the applicant's health, personality, education and training, experience and resources as will throw light upon the probabilities of his becoming a useful and desirable member of our community.

In these connections, information is desirable as to his close personal contacts in the country or countries where he has already resided, and in the event of his application being granted, as to those with who he would be in immediate touch in this country.

It should be noted that in the case of all enemy aliens the terms of the Presidential Proclamations prescribe, as a condition to the granting of the visa, that the record shall furnish satisfactory assurance not only of safety, but also of benefit to the United States.

Witnesses who are not themselves American citizens are requested, if possible, to bring with them the passports on which they entered the country.

While it is not in any way obligatory for him to do so, the witness may introduce his testimony by presenting six copies of a brief typewritten statement covering the points already mentioned (one copy for each member of the Committee and one for the stenographer). Experience has shown that such statements serve as a useful basis for such discussions as the members of the Committee may wish to initiate, are likely to ensure a more satisfactory permanent record, and operate to save the time and energy of all concerned.

May 11, 1945

Hebrew Immigrant Aid Society

1317 F Street, NW

Washington 4, DC

Gentlemen:

Attn: Mr. Abraham Rockmore, Counsel

Re: Abraham, Matilde BARKI et al

We are in receipt of your letter of May 8th and have communicated with Mr. Capeluto at once.

In accordance with your wishes, Mr. Capeluto will contact your Office by 12:00 noon on June 7th in order to attend the hearing scheduled for 1:30 p.m. on that day, together with you.

Thanking you again, we remain,

Yours very sincerely,

Frances Pick

Secretary

HEBREW IMMIGRANT AID SOCIETY

May 14, 1945

Miss Dorothy Spielberg

Migration Department

National Refugee Service, Inc.

139 Centre Street

New York 13, NY

Dear Miss Spielberg:

RE: BARKI, Abraham & Family

Tangiers Case #A38812

We are in receipt of your letter of May 9th.

Please note that upon advice received from Washington that a hearing would be called, Mr. Capeluto communicated with a close personal friend of his who is residing in Washington, asking him to attend the hearing in his place since it was very doubtful at that time that Mr. Capeluto would be able to be present at the hearing himself.

However, Mr. Capeluto's friend did not think it would be advisable to do so and he got in touch with HIAS, Washington, asking them to enter their appearance. Therefore, upon a very strong recommendation made by his friend, Mr. Capeluto sent the IVRC form through HIAS, Washington.

We trust the above explanation will be found satisfactory by you, the same as that given by us on May 8th in connection with the Nussbaum case. In connection with the letter we like to add that we have gone through this quite voluminous file and beg to state this case was first handled by HIAS as early as 1940, and the overwhelming majority of letters were exchanged by this office with that agency.

Assuring you that we are just as anxious as you are to have our very pleasant relationship continue and thanking you for your cooperation, we remain,

Yours very sincerely,

Frances Pick

Secretary

WASHINGTON EMIGRE BUREAU, INC.

May 23, 1945, Wednesday [Seattle]

Dear Claire,

Received your letter of April 2nd and was pleased to hear from you. Today I also received your note of April 24th and a copy of the letter sent to you by the National Refugee Service.

No doubt you will be glad to know that we have already made our reservations and are leaving on May 30th for Washington, DC. The hearing has been set for June 7th at 1:30 p.m., at which time I am to appear before an Interdepartmental Visa Review Committee at Washington, DC. I hope that the results of all our efforts will be entirely favorable. Rachel is going to accompany me as after we have finished my work in Washington, DC, we are going to New York for our 15th wedding anniversary. It will, of course, be difficult to leave the kids here at home, but the importance of my appearing at this case makes this trip necessary, and I hope and pray that we will be successful in bringing you all to the United States. That is why we are sacrificing. And, however, our minds will be at ease knowing that the kids will be well taken care of by my mother-in-law and sister-in-law, and our friends and relatives have assured us that they will keep an eye out for them.[60] The day that I received your letter of April 2nd I also received letters from Mathilda and Rachel in Cairo. I was very glad to hear from them both, and they are getting along fine, with the exception that they are extremely worried over the whereabouts of their father, mothers, and sisters. I hope [to G-d] that everybody will be all right.

We are indeed glad to learn that the war in Europe has come to an end at last, and soon we may be able to hear some news from our loved ones there, which we hope will be good news. Now we must hope that it will not be too long before we can clean up the Japs at which time the entire world will again revert to normal peacetime living, although the change cannot come overnight.

Regards from Rachel and the kids. I will keep you posted while on my trip to Washington, DC, and New York, and let you know just what is going on. Mary received your letter of the 24th today and was very happy to hear from you. As soon as she has some time, she will write you again.

Love,[61]

---

[60] In Ladino, "el dio que tenga cargo de ellos."

[61] This letter is from Ralph Capeluto.

May 23, 1945

Dear David,

I wonder if you already know that the date for my hearing from an Interdepartmental Visa Review Committee has been set for June 7th at 1:30 p.m.

Please note that we will leave Seattle May 30th, and I believe we should arrive in Chicago on June 2nd at 8:30 a.m., at which time we will wire you as to the exact time we will arrive in Washington, DC.

In the meantime, Dave, please see if you can get us some hotel accommodations for we do not like to impose on your family.

I am sending today via parcel post a small gift for your child, and I hope she will enjoy it.

Regards to your family and regards from my family, Emma, my mother-in-law and father-in-law. I hope to see you all soon in good health.

Sincerely,

RC/mi

FEDERAL SECURITY AGENCY

OFFICE OF VOCATIONAL REHABILITATION

Washington 25, DC

6309 3rd Street NW

Washington, DC

May 25, 1945

Dear Ralph:

I was glad to hear that you have already been advised of the coming hearing and especially to know that we will see each other again soon. Two weeks ago my wife presented me with another daughter. Since then I have been so excited that I haven't had a chance to write to you. So, will you pass the news along? The mother and baby are doing nicely, and the father is recuperating too.

I had hoped to take care of you in our home when you came. But we have another Capeluto visiting us — Morris Capeluto and his wife from Los Angeles. I believe they will be here until the 11th of June. If you plan on staying in Washington beyond that date, of course you will have to come and stay with us. I have already made a reservation for you at the Ambassador Hotel, 14th and K Streets NW, starting June 3.

We're looking forward with a great deal of anxiety to see you and your charming wife. Please let me know the exact time you will arrive so that I can arrange to meet you.

Regards.

Sincerely,

David

WESTERN UNION

WT137 8_NFW NEWYORK NY 5 356P

MR. AND MRS. CAPELUTO

AMBASSADOR HOTEL 1459 June 5 PM 4 06

Reservation made Hotel McAlpin for Friday, June 8th. Harte and Co.

CAPELUTO

TRANSLATION

Tangier, June 6, 1945

Dear Uncle and Aunt:

Without having the pleasure of answering any of your letters, I inform of our news which I think will be as well received as yours are by us.

Your last letter is dated February 17 and it is strange you have not written further. I assume that you have nothing important to relay, but we are always pleased to receive a few lines from you. If you wait for something to happen in order to write to us, one must assume that if we did not have the business of the trip about which you impart us some news that we would not hear from you.

Dear ones, it is not my intention to make any remarks, but we would wish you write more often, our relations being unfortunately limited only with you. We have relatives everywhere, but no regular correspondence. Some are lazy; others find the pretext that letters go astray. Others say they are busy. Those who would write the most are unfortunately impeded by circumstances. Thus, it is with you that we have more opportunity, and it is a pity not to profit by it. It is not in vain that they say that gradually relatives become strangers. When in Rhodes I was not aware of it because we were all together. But now I really understand the statement. When one moves away, it appears at first that he will never get over the separation; later, gradually the saying "out of sight, out of mind" comes into play. And if by chance one of the parties is "*pinti*"[62] as we say in Rhodes, oblivion is the result. With the pretext of having to receive a letter in order to answer it, one can wait and wait and never write. This, thank God, does not happen to me. If it were not so, I would not write. This would be imitated by everyone to everyone's satisfaction. Sometimes I wonder: "What is the opinion of others about me? Would they label me annoying?" But when I receive your so affectionate letters, I think otherwise and do not alter my ways. As a matter of fact, without exaggerating, for each of your letters I write three.

Well, this is the past, and from now on, we will always have your news, be it from you or whomever, even Morris can very well write to me, and I will derive much pleasure.

Dear ones, allow me to get back to the matter of us going to the United States. Is there anything new? We have no news from anywhere. Besides what I wrote in my letter of April 24, nothing special. What have you done yourselves? I supposed that now that the hostilities in Europe have ended with the complete victory of the Allies, for which we are so happy here, things will get easier, even though the other fanatics in the Pacific still remain; but this, with God's help, will not last long. It is madness on their part to continue the struggle. It is because they are blind to what happened to the one that one might say was their father. Too

---

[62] miserly

bad for them. What will he attain except their destruction to the point of never being able to recover. What is to be lamented is the fact that more people will die, but God will protect the latter and will shorten the remaining period on account of the noble and just cause they defend.

You cannot imagine how much we suffer here, seeing all the horrors of the concentration camps in Germany. Many illustrated magazines are published here and they show many newsreels. We do not know if any of our (relatives) had the bad luck of being deported and having suffered these inhuman tortures. Thank God, everything has passed, and little by little the monstrous authors of the horrors are disappearing. But at what price? How many dear beings have disappeared, how many mothers, spouses, sons have suffered? We are still in a dream, living in hope, and we pray that upon awakening everything will be all right. But this will be a miracle. May God help us, due to the *"zehut"* that they are all innocent.

Dear ones, this week we received a letter from Palestine from Aunt Sarina, telling us that everything is okay and that her sons are working in a shoe factory, but that her husband is still idle. The letter was dated April 20, but a letter received by some friends of ours from Palestine written at a later date mentions that Chelibon is working. We hope it is true for it is not only a matter of earning a living, but because it is difficult to have a man like Chelibon constantly around the house. It is better for him to be busy in a shop, for the sake of Aunt Sarina. She also tells us she is exchanging letters with the daughters of Aunt Behora, Mathilda and Rachel, who wrote to her about their having Leon, the son of Aunt Marie, as a guest the eve of Passover. As I believe I have written to you, Leon Levy left Tangier for Palestine in the same boat as Aunt Sarina. He had always in his head to join the Allies. He was unable to do so from here, and when he arrived in Palestine, he took advantage and joined them. It must be that he happened to be in Cairo on Passover. According to another fellow who left for Palestine and who wrote to his brother, Leon is at present in Italy. He was lucky in that the war in Europe is over and perhaps he can investigate and search for his family.

Dear ones, regarding the money you had sent and was returned, one payable to Aunt Esther and one for Papa, we received in exchange two other remittances payable to Aunt Esther, one on March 26 and one on April 9. To avoid confusion and loss, I would like to know if these two remittances correspond to the previous returned ones. As the two were payable to Aunt Esther, perhaps you have not received the one payable to Papa. To straighten things out, please advise if it involves the same ones or if there is a third one. Perhaps the one payable to Papa is lost and it is a pity.

Nothing else to add other than to say that we are all well. We hope you are, too.

Kisses from everyone, particularly Aunt Esther.

Dear Uncle Raphael, and I say it confidentially, never blame Aunt Esther for not writing. Although she is somewhat lazy, I admit, she does not feel like doing anything. She is very sad not knowing about her sisters. Believe me, she loves you very much and her only wish is to know about the people from Rhodes and to see your faces. This, Uncle Raphael, is between us, and do not mention it in your answer.

Many kisses to dear Jamila and her husband. Fond regards to Mary Israel, and please tell her that I hope to have the pleasure of receiving soon a letter from her. Affectionate regards and kisses to the kids and you. Your niece who wishes to see you soon,

Claire

P.S. Upon finishing this letter, I received yours dated May 23, and you can't imagine the joy we felt upon reading its contents. We pray now that the results of your activities will bear fruit. Keep us abreast of everything as soon as possible.

[Letter addendum]   June 6, 1945

Dear Uncle, I was glad to know that Aunt Rachel will accompany you on your trip. She will bring luck. I wish you a good trip and have a good time and spend little. I have also received the letter from Mary. I did not have the chance of reading it in its entirety as I want to finish this one and send it. It is very late, and I fear it will miss the plane. I will answer her very soon. I am looking forward to your favorable news, and meanwhile I send you kisses from my heart.

Claire

WESTERN UNION

WM22

W.NF25 12 COLLECT=NF WASHINGTON DC 30 1105A   1945 JUN 30 AM 8:15

RALPH CAPELUTO SEATTLE CURTAIN MFG CO=$229.32

1562 PREFONTAINE BLDG THIRD AND YESLER WAY SEATTLE WASH=

STATE DEPARTMENT GRANTED ADVISORY APPROVAL VISA APPLICATION BARKI FAMILY. LETTER FOLLOWS.

HEBREW SHELTERING AND IMMIGRANT AID SOCIETY HIAS

HIAS ALSO VISA BARKI.

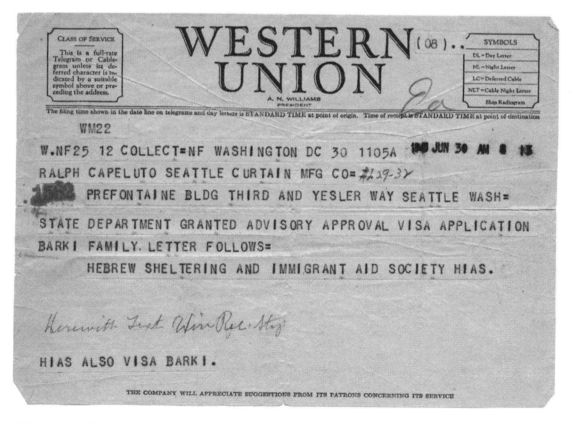

Telegram dated June 30, 1945. Telegram from Hebrew Sheltering and Immigrant Aid Society (HIAS) to Ralph Capeluto notifying him that advisory approval for visa application was granted.

Washington Office

HEBREW SHELTERING AND IMMIGRANT AID SOCIETY

(HIAS)

June 30, 1945

Mr. Ralph Capeluto

Seattle Curtain Manufacturing Company

Prefontaine Building

Third and Yesler Way

Seattle, Washington

Dear Sir:

We are very pleased to confirm herewith our telegram of even date indicating that the Department of State has granted advisory approval to the visa applications in behalf of Abraham Barki and family. Appropriate notification of this action has been forwarded by the Visa Division to the American Consul at Tangier.

Please be assured that we are most happy at the successful outcome of this case and sincerely hope that the aliens will not encounter any further difficulties in obtaining their visas and proceeding to the United States for permanent residence.

Sincerely yours,

ABRAHAM ROCKMORE

Counsel

vrp

Tanger, el 4 de Julio 1945.

Queridos tios,

Por mas que os lo escriba, nunca podré deciros con precision, la alegria que consentimos en recibir vuestro telegrama del 30/6 como sigue

"HEREWITH TEXT WIRE RECEIVED STOP STATE DEPT. GRANTED ADVISORY APPROVAL
"VISA A-PPLICATION BARKI FAMILY LETTER FOLLOWS HEBREW SHELTERING AND
"IMMIGRANT AID SOCIETY - Ralph Capeluto -"

Por no se que milagro, porqué los telegramas tambien tardan en llegar, le recibimos el 2/7 Lunes à las 8 de la mañana. Era tan temprano que nunca nos habriamos imaginado que era por esto que llamaban à la puerta Ademas que el Sabado 30/6 recibimos la carta de la tante Rachel del 13/6 diciendonos que teniamos que esperar 4 semanas para tener la contestacion. Asi es que verdaderamente nos cogio de sorpresa, pero sorpresa agradable.

Queridisimos tios, no se como agradeceros de todo lo que habeis hecho por nosotros, gracias que no fué en balde y con favor de Dios, pronto tendremos la suerte de demostraros nuestro agradecimiento. Ahora es de esperar que lleguen à la Legacion de los Estados Unidos en Tanger, los visados, que creo no tardaran y que empesemos aqui à correr, porqué tambien aqui hay muchos pasos que dar. Por esto no hay que preocuparse, lo principal ya está hecho.

Queridos tios, parece que esta es una de mis ultimas cartas que os dirigiré. Parece mentira pensa-r que dentro de breve nos veremos y conoceremos. Lo que hayais reuscido aqui les parece à todos un milagro y cosa que no se puede creer, porqué la verdad que os diga como mashalà somos muchos os exigirian muchas cosas. Todos aqui estan contentos por nosotros, porqué iremos à un sitio donde podremos hacer algo, pero no os podeis imaginar cuan tristes estan todos, los conocidos, los amigos, los patrones, todos por separarsen de nosotros.Nos habian tomado tanto cariño, cada uno de nosotros en el lado que iba. Enfin que se va à hacer. Mas deseamos ajuntarnos con vosotros, ya que aqui no nos queda ningun querido.

Queridos tios, ahora q-uiero que presteis mucha iatencion à lo que os escribo y que me contesteis en seguida à lo que os pregunto. Primeramente me gustaria saber todos vuestros pasos, que estoy tan curiosa de conocerlos, pero este gusto lo dejaré para cuando nos encontremos. A-hora lo q-ue mas me interesa es que me escribais sobre las cosas que tenemos que llevarnos de aqui. Ya sabeis que no es facil desazeram una casa, aunque aqui nunca hemos asentado la cabeza y arreglado nada porqué ni teniamos gusto ni pensabamos quedarnos.definitivamente, pero ya sabeis que una casa es una casa y no hay mas remedio que tener de todo. Asi es que empesando por :

I°) el algodon de la-s camas. Es necesario que no lo llevemos ? Pensamos hacer una bala de unas colchas que tenemos y dos minderis de algodon. Que décis ?

2°) De cocina, hace falta que nos llevemos algo ? Por ejemplo los aluminios el cobre. Si es que no vale la pena y que ahi es barato, aqui podemos vender lo que tenemos y comprar ahi otros nuevos. Es tan largo el viaje que seria ridiculo si nos llevamos cosas que no valen la pena y que ahi podremos comprar mas barato. Hoy en dia se paga tanto de flete

Letter dated July 4, 1945. Letter from Claire Barkey to Ralph Capeluto rejoicing notification that immigration visa had been granted.

- 2 -

que seria mejor asegurarse antes que hacer nada. Queridos tios, nosostros ya estamos tan adeudados con vosotros por lo que habeis hecho hasta ahora que no quisieramos añadir mas deudas, ni atangantaros mas, pero comprendereis que es una cosa razonable el preguntaros estas cosas. Como todavia tendremos 2 o 3 meses que estar aqui, os ruego nos contesteis en seguida al recibir la presente, sobre todo lo que os pregunto para quepodamos hacer las cosas con tranquilidad y no dejar todo hasta el ultimo momento.

3°)Tambien desearia saber, si llegando ahi, supongamos que estemos aqui 2 o 3 meses mas, en fines Septiembre/ Octubre, que ropas necesitaremos. Tendremos que llevar ropas de invierno, de verano o de media estacion.

Estas son las cosas principales que me interesan saber lo antes posible, para poder arreglar todo con tiempo. Mashalà somos numerosos y para todos habrà que preparar algo.

Me voià à excusar si no os alargo mas, pero estoy hasta la cabeza de trabajo y hace tanto calor.

Ya os estaré escribiendo al corriente porqué siempre tendré algo que preguntaros. Os ruego por empezar me contesteis en seguida sobre lo qué os pregunto por la presente.

A la querida Mary Israel, os ruego lex digais que estoy verda-deramente avergonsada de no escribirle pero que le ruego me excuse y me comprenda. Todo lo que tengo que escribirle, se lo diré cuando nos veamos, que espero serà dentro de poco tiempo. Y asi serà mejor, tendré mas cosas que contarle.

Tambien à todos vosotros. Y à los niños ? esto si que me parece un sueño, que veré dentro de poco à mis queriditos primos. Como yo, todos en casa estàn asi, locos de contentos. Ya vereis cuando os lo cuenten ellos mismos.

Enviandoos a todos muchos besos de toda la familia, y rogandoos me contesteis en seguida, os beso y os abrazo vuestra querida sobrina que espera veros muy pronto.

Claire

217

TRANSLATION

Tangier, July 4, 1945

Dear Uncle and Aunt:

No matter how much I write, I cannot describe the joy we felt upon receiving your telegram of June 30, as follows:

"HEREWITH TEXT WIRE RECEIVED STOP STATE DEPT. GRANTED ADVISORY AP-PROVAL VISA APPLICATION BARKI FAMILY LETTER FOLLOWS HEBREW SHELTERING AND IMMIGRANT AID SOCIETY—Ralph Capeluto"

I don't know by what miracle, because telegrams also take a long time to arrive. We received it Monday, July 2, at 8 a.m. It was so early we could not figure out the reason they were knocking at the door. Besides, on Saturday, June 30, we received a letter from Aunt Rachel dated June 13, stating that we had to wait four weeks to receive an answer, so that we were really surprised, but pleasantly so.

Dear ones, I don't know how to thank you for everything you have done for us. Thank God it was not for naught and God willing, we will have the chance to show our gratitude. Now, we have to wait for the visas to reach the U.S. Legation in Tangier, and I believe they will not take long. And we will then start getting busy because here also there are steps to be taken. This is less of a worry, the main thing is done.

Dear ones, it seems that this is one of the last letters I will address to you. It seems incredible to think that within a short time we will see each other and get really acquainted. The fact that you succeeded seems a miracle and unbelievable to everyone, as, we are being numerous, they must have demanded many things. Everyone here is very glad for us because we will go to a place where we will do something. But you cannot imagine how sad everyone is, acquaintances, friends, bosses, to part company. They became very fond of each of us. What can be done? We prefer to join you since no dear ones remain here.

Dear Uncle and Aunt, please take notice of what I write and answer right away. First of all, I would like to know all the steps you took as I am curious to know them, but this can wait until we meet. What concerns us now is to know all the things that we must take from here. You know, it is not easy to "dismantle" a house, although we never had completely settled here nor put everything in order. We were not in the mood nor we thought of staying permanently, but you know, you need a little of everything, regardless. So, let us start with the following:

1) The cotton from the beds, is it necessary for us to take? Perhaps making a bale of some quilts and two cotton blankets. What do you think?

2) For the kitchen—do you need to take something, as for example, copper pans? If it isn't worthwhile and if cheap over there, we can sell whatever we have and buy new ones over there. The voyage is so long that it would be ridiculous to take useless things. Nowadays, you pay a great deal for freight and it would be better to make sure before doing anything.

Dear ones, we are so indebted to you for what you have done so far that we don't want to add more debts or to pester you, but you will understand the reasonable questions. As we will be here for two or three months, please answer immediately all my questions so as to allow us to do things with ease and not at the last moment.

3) Also, we would like to know if upon arriving there, assuming in two or three months, at the end of September or October, what type of clothing will we need? Do we have to bring winter, summer, or mid-season clothing?

These are the main things we are interested to know as soon as possible to be able to arrange everything in time. We are many and must prepare something for everyone.

You must excuse me if I don't prolong this letter as I am up to my neck in work and it is so hot. I will keep you posted because I will always have some inquiry to make. Please start answering me concerning what I have asked so far.

Please tell Mary Israel that I am shamed not to have written and to excuse and understand me. Whatever I must write, I will relate when we see each other, which I hope will be shortly. And that will be better, and I will have more to say. The same with regard to all of you. And the children, how are they? It really seems like a dream that shortly I will see my dear little cousins. Including me, everyone is going crazy from happiness. You will see when they will tell their own story.

We send kisses from the whole family and please answer right away. A kiss and a hug from your dear niece who hopes to see you soon.

Claire

July 10, 1945

Dear Claire,

Enclosed you will find copies of correspondence I have received from Washington, DC, in regard to your visa. Now that I have done all I can from this side, I hope you will not lose any time in contacting the American Consul at Tangier for their approval.

Also contact the Hebrew Immigrant Aid Society (HIAS) and the Jewish Refugee Committee in Tangiers and see what assistance they will be able to render to speed up your departure to the United States.

If there is anything I can do for you, do not hesitate to wire or write me.

Regards from the family and regards to Papa, Mama, and the kids and to Auntie Esther. I hope I will be seeing you all soon.[63]

---

[63] This unsigned letter is most likely from Ralph Capeluto.

CABLE

NA268 INTL=CD TANGER VIA RCA 34 24

NLT RAPHAEL CAPELUTO=

PREFONTAINE BLDG, SEATL

VISAS NOT ARRIVED INQUIRING AMERICAN CONSULATE TANGIER SAID TO OB-
TAIN VISAS INDISPENSIBLE PRESENT AFFIDAVITS STATEMENT YOUR BUSINESS ACCOUNT
AND OTHER GUARANTEES SHOWING YOU MAY SUPPORT US.

ABRAHAM BARKI

National Refugee Service, Inc.

139—Centre St.

NY City   4 copies[64]

---

[64] This wire dated July 24, 1945.

TRANSLATION

Tangier, July 25, 1945

Dear Uncle and Aunt:

We acknowledge receipt of your telegram dated July 5, as follows:

"APPROPRIATE NOTIFICATION FORWARDED BY VISA DIVISION TO AMERICAN CONSUL TANGIER STOP PROCEED TO OBTAIN VISA FROM AMERICAN CONSUL WIRE RESULTS"

by which we understand that after having been granted, the visas have been sent to the American Consulate of Tangier. We also understand that you ask us to try to obtain the visas from here.

Upon receiving the above-mentioned telegram, Papa and I presented ourselves to the American Legation here. After having read the telegram, the Consul gave us a request for a visa to be filled in. Among the many questions appearing on it, ages, professions, birth place, nationality, the most important was the following: If we have resources to live in the U.S. or if we go under someone's responsibility.

I wrote down that we were under your care. Eight days after having sent them properly filled, they sent us a letter summoning us, but we were disappointed when he told us that referring to the above-mentioned question, that is, the means we count on to live in the U.S., they need proof that you can support us. Proof, such as bank statements, a report on your business, names of firms you deal with; in other words, as many guarantees as you can possibly send to show that you can take care of us.

This, dear ones, puts us in a confusing situation. We don't understand what these people want. If Washington has given the visas, surely it must have been after you showed them of the proofs of guarantee. I remarked that to the Consul, but he told me that there are new laws stating that each U.S. Legation in a foreign country must decide by itself the question of visas to enter the U.S. This is a law that appeared in the Tangier newspapers and had the following text:

"Washington, July 22, 1945—The matter of visas to enter the U.S. will soon revert to the pre-war system. The review of requirements announced by the U.S. State Dept. gives to the diplomatic and consular authorities overseas the possibility to act according to the pre-war principles exercising their own initiative in the matter of visas. The State Dept. will not accept sponsorship of documents nor will initiate action in visa cases."

We do not know if the law concerns us since our case has been solved, as you wired us. Did we deceive ourselves or have we misinterpreted your wire? I hope it is not that for what a disappointment it would be!

Assuming the above, and not having had the luck of obtaining visas in Washington, and thinking that you are awaiting the results of our steps here, I thought it timely to wire you as follows: "VISAS NOT ARRIVED INQUIRING AMERICAN CONSULATE TANGIER SAID TO OBTAIN VISAS INDISPENSABLE PRESENT AFFIDAVITS STATEMENT YOUR BUSINESS ACCOUNT AND OTHER GUARANTEES SHOWING YOU MAY SUPPORT US"

Also, to gain time for your immediate preparation of affidavits and necessary documents, exactly like those you had sent us when we were in Rhodes. Everything will be as before the war.

I think it would be advantageous and useful to get some support of the Hebrew Sheltering and Immigrant Aid Society.

Dear ones, I greatly regret that we still have to bother you when we thought we would be at your side and that everything had ended satisfactorily. It is the bad luck and everything is fate. Yet, I have the hope that our visas had been granted in Washington before the enactment of these laws.

Dear Uncle and Aunt, I swear that after this, in order not to trouble you anymore, we would desist from our going to the U.S. but how can we take this decision if life is impossible here? Until now, the Refugee Committee has helped us somewhat, but there is talk that it will not last and with justification, because there are more unfortunate people than us to succor, in so many countries recently liberated in Europe. Thus, please make a last effort and send us the earliest possible what I ask. Let us see if, once and for all, they are sufficient. It would be great if all these guarantee papers would arrive at Tangier with the visas.

Dear Uncle and Aunt, it is impossible to tell you how we recognize your efforts and work in you're trying to help us, but I can't find the words to tell you what we will always be grateful. We wish we would succeed in doing something and be able to pay our debt.

We await anxiously your news and meanwhile Papa, Mama, Aunt Esther, my brothers and sisters requested me to send their hugs. Regards to dear Mary Israel from me. Tender kisses to Morris, Betty, Marlene, and Amelia. Regards to Aunt Jamila and her husband. To you, dear Uncle and Aunt, a strong and affectionate hug from your niece.

Claire

SEATTLE-FIRST NATIONAL BANK

SEATTLE 14, WASHINGTON

July 30, 1945

American Consulate

Tangier

Morocco

Gentlemen:

Mr. Ralph Capeluto, who has been a valued customer of ours for a number of years, informs us that he is negotiating to bring in to this country a number of his relatives who are now residing at Tangier, Morocco.

At his request we are pleased to inform you that Mr. Capeluto is carrying a good personal account with us. He is one of the partners of the Seattle Curtain Manufacturing Company, which firm has also been a client of ours ever since it commenced business in 1930. They are carrying a very desirable account with us, and in the past we have granted the company credit accommodation in connection with its business up to $40,000, most of which has been upon an unsecured basis. And in addition to this, we have also made them substantial loans for the purpose of purchasing United States Government Bonds. The financial statement of the Seattle Curtain Manufacturing Company as of December 31, 1944 indicates a net worth in excess of $140,000 with an excellent position of affairs reflected. Mr. Capeluto owns one-half of this business, and we understand that he also has other assets, which, in our opinion, would bring his personal net worth over $100,000. We regard him as being a man of excellent character and reliability, and believe that he is in a position to fully protect his reasonable commitments.

Very truly yours,

F. E. Jerome

Vice President

FEJ:MB

SEATTLE-FIRST NATIONAL BANK

SEATTLE 14, WASHINGTON

July 30, 1945

American Consulate

Tangier

Morocco

Gentlemen:

We understand that Mr. Charles D. Alhadeff has made application and has issued his guaranty on behalf of the nine relatives of his cousin, Mr. Ralph Capeluto.

Mr. Alhadeff has requested that we write you for the purpose of vouching for his ability to carry out the commitments he has made in the application.

We are pleased, therefore, to inform you that he has been known to us for many years, and we consider him to be a man of excellent character and reliability. He is one of the partners of Whiz Fish Products Company and the Palace Fish and Oyster Company, and in connection with the business operations of these firms we have granted them a very substantial line of credit which has always been handled in a most satisfactory manner. In Mr. Alhadeff's application he mentions that he has an annual income of over $25,000, and that he has additional assets valued at $150,000. We are pleased to confirm these representations. In our opinion he is well-qualified to execute the guaranty under discussion and we consider his abundantly responsible for much obligations as he may incur there under.

Very truly yours,

F. E. Jerome

Vice President

FEJ:MB

IN THE MATTER OF THE APPLICATION

     -of-

FOR IMMIGRATION VISA TO THE UNITED STATES

STATE OF   )   Washington

CITY OF   )   SS Seattle

COUNTY OF   )   King

I, Ralph Capeluto, being duly sworn, deposes and says:

That I was born in Isle of Rhodes on Jan. 10th. 1900.

That I am a citizen of the United States by birth _____, or by naturalization _____x_____, certificate #2393226, issued by New York Federal Court, on Feb. 21st. 1927.

Vol 295 No. 81931

That I am concerned about the welfare of Relatives on attached list, who was born in (see list) on (see list) and is residing at (see list) and who is anxious to immigrate to the United States to join me.

That I am a blood relative of Eight of the nine applicants. I am very much concerned about his welfare and have a strong sense of moral responsibility for him. That I hereby give assurance that I will properly receive and care for the said applicants upon his arrival in this country and I will not permit him to become a public charge upon any community or municipality (Explain Relationship)

That as proof of my financial ability, I allege as follows:

(documentary proof is hereto attached)

1. That I am (give occupation) Curtain Manufacturer

2. That I have an annual income of $ see statement attached

3. That in addition I have assets valued at $ see statement attached

     Insurance $_____ Cash surrender value $_____

     Bank Saving $_____

     Other Assets (including personal property such as bonds, etc.)

4. That I have dependent upon me for support: (State relationship and degree of dependency) Wife and four children the eldest child being fifteen years old

That this petition is made by me in order that the Honorable American Consul abroad will visa the passport of the said Relatives

Sworn and subscribed before me.   <u>Ralph Capeluto (signed)</u>

this 30th day of July 1945

(signed)

Notary Public in and for the State of Washington,

Residing in Seattle

IN THE MATTER OF THE APPLICATION
FOR IMMIGRATION VISA
SCHEDULE OF PERSONS FOR WHOM APPLICATION IS MADE

Name	Date of birth	Place of birth	Present address	Relationship
Esther Capeluto	March 10th 1909	Isle of Rhodes	Tangiers Morocco	Sister
Abraham Barki	Feb 20th 1891	Aidin, Turkey	"	Brother-in-law
Matilda Barki	March 5th 1895	Isle of Rhodes	"	Sister
Claire Barki	March 14th 1921	"	"	Niece
Rachel Barki	March 5th, 1923	"	"	"
Hain Barki) twins	March 27th 1925	"	"	Nephew
Moise Barki)	"	"	"	"
Jacques Barki	March 3rd 1928	"	"	"
Regina Barki	Jan 9th 1932	"	"	Niece

Statement of annual income

	Calendar year		
	1939	$2,641.64
	1940	6,349.00
	1941	10,270.83
	1942	12,733.85
	1943	29,638.30
	1944	45,728.62
	1945 estimated	45,000.00

Statement of Assets

Insurance carried $21,595.00 of which	
One $5,000.00 policy fully paid up surrender value	$3,165.00
Bank Savings	2,000.00
Home free and clear of all encumbrance	10,000.00
Defense bonds	10,000.00
***Net worth of 50% equity in Seattle Curtain	
Manufacturing Company a two man partnership	85,000.00
	$110,165.00

I Llewellyn A. Roberts a certified public accountant by examination in the State of Washington do hereby certify that the statement of annual income is taken from the Federal income tax returns prepared by myself, that policies of insurance covering $16,595.00 are in the Company's safe and the net worth of equity in the Seattle Curtain Co. is computed from the ledger balances as at June 30th 1945.

(signed)
***Curtain Co. owns $130,700 U.S. Treasury bonds

IN THE MATTER OF THE APPLICATION
     -of-
FOR IMMIGRATION VISA TO THE UNITED STATES

STATE OF   ) SS   Washington
CITY OF   )   Seattle
COUNTY OF   )   King

     I, Charles D. Alhadefff, being duly sworn, deposes and says:

     That I am a resident of the State of Washington, City of Bellevue, residing at Route 3 Box 588 in the County of King.

     That I am a citizen of the United States by birth May 6, 1909, or by naturalization _____, certificate #_____x_____, issued by _____ Court, on _____.

     That I am concerned about the welfare of nine relatives of my cousin Ralph Capeluto and is residing at Isle of Rhodes, Tangiers, Morocco and who is anxious to immigrate to the United States to join me.

     That I am a blood relative of _____. I am very much concerned about his welfare and have a strong sense of moral responsibility for him. That I hereby give assurance that I will properly receive and care for the said nine relatives of Ralph Capeluto upon his arrival in this country and I will not permit him to become a public charge upon any community or municipality (Explain Relationship)

     That as proof of my financial ability, I allege as follows:

(documentary proof is hereto attached)

1. That I am (give occupation) Fish business - Wholesale, canners and producers
2. That I have an annual income of $ over 25,000.00
3. That in addition I have assets valued at $ over 150,000.00

     Insurance $ 50,000.00   Cash surrender value $ 150,000.00
     Bank Saving $ over 10,000
     Other Assets (including personal property such as bonds, etc.)
     Bonds - $50,000.00   Business interests (over $100,000.00)
     Property $25,000.00

4. That I have dependent upon me for support: (State relationship and degree of dependency) Wife and three children

That this petition is made by me in order that the Honorable American Consul abroad will visa the passport of the said nine relatives of my cousin Ralph Capeluto

Sworn and subscribed before me.   Charles D. Alhadeff (signed)
this 30th day of July 1945
(signed)
Notary Public in and for the State of Washington,
Residing in Seattle, Wash.

July 31, 1945
AIR MAIL   REGISTERED   SPECIAL DELIVERY
Miss Hortense Ginzbourger
Migration Department
National Refugee Service, Inc.
139 Centre Street
New York 13, NY

>   RE: BARKI, Abraham and
>   Family, Tangiers
>   Your #A 38812

Dear Ms. Ginzbourger:

We beg to refer to your letter of July 12th and ours of July 19th. In the meantime, Mr. Capeluto has received a cable from his relatives in Tangiers advising him that new affidavits are required as per information received from the consulate.

We are, therefore, enclosing herewith the following papers:

Affidavit of Mr. Ralph Capeluto in four copies

Letter of Seattle First National Bank in duplicate

Affidavit of Mr. Charles Alhadeff in four copies

Letter of Seattle-First National Bank in duplicate

Will you kindly forward these documents at once by airmail to Tangiers, advising us of the postage so that Mr. Capeluto may reimburse you without delay. The address of Mr. Abraham Barki and his family is 77 Paseo Cenarro, Tangiers, Morocco, and we leave it to you to send the documents to the applicants or to your committee abroad whichever way you consider faster. Mr. Capeluto is very anxious to expedite matters in any possible way, and if you believe it will be helpful if he deposits with you funds to cover the cost of transportation from Tangiers to a USA port, he will be very glad to do so. May we mention that Mr. Capeluto bears a very fine reputation in our community and is well thought of personally by everyone who knows him. Furthermore, Mr. Capeluto was very helpful to our community at a time when it was very difficult to obtain positions for our new arrivals, and we know that he will help again if the occasion should make it necessary.

Mr. Capeluto has cabled his relatives today that the documents are going forward, and we thank you in advance for doing everything in your power to assist in this case.

Yours sincerely,

Frances Pick
Secretary

WASHINGTON EMIGRE BUREAU, INC.

Aug.14,1945

Mrs. Dorothy Spielberg
Migration Department
National Refugee Service, Inc.
139 Centre St.
New York 13, N.Y.

Dear Mrs. Spielberg: Re: BARKI, Abraham
                                            and family
                                        Tangiers
                                        Case #A 38812

Immediately upon receipt of your letter of August 7th
we communicated with Mr. Capeluto who is very glad indeed that the documents are on their way.

Please accept the sponsors' and our own best thanks
for your assistance.

If there is anything further you can do to expedite
matters we would greatly appreciate it. As you know
Mr. Capeluto is most anxious to have his relatives
come to this country without any further delay.

In accordance with your suggestion, we have written
to Hias, New York in regard to depositing money for
the family's transportation.

Mr. Capeluto will thank you to send a port and dock
notice to Hias and has asked us to give you the following address of his relative in New York:

    Mr. Harry Benater
    1113 Blake Court
    Brooklyn 23, N.Y.

Mr. Capeluto has written to Mr. Benater that you will
get in touch with him.

Hoping that you will soon be able to let us have some
more news, we remain,

                            Yours sincerely,

                            WASHINGTON EMIGRE BUREAU, INC.

CC Mr. Capeluto   Frances Pick
                                Secretary

Letter dated Aug. 14, 1945. Letter from Washington Emigre Bureau to Migration Department, National Refugee Service, helping to smooth the way for the Barkey family's immigration.

August 14, 1945
Mrs. Dorothy Spielberg
Migration Department
National Refugee Service, Inc.
139 Centre Street
New York 13, NY

RE: BARKI, Abraham and family

Tangiers

Case No. A-38812

Dear Mrs. Spielberg:

Immediately upon receipt of your letter of August 7th we communicated with Mr. Capeluto who is very glad indeed that the documents are on their way.

Please accept the sponsor's and our own best thanks for your assistance.

If there is anything further you can do to expedite matters, we would greatly appreciate it. As you know, Mr. Capeluto is most anxious to have his relatives come to this country without any further delay.

In accordance with your suggestion, we have written to HIAS, New York, in regard to depositing money for the family's transportation.

Mr. Capeluto will thank you to send a port and dock notice to HIAS and has asked us to give you the following address of his relative in New York:

Mr. Harry Benater

1113 Blake Court

Brooklyn 23, NY

Mr. Capeluto has written to Mr. Benater that you will get in touch with him.

Hoping that you will soon be able to let us have some more news, we remain,

Yours sincerely,

Frances Pick
Secretary

WASHINGTON EMIGRE BUREAU, INC.

cc: Mr. Capeluto

WESTERN UNION

August 27, 1945

Claire Barki

77 Paseo Benarro

Tangiers, Morocco

Why long silence wire collect regarding visas remitted HIAS 3000 dollars advance transportation.[65]

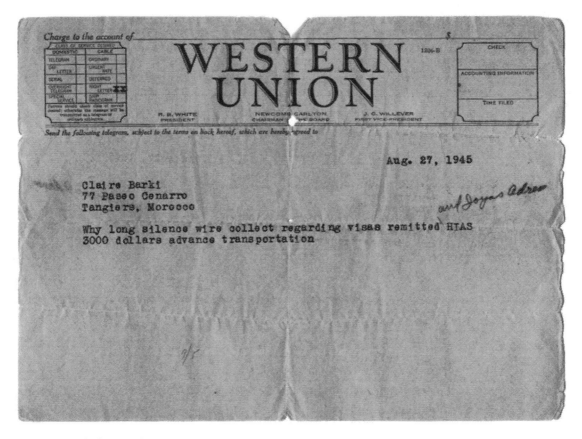

Telegram dated Aug. 27, 1945. Telegram from Ralph Capeluto to Claire Barkey.

---

[65] From Ralph Capeluto.

HEBREW SHELTERING AND IMMIGRANT AID SOCIETY

425 Lafayette Street

New York 3, NY

September 12, 1945

Mr. Ralph Capeluto

807—30th Avenue South

Seattle, Washington

RE: Abraham BARKI and Family

77 Paseo Cenarro

Tangiers, Morocco

Dear Mr. Capeluto:

We are in receipt of your check in the amount of $3,000 which we have cabled immediately to our appropriate European Agency to arrange transportation in this particular matter.

However, you failed to include $3.00 cable charge and will you kindly comply with this request and remit by return mail.

We shall, of course, keep you advised of any and all developments.

Very sincerely yours,

Abe Grossman

CONSULTANTS DIVISION

AG:rm

cc: HIAS

320 Smith Tower Annex

Seattle, Washington

TRANSLATION

Tangier, September 18, 1945

Dear Uncle and Aunt:

We received your esteemed letter of August 23 and were glad to know you are in perfect health. We are all well and glad we will join you soon.

Dear ones, when everything seems to come to an end, more difficulties crop up. After having received copies of the guarantee papers from the National Refugee Service of New York, we appeared before the local American Consul. Without having a need to hand them to him, he told us that they had already received directly the originals and that everything was in order, that the guarantee was sufficient and as far as the "support" is concerned, they would allow us to enter the U.S. They gave us a list of what we have to prepare here, be it photographs, birth certificates, certificate of good conduct, medical certificate, and the most important, a letter from steamship companies in Spain or Portugal, stating the date of departure of liners for the U.S, and if there are nine tickets available for us.

We prepared all these papers ourselves, except that we had the Tangier Committee write to the steamship company. The local Committee must have written to the Lisbon Committee, for after almost a month, on Friday, September 14th, they called us to advise that they had a wire from the Lisbon Committee stating they had communicated directly with the American Consulate of Tangier. We appeared before the latter with all the documents, including the passports from the Italian Consulate valid for the U.S. and renewed for one year. They told us that everything from our side was in order and that they would ask for eight spots in the Italian quota and one in the Turkish quota. Upon receiving them, they will notify us to tell us that we can definitely obtain the visas. Then we would make reservations on the boat and after showing the steamship tickets, the Consul would grant us the visa.

All these complications and delays are due to the fact that, according to what the American Consul said, there were many cases in which visas had been granted for four months but had expired because there were no boats for the U.S. or accommodation left in them. As we have to pay again $10 for each one to renew them, we are waiting for them to call us, granting definitely the visas, in order to call the Lisbon Committee so that they may make reservations. We would have preferred everything to be ready to be able to embark before the rains start, but what can we do? Everything is for the good. We have waited so long, we will wait a little longer. These are government matters, and, as you said, we must have patience.

Dear ones, today is Tuesday, and we have just concluded Yom Kippur. Yesterday, all our prayers were directed on behalf of the unfortunate relatives, for we are uncertain whether they are still alive. We have no lists here. We only know about six girls from Rhodes who met in Paris or in Holland and this information came from America, where they read the list in the communities over there. It is most likely that you know something about them and you should let us know.

As far as Eliezer Jacob Surmani is concerned, he must be the son of Jacob Surmani, our cousin, son of Tia Tamar[66], because there was no other Jacob Surmani in Rhodes and Eliezer was his son. It must be that of this unfortunate cousin, two sons survived because about a year and a half ago, Salvator Levy of Belgian Congo, son of Aunt Rizula, wrote to me stating that he had received a letter from his mother who had gone to Palestine on an unfortunate voyage which would take long to relate and of which I will tell you when we are together, stating that Moshe, the twin, son of Jacob Surmani, had fled Rhodes, I don't know how, and was in Palestine. This occurred when they were not receiving letters from Rhodes and when the Germans were there. Salvator suggested that I write Jacob Surmani through the Red Cross to let him know that his son was safe and sound. I did this soon after, but I do not know if his father had the joy of receiving the news. Salvator also told me that the boy had related that Tia Tamar had died from the suffering and deprivations.

Also, Aunt Sarina wrote to me saying that she saw him in Palestine and he was attending the same school as Shelomo, her son.

Of all the places stepped on by the wicked Germans, the one that suffered most of the consequences, I believe, must have been Rhodes, an island that produces nothing. If hunger did not liquidate them, the suffering inflicted upon them must have done it. It is preferable to have been taken to other places to work, but at least having something to eat. We hope to find out more about them some day.

Dear ones, as to what refers to Behor of Aunt Behora, as I told you, I have written to him several times and he never deigned answering me. He is a strange one! Even so, I will write to him this week and I will see if I am luckier. I will also write to Cairo. It is very likely that they have engaged themselves to search their relatives. As soon as I find out, I will let you know.

Nothing else to add. We hope that all the difficulties will tumble down and we see each other soon. Affectionate kisses from all of us and greetings for the New Year and may it bring us all happiness and may we have good news from everyone.

A strong hug to my little cousins from your niece who loves you very much.

Claire[67]

---

[66] Mathilda Barkey's aunt.

[67] Claire's maternal grandmother Rachel (whose maiden name was also Capeluto), who was married to Mussani Capeluto, had several brothers and sisters. They were: Diamante Benatar (the mother of Harry Benatar who received us in NY upon arrival) Tamar Surmani (referred to above), Rizula Levy (mother of Salvator Levy, also referred to above), Rahamin Capeluto, Mussani Capeluto, Abraham Capeluto, and a half-sister Bohora Hasson.

"Tia" means "Aunt" in Spanish. The Sephardi of Rhodes and Turkey gave this title to older people out of respect.

As previously referenced, Salvator Levy is the brother of Rahamin, presently living in Toronto, Canada.

Spanish[68] Protectorate

of Morocco

Region of Tangier

Police Station   <u>Safe Conduct</u>

Section:

No. 2587

We grant authorization to move to the United States via Spain and Portugal

to: Moise Barki

Native of Rhodes, 20 years of age, son of Abraham and of Matilde, residing at Paseo Cenarro, 77, provided with Passport No. 2588288 issued by the Italian Consulate at Tangier, April 14, 1944.

Tangier, September 22, 1945

For the Regional Superintendent

THE LOCAL CHIEF OF POLICE

VALID FOR: One-way trip

---

[68] Tangier became an international district in 1923 and was occupied by the Spanish from 1940 to 1945 under the Franco regime. According to Wikipedia, it "was restored to its pre-war status on August 31, 1945. Tangier joined with the rest of Morocco following the restoration of full sovereignty in 1956."

TRANSLATION

Tangier, October 3, 1945

Dear Uncle and Aunt:

I have before me your telegram of September 29 stating:

"WHY LONG SILENCE WIRE COLLECT REGARDING VISAS AND GIOIA'S ADDRESS REMITTED HIAS 3000 DOLLARS ADVANCE TRANSPORTATION"

which I answered on October 1, as follows:

"CONFIRM LETTER 18/9 (Sept. 18) PASSAGES RESERVED AWAITING COMMUNICATION DATE NEXT STEAMER WILL SAIL FROM LISBON ADDRESSES LETTER FOLLOWS"

I was unable to answer before because since it was Passover and the Committee was closed, I preferred waiting for it to be open to see if meanwhile they had received any notice.

As a matter of fact, as I said in my letter of September 18, which I hope you already have received and a copy of which I am enclosing, the only thing we are waiting for is the number of the American quota and a boat which is the main thing. There is a gentleman here who had been waiting I don't know how long for an ocean liner to sail from Lisbon. For us, it is even more difficult because we are so many

Dear ones, you know how great is our interest in leaving, and as soon as possible. We will thus be more patient until the appointed time. The steamship company which is the Companhia Colonia de Navegacao of Lisbon, stated on the telegram which I saw and which was sent to the American Consulate of Tangier, "PASSAGES RESERVED FAVOUR ABRAHAM BARCHI AND FAMILY: MATILDE (Mazaltov), CLAIRE, RACHEL, HAIM, MOISE, JACQUES, REGINA, ESTHER CAPELUTO FOR NEXT STEAMER SAILING FROM LISBON TO UNITED STATES," so that we need to be definitely advised in order for us to leave. We would like it to be as soon as possible on account of the rigid winter starting from Lisbon to all the stops, but we must be patient. If we receive any news, we will let you know and when we are about to leave Tangier, I will wire you. Also when we leave Lisbon which is the main thing, as we do not know if we will remain a few days in Lisbon or if we will embark right away for the U.S.

Dear Uncle and Aunt, on your telegram you ask us the address of Aunt Gioia. I'll tell you that the only one we have is Aunt Sarina's which is as follows:

Chelibon Maish, Rehov Zebulun 3, Tel-Aviv (Palestine)

We received three or four letters which for sure were delayed and in each of them they said they had no news for us. We did not fail writing them. We do not have Gioia's address because on the single letter we received, she told us to write to her care of Aunt Sarina as they were not completely settled. I did always forget to send you Sarina's address as I would leave it at home and as I always write my letters at the office, always at the last moment when the plane was about to leave. My head is turning in so many directions; i.e., leave everything in order at the office, bring the new employee up to date, etc. This very day I had to send the porter's daughter home to bring Sarina's address.

I cannot delay any longer. I hope everyone is very well, as we are, and impatient to be reunited.

Papa, Mama, Aunt Esther, Rachel, Haim, Morris, Jacques, Regina, send you kisses and hugs. Kisses to Aunt Jamila and her husband from us. Give regards to Mary Israel and tell her that I count on her friendship from now until we are together. Regards to all the relatives.

To my dear little cousins whom I love so much and long to see very shortly, many kisses from me. And to my dear Aunt and Uncle many hugs from your niece.

Claire

TRANSLATION FROM FRENCH

CABLE

Milan, Italy, October 24, 1945

TO: Ralph Capeluto

        5th Floor

        Prefontaine Bldg

        Seattle, Washington

MAMA MARI, PAPA SADIK, MOISE DECEASED

RACHEL AND I IN MILAN—DESPERATE—WE NEED

URGENT HELP. WE IMPLORE REMIT RHODES SURVIVORS

AID COMMITTEE, SUITE 3100, 1441 BROADWAY, NY, WIRE.

LEA LEVY[69]

---

[69] Rebecca Levy, Lea's sister, and Morris and Vida—Lea's cousins—came across the ocean together on the same steamship.

TRANSLATION

Tangier, October 31, 1945

Dear Uncle and Aunt:

After my last letter I wanted very badly to write to you, but having a very bad cold it was impossible. How days, weeks, months, pass, I do not know. What I know is we are all very impatient. Winter is upon us and without news about our departure. To each of my letters that I send to the Lisbon Steamship Company, they answer that they do not have any set date for departure, and the strikes make things worse. But it is not in our hands whatever depended on us has already been done, whether it be from your side or ours, and now everything is in the hand of God. When I find out something for certain, I will wire you.

Meanwhile, the Tangier American Consulate cannot ask for the quota numbers from Washington to gain time without having the exact date of departure of the boat from Lisbon as Washington issues quota numbers valid for one month. And if they ask for them now and they give them, let us say, for November and there is no steamship in November, it is a useless effort. Thus everything depends on the Lisbon Steamship.

Dear ones, the reason that we did not write after my last letter was also motivated by our having been struck by a misfortune which we had foreseen, but which we hoped would not happen. Last week, I received surprisingly a letter from Milan from Rachel Levy, daughter of Aunt Marie. You cannot imagine my surprise when the mailman handed it to me in the street. I could not believe my eyes at first, and I don't know how I opened it. As I started to read it, tears filled my eyes and passersby would stare at me until I realize how ridiculous I looked, and I entered the portal of a house and started reading carefully. After having finished it, I did not know whether to keep walking home to inform Mama or to go I don't know where. I later thought since I had to tell her anyway that it would be better to do it immediately now that I felt more courage.

The letter was written in Italian with all the details, dates, places, everything relating the sad odyssey that the unfortunate people from Rhodes experienced from July 20, 1944 until April 1945 when they were liberated. I would like to send you the letter such as I received from Rachel, but I don't want to cause you such an emotion and I thus confine myself to summarize somewhat what our dear ones went through.

On July 7, 1944, all the Jews of Rhodes were interned by trick by the wicked Germans as political prisoners. Without being able to take along anything and having taken away from them money, clothing, they put them in a boat built to carry coal. They stayed nine days in the open sea from Rhodes to Piraeus [Greece, usually a trip of about 12 hours] under the bombing and ground mines, fighting the storms and bad weather. When they arrived at Piraeus, after having been stripped naked without distinction, you can imagine the fate of these girls, were by force of blows shaven from head to toe, like a pumpkin. They filled two rail boxcars, one of men, one of women, cars full of lice, where many died asphyxiated or from typhus on account of the lice and filth.

After a terrible trip and long stretch, they were taken to Auschwitz.[70] They were separated in the camp without distinction, all married women of any age with their own children, and taken to gas chambers to be asphyxiated and as a matter of course, cremated. The same fate fell on the older men and the children, thus, of 2,000 persons 500 (250 young men and 250 young women) remained. Included in the unfortunate group, dear Aunt Behora and Marie and their husbands met the same fate. Vida and Rosa Capeluto, Lea and Rachel Levy and Moshe Levy were among the 500, separated because they were able to work. Hard labor with 80 grams of black bread daily and 10 grams of margarine, something dreadful. Awakened at three in the morning with blows with hands and stick, they were forced to walk five kilometers carrying a load and working in the streets. After this wretched work, they were taken to ammunition factories at the time when the Allies were approaching. But Rachel Levy, who was very thin, and to get rid of her faster, was left working on the highway, naked, hairless, and in the snow. She, herself wonders how she was able to endure. Moshe Levy, a 21-year-old young man, how much he must have suffered, died one month before the liberation. Moshe was assigned like the young men of Rhodes to work in the coal mines of High Silesia. There lay the Hell for all the young men of Rhodes, hell conceived by Dante and put into effect by wicked Hitler. Rachel and Lea never saw Moshe during the time he spent in the camp because they were separated from the men.

Dear Uncle and Aunt, this is the sad odyssey of our dear relatives and of all the acquaintances from Rhodes. Of the 500, barely 100 survived, approximately 80 young girls and 15 young men. Rosa Capeluto was in Milan with Rachel and Lea Levy, but a few days before Rachel wrote the letter, she was transferred to Modena, near Milan. A letter that a girl who is in France wrote to a cousin who is here states that Rosa is ill. Rachel has no news about Vida. How strange and sad as Vida was stronger and more hardy than the other cousins. Upon receiving her letter from Rachel, I wired her with paid reply because all wires are sent at the sender's risk, and upon receiving an answer I would be sure that she received it. I gave her your address as she asked me in the letter, entreating at the same time to write to you and to ask if you can do something for them. She told me this because I exchange letters more often with you and that it would be easier and because the means of communication from here are better.

Dear Uncle and Aunt, we would have liked to send them what we have, but unfortunately after having all the post offices and the Red Cross, there is no way that one can send anything to Italy. Besides the matter of food, they must be badly off concerning clothing, because even those who remained in Italy must not be able to find anything. And what can be said about these unfortunate people who came naked and hungry from the camps, especially ours who are not accustomed to the Italian climate, rigorous as compared to the mild climate of Rhodes? In Italy there is much snow and from September one suffers from cold as if it were January. Therefore, dear ones, I don't know how to beg you, perhaps you can do something for these unfortunate girls, being that for the moment nothing can be done from here. Clothing is of great concern.

---

[70] The worst of all the Nazi extermination camps, made worse for Rhodeslis and other southern European Jews who lacked language skills to communicate with other prisoners or to understand guards.

This is the address of Rachel Levy in Milan, "Miss Rachel Levy-Scuole Sinistrati—Via Monviso, No. 2, Milano (Italia)

I have not written yet to Aunt Behora's daughters in Cairo because really I do not know how to go about it. If I knew that Vida was alive, it would be something. By informing them about the unfortunate Aunt Behora and Uncle David and the other relatives, it would already be enough to bear. As far as Vida is concerned, it would be a fatal blow for these sisters who loved each other so much.

In spite of this painful situation, we must consider ourselves a little lucky because in proportion, three remain alive. There are families who have completely disappeared and all of them young. I do not know the fate of hundreds of friends of mine, strong and young. Something frightening!

Dear ones, as Rachel states in her letter, thank God that we were spared miraculously from this barbaric act. I don't know what kind of miracle was performed for us. And to think that we were complaining continuously when we were here like kings. We will never have a notion of how much these people suffered. Many of them wonder how God allowed these things to happen and why they did not die, because to live these sad memories will consume them little by little. They are completely demoralized without hope, alone in this world, completely deprived of health and everything else. What a sad fate!

Dear ones, I have now a headache. We are experiencing a week of insanity. There remains no one among the refugees who are not coming to read this unpleasant letter, and they all wonder how this young lady had such courage to relate these sad facts.

I will not prolong this letter any further. Please write to me and excuse this sad letter, but I could not help it, because you too were as concerned as we were about them.

I hope you are all well. Don't stop writing. Hoping you will busy yourself with doing something for our dear helpless survivors, I send you kisses from the bottom of my heart.

Your dear niece,

Claire

TELEGRAM

Rome, November 7, 1945

FROM VIDA AND ROSA CAPELUTO

TO UNCLE RALPH

> PARENTS MARY, SADIK, MOSE DEAD—LEA AND RACHEL IN ROME
>
> Hugs

THE REALITY OF WAR

Despite the hardships of the war, the family in Tangier was blissfully unaware of what was happening to their Jewish brethren who had stayed in Rhodes or who lived elsewhere in Europe.

Although they lost contact with the relatives in Rhodes, they had no idea until after the war when they received the letter from Rachel Levy telling them about what had happened when the Nazis invaded Rhodes.

"When I read it, Claire got us all together," recalls Jack. "She read it out loud to everybody. Not only us, but also neighbors. That was the first I heard it was happening. My reaction was 'damn Germans.'"

"I didn't realize it," Victor said. "I just lay in bed and cried. The Germans were mortal enemies. They killed a lot of my friends, people I went to school with. Parts of the family were gone. I have almost eternal hate towards the Germans."

Morris followed the progression of the war—especially in Italy—at school and through the newspapers. At school, he would pin little flags on a map to mark the advances of the Allied troops. Yet he too had no idea what had happened to the Jews.

"We were absolutely not aware of the Jews and the concentration camps until they got back and we got letters from Rachel," he said. "Who else knew about it? Even the United States didn't know what was going on."

Regina recalls an uneasy feeling because her mother had not heard from her sisters in Rhodes for a long time. They were completely unaware that Jews were being killed. When they did find out the truth, they feared the Arabs in Tangier might be allied with the Germans and that their lives too would be threatened.

"It was that awful feeling of being afraid," Regina said.

At times the family members gave up hope that they would ever get to the United States. They didn't want to go to the Belgian Congo because as Jack said, they had to take quinine every day for malaria, and they wouldn't get a good education there.

Abraham left it up to the children to decide whether they wanted to go to Palestine or the United States. Although two of Mazaltov's sisters and their families left for Palestine in 1945, the Barkey family decided to wait it out in Tangier in the hope that they would eventually get to America.

"We thought everybody was rich. That's all you heard, that everyone was rich (in America)," Regina said. "We thought Uncle Ralph was rich. He was not rich. He was comfortable."

TRANSLATION

Tangier, November 7, 1945

Dear Uncle and Aunt:

Without having the pleasure of having your news, I confirm my last letter of 31 October '45, a copy of which I am enclosing.

I am hurrying to send you this letter to give you the good news we have just received. It deals with a letter from dear Vida and Rosa Capeluto, daughters of dear Uncle David and Aunt Behora. The letter is dated October 13, 1945, and comes from Rome. After relating all the misfortunes about which Rachel Levy wrote to us and that I am informing you that in the enclosed letter, Vida tells us that she arrived at Rome on September 8, 1945, and as she learned that Rosa was in Modena, she asked the latter to join her.

Dear Uncle and Aunt, I don't know how these unfortunate ones are alive after what they have just related. Rosa, after the liberation in April, weighed 30 kilos [66 lbs.] contracted typhus, and had her head shaven. She tells now that she weighs 50 kilos [110 lbs] thanks probably to the treatment ministered to her. As I mentioned in the enclosed letter, what my friend wrote to her relatives that Rosa was ill was not a lie. Imagine what 30 kilos represent, just a little bundle. Vida says that she was so frail that she was separated from Rosa in October 1944 for the purpose of sending her to the crematorium. She doesn't know herself how they saved her. From that date she and her sister did not see each other and imagine, she writes us, when they saw each other again, it seemed impossible and felt like being born again. Yes, dear ones, each one that reappears is one born again, and one gained. In their letters they confirm the tragic death of their parents and Uncle Sadik and Aunt Marie and Moshe Levy.

Knowing Mama and how much she loved them, the poor little things sent us a photo to console us. I am going to reproduce six, so I can send them to you, Cairo, and Congo. As you will see, they do not appear in bad shape, but what a sad face Vida has, and Rosa is puffed up as if she were force-fed. According to Vida, her brother residing in the Congo sent a wire to the community of Milan, inquiring about them and the Community advised them and they in turn also sent a telegram. They also wrote Cairo. As I believe that communications are better from here, and to act promptly, I sent a wire to Matilde and Rachel relating everything and asking them to reply by wire as we are very concerned. We pray that everything over there is okay. What a mess! Everyone is uneasy!

Dear ones, the following is the address of Vida and Rosa in Rome—Signorina Vittoria Capeluto, Via Condotti No. 5, Roma (Italia).

For them as well as for Lea and Rachel, I take the liberty of begging you to try and be of some assistance. We, as we told you, unfortunately cannot do anything for the moment. I believe and I hope that it would be easier for you.

Dear Uncle and Aunt, what is new with you? Why do you not write? We are very worried and would like to receive your news. No news from us, and we are awaiting notification from the steamship company. What can we do? We must be patient for without it nothing can be obtained. Against my will I am always in a hurry.

Papa, Mama, Esther, my brothers, my sisters send you kisses. Kisses to all of you from me. Awaiting your very prompt answer and with much affection, I send you kisses.

Your niece,

Claire

P.S. One photo is for you and one for Aunt Jamila.

TRANSLATION

CABLE

Rome (around November 15, 1945)

TO: RALPH CAPELUTO

        PREFONTAINE BUILDING

        SEATTLE, WASHINGTON

"ADDRESS CONDOTTI 5—NEED URGENT HELP—APPRECIATED—LACK SHOES—SIZE 35—THANKS—KISSES

Vida and Rosa Capeluto

TRANSLATION

Tangier, January 10, 1946

Dear Uncle and Aunt:

This time, contrary to my habit, I have delayed answering your dear letter, for which I hope you will excuse me. It did not depend on my will, but I have been busy these final days of the year and have been in bed with a cold.

Dear ones, besides all the reasons for which I would have liked to leave Tangier, I add the accounting of end of year. It is a job somewhat hard and tiresome and as I have not left my job and remaining in the office, it fell upon me to close the books. Well, what can we do? We wait until God wills. I must tell you that the steamship company of Lisbon, to which I write continually inquiring if there is anything new, sent us a letter on December 20, 1945, advising us that there was no boat leaving for the United States. Tired of much waiting, I went to the Refugee Committee of Tangier and spoke to the head. I showed him the letter and told him that there was no way of waiting any longer. He replied that he would write to this Company, that it seems difficult to go through Lisbon, and that he had wired for a possibility of going through Spain. And according to him, we will leave in March or April. As soon as he receives an answer to the wire, he will notify us.

We learn elsewhere in the press that a big Spanish company has resumed its service to the U.S. We hope there is something to it. As I already told you, I will advise you without fail.

Dear ones, enclosed with your letters we received some pictures. Are these the dolls with whom we will be upon arriving at Seattle? And the handsome young man, who is he? What a difference between the previous photos and these! It is true that they are in the growing stage, and they are indeed a sight for sore eyes.[71] Dear Morris hiding all of you. We wish to be near you and get acquainted. At home, it is something incredible, going or returning from the office, I find them holding the photos. I put them away to keep them from being mishandled. If this is for just the photos, what would be when having them near?

Dear ones, we received this week letters from Italy from dear Vida and Rosa, Lea and Rachel. You cannot imagine how grateful they are for what you are doing for them. They also have received eight parcels and it seems all of them will meet in Rome. Also Behor sent them money and they will be able to buy some clothing.

We also received letters from Cairo and from Palestine from Aunt Sarina. They all are well. Aunt Sarina also wrote about Aunt Gioia and says that she is very well and that they see each other once a week. Our cousins from Italy tell us that they wrote to you several times and would wish to receive your news. They requested me to write to you to that effect.

We are all well here and very anxious to leave and be at your side. All the acquaintances send you regards. Kisses to Aunt Jamila and her husband. Many kisses to the dear little cousins from her uncle, aunt, and cousins. Affectionate regards to Mary Israel from me. Kisses from Mama, Papa, Aunt Esther, my brothers, my sisters. With all my affection, your dear niece who loves you very much and wishes to see you soon.

Claire

---

[71] Liberal translation.

TRANSLATION

Cairo, February 8, 1946

[From Mathilda Cherez]

Dear Uncle Raphael and Aunt Rachel Capeluto:

The present letter is to let you know that, thank God, we are all well. We hope to always receive good news as well. We have not received a letter from you and are worried. We hope you are all well.

Dear Uncle, we are receiving letters from dear Victoria [Vida] and Rosa, letters so sad, and we are unable to offer consolation; surely, they must have written to you. It is such a great sorrow that we will never forget them. It is bad enough what we have lost. It is worse for what they are still suffering and not knowing where they are going, whether to Rhodes if they can go. But if they want to leave, they do not let them. They are just waiting for God to open doors for them. It would be a great joy if they allow them to enter this country, but there is no hope for this. Dear Haim[72] wired us advising them to go to Palestine because they do not let them enter the Congo for now. They do not want to go to Palestine as they are tired of being dragged and of being strangers. They want to be at the side of a dear one to be consoled, for what they went through is not a trivial matter. To see what they write, even the stones could cry. What a terrible fate to have suffered by people who are so good! We cannot rationalize this. We are ill to think about them, a father and mother so good and full of love. We will never forget them. You certainly must remember them, above all, he (her father) was the one who shined the most in the family. We pray God that these young ladies leave these places and find solace from now on.

Dear ones, they wrote to us saying that they received many things from you. May God reward you for this. While writing this letter, I received one from them saying that they received your letter and photos of your kids, and they were so happy. They have received the money you sent as well as Haim's. Everything will be restored except there is no remedy for those who are gone. We have also received a letter from Lea who went to Rome to see the dear ones. We further wept with the letter we read. It is such a great tragedy that we will never forget. We pray the Lord not to bring us any more deaths.

I have nothing further to add other than to start sending regards. Please remember me to dear Amelie [Jamila] with her husband. Kisses to the kids from all of us. Dear Albert (Israel), Rachel, and the kids. Albert [Mathilda's husband], dear Maurice hugs you. I send you hugs from the heart. Your dear niece who begs you to write.

Mathilda A.[73] Cherez

P.S. If you meet the son of Ruben Avzaradel, Bohor, tell him that he has his sister Laura in Rome and to have pity on her.

---

[72] Also called Behor, Mathilda Cherez's brother. Mathilda is a cousin who is referenced in an earlier letter on page 137.

[73] The "A." stands for her husband Albert.

TRANSLATION

Tangier, February 19, 1946

Dear Uncle and dear Aunt:

I hope this letter finds you in good health together with our dear cousins. We are all well and are waiting to be at your side.

Dear ones, it appears the long awaited moment has arrived. Last week we were called in by the American Consulate and they showed us a letter from the Steamship company "La Compania Transmediterranea," which stated that we had the ticket reserved for the Steamship "Marques de Comillas" which leaves Bilbao (Spain) on the 5th of May 1946. With this, everything is in order. What remains is the number of the quota which has been requested by the American Consulate for the month of April. It is eight numbers for the Italian quota, and one for the Turkish quota for Papa. We hope the last step will succeed and that we will leave Spain at the appointed date.

Dear ones, according to the information given to us by the agent of the above-mentioned company, the steamship stops at La Uayra in Caracas, Puerto Rico, Havana, Philadelphia, and New York. The voyage will be somewhat long, they say 20 to 22 days, but since the weather is good in May, we hope to have a good trip. We beg you to get in touch with Heskia Benatar to advise him of what I write, and it would be useful if you sent me his address. When we leave Tangier, which will be at the beginning of May, because to go to Bilbao we have several traveling days across Spain, we will write you. I ask that you take certain measures not to leave us without a guide in New York, which is the only thing that concerns us. As far as the boat is concerned, nothing to worry as we can use Spanish, a language that we all know well.

Dear ones, you can't imagine the joy we felt upon receiving your news, and we hope everything will go well until the end. As the saying goes, "there is no absolute happiness." The dear ones who disappeared should have shared it as they always wanted our well-being and happiness, Mama having been the dearest of all sisters to all of them.

Dear Uncle, Aunt, this week we received a letter from Aunt Sarina. She is very well and tells us that Aunt Gioia is all well. We receive regularly letters from Italy from our cousins. The word "well" cannot apply in this case, having suffered so much and missing the dear ones, but they feel more encouraged. Unfortunately, they have no choice but to face life as it presents itself. Vida and Rosa are still in Rome, Rachel in Padova, and Lea, after having returned from Rome, is in Milan where life is cheaper and where one can eat in the "cantina."[74] In Rome life is very expensive and she says that Vida and Rosa can subsist there because Behor sends them something. But since she [Lea] has no one to help her, she prefers to be at the charge of the Committee. Lea received 30 lbs. sterling from Salvator Levy to whom I wrote to ask if he could help them enter the Congo. Salvator states that to bring them in is difficult as immigration is prohibited, and besides he intends to go to Palestine in June. As soon as he is advised of their having received the 30 lbs. sterling, he will send more money. We also received several letters from Belgium from Leon Levy. He says that he has asked permission to go and see his sisters in Italy. It seems he is on a world tour with the Jewish Brigade.

Nothing else today. Many kisses from everyone.

Receive a strong hug from, Claire

PS: Warmest apologies for sending this letter late because we are waiting for an answer from the American Consulate. Unfortunately we have still to wait.

---

[74] Probably a welfare kitchen where they feed the indigent.

Tangier, March 2 1946

Dear Morris,[75]

We have received with pleasure your kind letter for which we thank you. And it causes an agreeable surprise to hear from you, and we were very glad to know you are all in good health. So we are.

We were very pleased to know you are making improvements at school; we shall be very obliged to write us how are the schools there; can some schools be attended at night by pupils who are working during the day? Because we intend to keep on studying and improve our knowledge.

We have learned English, a little at school, and the rest from an English teacher for a few months. We have done also bookkeeping, French shorthand, and typewriting examinations.

And what about books? Can you get them of all kinds, and good dictionaries? Please let us know about it.

We were very happy to read you are interested in mechanical drawing, art, and trumpet playing. We also play a little violin for we are learning it now. So, we hope to organize with you a little and familiar orchestra so as to enjoy ourselves from time to time and to spend the leisure time agreeably.

What are your hobbies? Are you collecting stamps, coins?

Dear cousin, we suppose we shall be on the way to the U.S.A. in May as we were told (*si dios quere*)[76].

Please give our kind regards to your Papa and Mama, sisters, Aunt Jamila and her husband, relatives, and to everyone who ask about us.

Our parents, Aunt Esther, sisters and brothers are sending you their best regards. Awaiting your prompt reply, we remain

Your loving cousins,

Victor & Morris Barki

---

[75] Victor and Morris wrote these letters to their Seattle cousin and aunt and uncle in English, which at the time was their second language.

[76] God willing.

Dear Uncle and Aunt,

We received with great gladness your esteemed letter and were very pleased to know you in good health.

We don't know how to pay you all the interest and kindness you show us. We are anxious to meet you and we hope it will be soon. We shall be very happy to see you. However, it seems like we already know you well.

We have to relate a great many things, have we not?

We were beaten with surprise to read that Miss Taranto is in Seattle. We thought she stayed at Rhodes, so we were very glad to know she is out of danger. How did she go to the U.S.A., because she was in the isle after our leaving, two months before the war.

Please give her our best regards and tell her our gladness.

It seems strange that Joe Fintz [sic] didn't write us. What is the matter with him? Is he quite well?

Dear Uncle and Aunt, we are glad our cousins are learning Spanish. Tell them not to mind; we'll do our best to teach them and they will make themselves easily understood in this language.

Please remember us to Aunt Jamila and her husband, to our cousins, relatives, and Joe Fintz. Papa, Mama, sisters, and brothers are sending to every one of you their best regards. Kind remembrances from Aunt Esther.

Hoping to meet you very soon and assuring you of our best consideration, we remain,

Your loving nephews,

Victor & Morris Barki

Abraham Barki
Paseo Cenarro N°77
T A N G E R

Tanger, le 8 Mars 1946.

Monsieur PAUL ALLING

American Diplomatic Agent and Consul General

Légation des Etats-Unis d'Amérique

T A N G E R

Monsieur le Consul Général,

J'ai l'honneur de vous exposer respectueu-
sement ce qui suit:

Depuis de nombreuses années, c'est-à-dire,
depuis 1939, année où moi et ma famille avons dû quitter notre domi-
cile de l'Ile de Rhodes, à la suite des persécutions raciales, nous
cherchons à émigrer aux Etats-Unis pour aller rejoindre mon beau frère
Ralph Capeluto, demeurant à Seattle, Washington.

En 1944, j'ai fait les démarches nécessaires
à cet effet auprès du National Refugee Service de New-York et en 1945,
mon beau frère Ralph Capeluto ainsi que Mr.Charles Alhadeff, ayant don-
né les garanties requises aux autorités compétentes de Washington, ont
obtenu du State Department, l'approbation pour la délivrance des visas,
par la Légation des Etats-Unis à Tanger, pour moi et pour ma famille.

La demande des visas en question a été dé-
posée en Juillet 1945, en même temps que les photos de ma famille,etc..
mais Monsieur le Consul chargé de la délivrance des visas, n'a pu me
les délivrer à ce moment-là, parce qu'il fallait que je produise en
même temps, la preuve de la réservation de nos billets de passage pour
l'Amérique, la Compagnie de Navigation portugaise par laquelle nous
comptions faire le voyage ne pouvant pas nous fixer ni sur la date, ni
sur le vapeur par lequel des places pourraient nous être réservées,
nous avons dû attendre et chercher en Espagne un autre moyen de transport.

Ayant réussi enfin à nous faire réserver des
places par la Compañia Transatlantica par le vapeur "Marques de Comilla
qui doit quitter Bilbao (Espagne) le 5 Mai 1946 pour l'Amérique du Nord
J'ai fait écrire, au mois de Janvier dernier, par la dite compagnie à
la Légation des Etats-Unis de Tanger, vous informant que les billets
de passage pour moi et ma famille, soit 9 personnes, étaient réservés
par le vapeur précité.

Avec la copie de cette lettre en mains,
nous nous sommes présentés à cette époque là,chez Monsieur le Consul
chargé de la délivrance des visas et lui avons demandé les visas si
longtemps et si impatiemment attendus, Monsieur le Consul nous répondit
qu'il devait d'abord demander les numéros des contingents pour le mois
d'Avril (8 italiens et 1 turque) et qu'il nous avertirait au moment
opportun.

Letter dated March 8, 1945. Letter from Abraham Barkey to American Diplomatic Agent & Consul General requesting that visas be issued for the other family members, but not for him since he is a Turkish national and all Turkish visas had been exhausted and were no longer available.

TRANSLATION FROM THE FRENCH

Tangier, March 8, 1946

From: Abraham Barki

Paseo Cenarro No. 77

Tangier

To: Mr. Paul Alling

American Diplomatic Agent &

Consul General

Legation of the U.S. of America

Tangier

Mr. Consul General:

I have the honor of respectfully setting forth the following:

For numerous years, namely since 1939, the year in which I and my family had to leave our residence in the Island of Rhodes, following racial persecutions, we have been trying to emigrate to the United States in order to join my brother-in-law, Ralph Capeluto, residing in Seattle, Washington.

In 1944, I took the necessary steps to that effect, with the National Refugee Service of NY. And in 1945, my brother-in-law, Ralph Capeluto, together with Mr. Charles Alhadeff, having given the required guarantees to the authorities of competent jurisdiction in Washington, have obtained from the State Department the approval for the issuance of visas by the U.S. Legation in Tangier for me and my family.

The request for the visas was filed in July 1945, and at the same time we furnished family pictures, etc. But the Consul in charge of the issuance of visas could not issue them at that time because it was necessary for us to show at the same time proof of ticket reservations for America. The Portuguese Company of Navigation on which we counted to undertake the voyage, being unable to give definite information as to date and the steamship from which places could be reserved, we had to wait and seek in Spain another means of conveyance.

Having succeeded finally in reserving passage by the Compania Transatlantica in the steamship "Maraques De Comillals" which is scheduled to leave Bilbao (Spain) on the 5th of May 1946 for North America, I caused said company to write last January to the U.S. Legation of Tangier, informing you that the voyage tickets for me and my family, that is nine persons, were reserved in the aforementioned steamship.

With a copy of this letter in hand, we appeared at that time there, at the Consul's in charge of issuing visas, and requested the visas for which we waited for so long and impatiently. Mr. Consul replied that he had to request the numbers of the quota for the month of April (8 Italian and 1 Turkish), and that he would advise at the opportune moment.

Last Tuesday, the 5th of the month, Mr. Consul summoned us and informed us that the quota of immigrants of Turkish nationality has been exhausted, and it was not possible to issue the visas. As you can imagine, Mr. Consul General, this answer stunned us and distressed us greatly.

But since adversity continues to overwhelm us, and must be resigned to the will of God, and to the laws in effect, I have abandoned momentarily the idea of going to America, myself together with my minor children Jack and Regina.

Being that the visas discontinued for the Turkish nationals does not affect at all the other members of my family who are of Italian nationality, having been born in the Island of Rhodes, I come, Mr. Consul General, to humbly entreat you to issue the visas corresponding to the members of my family as follows:

1) Esther Capeluto, born on March 10, 1909, in the Island of Rhodes (my sister-in-law)

2) Mathilda Barki, born on March 5, 1895, in the Island of Rhodes (my wife)

3) Claire Barki, born on March 14, 1921 in the Island of Rhodes (my daughter)

4) Rachel Barki, born on March 5, 1923 in the Island of Rhodes (my daughter)

5) Haim Barki, born on March 27, 1925 in the Island of Rhodes (my son—twin)

6) Moise Barki, born on March 27, 1925 in the Island of Rhodes (my son—twin)

I dare hope, Mr. Consul General, that you will kindly grant my request and issue the visas above-mentioned as soon as possible in order to enable me to take the necessary steps in time and not miss the voyage in the S/S Marques de Comillas, which as we mentioned, will depart for America on the 5th of next May.

I express in advance my deepest thanks and respect.

TRANSLATION

Tangier, March 15, 1946

Dear and esteemed brother, sister-in-law, and nephews, Raphael, Rachel and family:[77]

We received your esteemed letter and had great pleasure in reading its contents and especially the letter of dear Morris which brought great joy to all of us. What will it be when we finally meet! We are very impatient awaiting that moment and every passing day seems like a year, thinking that you are doing so much for us. May God reward you with good health and long life and everything good. No matter how much we want to repay, we will never be able to repay you for your good heart and good deeds. We pray now, dear ones, that God will not leave our wish unfulfilled and that we meet soon and that no new difficulties arise. We are all prepared, but are waiting for the numbers of the quota which we thought would be of little difficulty. But now the consulate informs us, to our displeasure, that we still have to wait because dear Avraham, who was born in Turkey, is under the Turkish quota, which is closed and has to wait until July when it will be opened. Dear Avraham would have been glad if dear Esther, me and the kids would leave and he would wait, but they tell us that he, being the head of the family, and we form a group, not individually nine persons. We hope you find out over there for certain as they may possibly make us wait longer, and the affidavits would expire and the Italian quota would close.

To know we have bothered you a lot, but since you are working so hard for us, let us hope it is not in vain. We are very thankful to you, dear Rachel.

Please know that we always received letters from dear Vida, Rosa, Lea, and Rachel, and they are so grateful and they bless you for everything you are doing for them. They are regularly receiving your parcels, and they hope you will write often. They were very glad to see you in the photos. We also thank you for helping these dear ones, orphans before their time.

Our unfortunate sisters were good and pious. They did not deserve such cruelty. We cannot console ourselves about these horrible deaths and our sorrow will last for the rest of our lives. We give thanks to God for having spared our nieces, and it seems a miracle after so many hardships. We pray God to prevent tragedies and to preserve us alive and healthy.

We also received a letter from Buenos Aires, from Mardoche Menashe of Cos.[78] We exchange letters all the time. He was glad you were trying to bring us over. He praises you a lot and remembers you very well, dear Raphael. He sends regards and hope you can write to him. He also sends regards to his Aunt Lea, wife

---

[77] This letter was written by Rachel Barkey on behalf of her parents.

[78] One of the Dodecanese islands.

of "Haham"[79] Nissim Mussafir, and to Marco Franco[80] and family, and tell them to write. His address is: Mardoche Y Menashe, Giribone 676 Dep B. Buenos Aires.

Please send regards to Mlle. Taranto and tell her we were glad to know that she is there with her sister. We thought she remained in Rhodes.

Regards to dear Jamila and her husband, to your father, mother, and family, Mr. Nissim Israel and family. Congratulations to Marie Israel. Regards to Mazaltov, wife of Jaco Pasha, and her family. Kisses to the kids. Dear Avraham sends you regards. He does not know how to thank you and is impatient to see you. Dear Esther, Claire, Rachel, Haim, Moshe, Jacques, and Regina send you kisses. We kiss you and hug you.

Your sister and brother-in-law,

Mazaltov and Avraham

---

[79] Literally, "wise,"; title for a wise and learned man or Torah scholar.

[80] Probably the father of Albert Franco, the lawyer.

WASHINGTON OFFICE

HEBREW SHELTERING AND IMMIGRANT AID SOCIETY

(HIAS)

27 March 1946

Miss Claire Barki

Pase Cennaro No. 77

Tangiers, Morocco

Dear Miss Barki:

We are in receipt of your letter of March 19.

We have carefully gone over the contents of same as well as of the enclosures. We then discussed the matter with an official in the Department of State, who confirmed our belief that the Turkish quota is over-subscribed for the rest of the quota year. However, there may be a quota number available for your father after July 1st.

Furthermore, we discussed with the State Department the possibility of having the other members of the family who are eligible to come under the Italian quota to come to the United States immediately and have your father wait for the Turkish quota. However, we were advised that since your father is the head of the family and the breadwinner, he naturally has to stay together with the whole family group.

You will, therefore, have to be patient a little while longer until the American Consul will have a Turkish number for your father. We sincerely hope that you will be able to proceed to the United States in July to be reunited with your family in this country.

Please be assured that we are always glad to be of service to you.

Sincerely yours,

ABRAHAM ROCKMORE

Counsel

AR:VRP:BGK

cc: Mr. Ralph Capeluto

HIA, Seattle

LEGATION OF THE

UNITED STATES OF AMERICA

Tangier, Morocco, April 1, 1946

Mr. Abraham Barki,

Paseo Cenerro 77,

Tangier.

Sir:

In continuation of my letter to you of March 13, 1946, I have to inform you that the Legation has just received a communication from the Department of State that Turkish quota numbers will not become available for you and members of your family for a considerable time. You should therefore take no steps in connection with your proposed immigration to the United States. The Legation will naturally inform you promptly upon the receipt of any news in this regard.

Very truly yours,

For the American Diplomatic Agent:

(signed)

A. David Fritzlan

Second Secretary of Legation

P.S. Your pasports and personal documents are returned herewith. They should be presented by you at the time you and your family make formal applications for visas.

Enclosures: As stated.

WESTERN UNION

Washington, DC 16, 2:56P, April 16, '46

TO: RALPH CAPELUTO

807—30 South, Seattle, Washington

State Department in touch with Legation at Tangier on Barki family visas. Have asked advice by wire. Will advise immediately on receipt reply.

Hugh De Lacy, MC[81],[82]

140p

---

[81] MC means Member of Congress

[82] Emerson Hugh De Lacy (known as Hugh), 1910-1986, was a Seattle native who represented the state of Washington in the U.S. House of Representatives as a Democrat from 1945 to 1947. He was an English teacher at the University of Washington before his election and, after a stint as editor of the monthly bulletin of the Machinists Union in Seattle and another attempt to run for president as a candidate of the Progressive Party, he turned to carpentry and eventually became a building contractor in California.

TRANSLATION

Tangier, written on 2nd day of Passover 1946

[Corresponding to April 17, 1946]

Dear brother and sister-in-law:

We received your esteemed letter and were glad to know that you are in good health. So are we.

Dear ones, you write that you are waiting impatiently. So are we. But, we see that it is somewhat difficult. They tell us that in about three or four months the quota for dear Avraham will be opened. We hope it is the truth. They did not want to give it to me (the number), but it was thanks to the efforts of Clara, even though it was for me, I received the visa 15 days before Passover. You can imagine what the displeasure was for all of us after having prepared everything, especially for the kids who are impatient and who look forward to the day when they will join you. And they want to repay Uncle Raphael and Aunt Rachel for what they are doing for them and for their cousins. Thank God you have such a good wife. May God grant her a long life for she is precious and may the good wishes of the dear nieces for you be fulfilled.

The delay was for the good. Dear Rachel has been suffering with the ear [pain] for a year, and the doctor told us she had to have an operation as the pain was great, and she was unable to sleep. We finally decided for the operation, and took her to the hospital 15 days before Passover and she was operated on. Now she is much better.

You can imagine our grief about our dear ones who suffered such horrible deaths, and think that our nieces are all alone and strangers, especially Lea who has bronchitis and is all puffed up. You don't know how grateful they are to you for your goodness, especially Lea and Rachel, who are more in need. I would like very much if you would write a letter once in a while to bring them some consolation and may God give them patience. We can only send them letters from here. And when I leave I will help them as much as I can.

Avraham and Mazaltov send you regards, and they don't stop thanking you. May God reward you for everything. All the kids send you regards. Give regards to Morris and tell him the hour of our reunion is approaching. Kisses to the girls. Regards to Jamila and her husband and the in-laws. Bye, your sister and sister-in-law.

Esther Capeluto

P.S. Today is the 2nd day of Passover. May we celebrate it together next year.

TRANSLATION

Tangier, April 23, 1946

My dear Aunt Rachel, Uncle Raphael, and cousins Morris, Betty, Marlene and Amelia (Mimi):

It is the first time that I write to you and do not know how to excuse myself for not having it done before. This letter is to let you know that we are all in good health. I hope we have similarly good news from you.

My very dear, I entered the hospital three weeks ago to have an operation on my ear which was giving me great pain. Thank God, I am well. I left the hospital on Saturday the 20th, happy to be healthy and from receiving the news that you will be happy to know.

They called from the American Consulate in order to give the visas to the following: Mama, Claire, Jacques, Regina and me. Dear Esther received it 15 days ago and she intends to leave on the 26th of April, and perhaps we will send Jacques with her if everything is in order. Tomorrow, they will give us the visas and within a month, God willing, we will leave. As you can imagine, we are very happy that finally we will be reunited, with God's help, and your goodwill and great heart, which we will never forget. Our wish is to be able to repay you, but this is something that money cannot pay, and we hope when you meet us, you will have the satisfaction of not being sorry for having worked so hard for us. We are only sorry that Haim and Moise did not receive the numbers of the quota, which is strange and can find no reason.

Papa also didn't receive it, but we were expecting that. We were thinking that he would be left alone with two young men, but we hope that they will be receiving their quota numbers soon and later, dear Papa, who is resigned to wait a little longer, provided with leave.

Dear ones, today is the last day of Passover, and we think about the dear ones who disappeared and with whom we spent happy Passovers, dear Aunt Behora, Aunt Marie, Uncle David, and Uncle Sadik, whom we will never see again. Our house was full of joy, and these are the days we mostly remember. We also remember the nights we spent together and for dear Mama and Aunt Esther, this is a sad remembrance which will last forever. We pray God not to bring us any more deaths and that dear Vida, Rosa, Lea and Rachel are healthy and in peace. We pray that next year we will celebrate Passover with you in America and with dear Aunt Jamila.

We always receive news from dear Vida, Rosa, Lea, and Rachel, and they always entreat us to send you regards and to say that they are grateful for what you are doing for them. There is a lot of poverty there and what you send is an act of mercy. Dear Lea is suffering a lot; may God heal her. They always hope you write to them for it brings them great consolation. But they complain about Aunt Jamila who has not even sent them a letter of condolences, and you know how much it means to them. Please tell Aunt Jamila to write to them.

Dear ones, I do not prolong this letter other than to say that we are very grateful and can find no words to express it.

Everyone sends regards. Regards to Aunt Jamila and her husband, Auntie Rachel, and all your relatives.

Regards to Mlle. Taranto. To you, Aunt Rachel, Uncle Raphael, cousins kisses and hugs. Your niece and cousin,

Rachel [Barki]

TRANSLATION

WIRE dated April 24, 1946

FROM TANGIER

TO: Raphael Capeluto

807 30th South

Seattle, Wash.

RECEIVED VISAS FOR EVERYONE EXCEPT ABRAHAM, HAIM, AND MOISE.

BARKI

TRANSLATION

RAPHAEL A.M. LAREDO

C P A

Tangier

PO Box 87

Tel #2965

CERTIFICATE

I, the undersigned Raphael A.M. Laredo, C.P.A. for the Courts of Tangier, hereby certifies that I have had the opportunity to audit the accounting work presented by Miss Claire Barki of various commercial enterprises for which I have been the administrative and accounting examiner since the year 1940. She has also assisted in my own field of expertise.

Of great intelligence and of an unwearying devotion, Miss Barki has always performed her task to the satisfaction of all her employers. Called up for family reasons to leave Tangier to settle in America, she will be greatly missed by all of those who have used her services and with whom she leaves a souvenir of excellent collaboration, of real competence, and honesty. I am very pleased to recommend her and to express my best wishes of success.

In testimony whereof, I issue this certificate for whom it may concern.

Tangier, April 26, 1946

[signed] Raphael A.M. Laredo

April 29th, 1946

Hon. Hugh De Lacy
House of Representatives
Washington D.C.

Dear Mr. De Lacy,

I have received a cable from
my brother-in-law, Abraham Barki in Tangier, stating
that visas have been issued for all except himself
and his two eldest boys.

I want to thank you most
sincerely for what you have done in this matter, it
has taken a tremendous load off my mind. I feel sure
that, with your help, the family will soon be
re-united and become prosperous and happy in their
new home and, in due course, law abiding citizens.

Again thanking you and
trusting that I may have the pleasure of seeing
you when you are in Seattle I remain

Yours sincerely

Letter dated April 29, 1945. Letter from Ralph Capeluto to U.S. Rep. Hugh De Lacy (D-Wash.)
thanking him for his help with the Barkey family visas.

April 29th, 1946

Hon. Hugh De Lacy

House of Representatives

Washington, DC

Dear Mr. De Lacy:

I have received a cable from my brother-in-law, Abraham Barki, in Tangier, stating that visas have been issued for all except himself and his two eldest boys.

I want to thank you most sincerely for what you have done in this matter. It has taken a tremendous load off my mind. I feel sure that, with your help, the family will soon be reunited and become prosperous and happy in their new home and, in due course, law-abiding citizens.

Again, thanking you and trusting that I may have the pleasure of seeing you when you are in Seattle, I remain,

Yours sincerely,[83]

---

[83] Not signed, but most likely from Ralph Capeluto.

WESTERN UNION

RALPH CAPELUTO C/O SEATTLE CURTAIN MFG. CO. 1946 MAY 2 A.M. 10:38

POSSIBLE ARRIVAL MARQUES COMILLAS 12 MAY NEW YORK = ESTHER JACK

807 30th 12.

Telegram dated May 2, 1946. Telegram from Jack Barkey and Esther Capeluto to Ralph Capeluto announcing expected arrival in New York on May 12. Jack and Esther were the first of the Barkey family members to arrive in the United States.

HUGH DE LACY
FIRST DISTRICT OF WASHINGTON
136 HOUSE OFFICE BUILDING
HOME ADDRESS:
SEATTLE, WASHINGTON
H. RICHARD SELLER
SECRETARY

MEMBER:
COMMITTEE ON NAVAL AFFAIRS

Congress of the United States
House of Representatives
Washington, D. C.

May 2, 1946

Mr. Ralph Capeluto
Seattle Curtain Manufacturing Company
Third and Yesler Way
Seattle 4, Washington

Dear Mr. Capeluto:

Thank you for your nice letter of April 29.
I am pleased to know that you have heard from your
brother-in-law in Tangier.

Mr. Travers has sent me the enclosed communication, confirming your report. If I can be of further
service in any way, I hope you will call on me again.
With best wishes,

Sincerely yours,

HUGH DE LACY, M. C.

hd:br

Letter dated May 2, 1946. Letter from U.S. Rep. Hugh De Lacy to Ralph Capeluto.

CONGRESS OF THE UNITED STATES

House of Representatives

Washington, DC

May 2, 1946

Mr. Ralph Capeluto

    Seattle Curtain Manufacturing Company

    Third and Yesler Way

    Seattle 4, Washington

    Dear Mr. Capeluto:

Thank you for your nice letter of April 29. I am pleased to know that you have heard from your brother-in-law in Tangier.

Mr. Travers has sent me the enclosed communication, confirming your report. If I can be of further service in any way, I hope you will call on me again.

With best wishes,

Sincerely yours,

HUGH DE LACY, M.C.

hd:br

TRANSLATION

CORIAT AND CO

Wire-Coriatco-Tangier

Damage Surveyors

etc.

Maritime Insurances

Representative

AGENTS FOR THE

TANGIER

Board of Maritime Insurers

of France

Head Office—Rabat

Branches:

Casablance—Port Lyautey

Tetuan & Tangier

R C Tangier 196

We, the undersigned Ancient Establishment Coriat & Co., Ltd., certify that Miss Claire Barki has been employed by us from April 1, 1940 until April 30, 1946 in the capacity of steno-typist secretary at the beginning and later as an accountant.

Remarkable employee, exerting zeal and diligence, she has given full and complete satisfaction as much by her intelligent collaboration as by her probity and honesty in every respect.

She is quitting us free from any obligation in order to settle in the United States of America, and it is with great sorrow that we part from her, and we wish her all the success that she deserves in the new country.

Done in Tangier, for whom it may concern, on May 12, 1946.

(Notarized by

the Tangier Chief of Police)

(COMPANY STAMP)

and signature

LIST OR MANIFEST OF ALIEN PASSENGERS FOR THE UNITED

ALL ALIENS arriving at a port of continental United States from a foreign port or a port of the insular possessions of the United States, and all aliens arriving at a port of said insular possessions from a foreign port, a port of continental United...

S.S. SPANISH "MARQUES DE COMILLAS". Passengers sailing from CADIZ, Spain, MAY 8th, 1946

No. on List	Head Tax Status	Family name	Given name	Age Yrs. Mos.	Sex	Married or single	Calling or occupation	Able to — Read	Able to — Read what language if cannot read	Nationality (Country of which citizen or subject)	Race or people	Place of birth Country	Place of birth City or town		Issued Place	Issued Date	Last permanent residence Country	Last permanent residence City
1		Cantieri Kibizeli	Tecs	20		S	H/W	Yes	Fr.Sp.Eng.	Yes	ITALIAN	ITALIAN	ITALY	Cremona		Barcelona	Apr. 20/46	Spain	Barcelona
2		Meyer	Helca	47		M	H/W	do	Gr.Fr.Eng.	do	SPANISH	GERMAN	GERMANY	Berlin		Tangier	do	Morocco	Tangier
3		Pizarro Salom	Alfonso	18		S	Student	do	Spanish	do	COSTARICAN	COSTARICAN	COSTA RICA-S.José			Madrid	do	Spain	Madrid
4		Erranquin Garrenqia	Pedro	25		S	do	do	do	do	SPANISH	BASK	SPAIN	Ondárroa			do	do	do
5		Carreras Coli	Adela	13			do	do	do	do	do	Pr. Rico	Santurce			do	do	do
6		Pérez Gerala	Angel	53		M	Business	do	Sp.Eng.	do	do	do	Spain	Cádiz		do	do	do
7		Labrador Fraile	Juan	61		S	Priest	do	Sp.Eng.	do	do	do	do	Buenavista		do	March 4/46	do	do
8		Santos Trujillo	Vidal	56		M	Merchant	do	do	do	do	do	do	Suchuantian					Tenerife
9		Diaz Gonzalez	Santiago	15		S	Student	do	Spanish	do	MEXICAN	MEXICAN	Mexico	Villahermosa		Madrid	do	do	Madrid
10		Ubanmo Lizarzaga	Maria de	44		S	do	do	do	do	SPANISH	SPANISH	Spain	Salamanca			do	do	Salamanca
11		Capeluto	Ester	35		F	S	H/W	do	Itl.Fr.Sp.	do	ITALIAN	ITALIAN	ITALY	Rodas		Tangier	do	Morocco	Tangier
12		Barki	Giacobbo	19		M	S	Typist	do	Sp.Fr.	do	do	do	do			do	do	do
13		Dragan Dudnyk	Anton	33		M	S	Farmer	do	Rus.Eng.	do	STATELESS	UKRANIA	KIEV			Madrid	do	Spain	Madrid
14		Ramos Martinez	Enrique	40		M	M	Laborer	do	Spanish	do	SPANISH	SPANISH	SPAIN	ALGIERS		Malaga	Jan. 30/46	do	Malaga
15		Ruedo Rincón	Concepción	28		F	M	H/W	do	Sp.Fr.Eng.	do	do	FRANCE	Paris			Madrid	Apr. 18/46	do	Madrid
16		Pérez Bachiller	Modesta	46		F	S	H/W	do	Spanish	do	SPANISH	SPAIN	Villaville			do	do	do	do
17		Rocca Sabel	Alfredo	34		M		Merchant	do	do	do	CUBAN	SPANISH		Oviedo		Havana	Nov. 24/45	do	do
18		Mendez Martinez	Carmen	30		F	M	H/W	do	do	do	CUBAN	CUBA	Havana			Madrid	April 25/46	do	do

MAY 12 1946

11		Capeluto	Ester JACQUES	35	F	S	H/W	do	Itl.Fr.Sp.	do	ITALIAN	ITALIAN	ITALY	Rodas
12		Barki	Giacobbo	19	M	S	Typist	do	Sp.Fr.	do	do	do	do	do
13		Dragan Dudnyk	Anton	33	M	S	Newspaperman	do	Rus.Eng.	do	STATELESS		UKRANIA	KIEV

Manifest from the Spanish ship Marques De Comillas, which brought Jack Barkey and Esther Capeluto to the United States from Tangier via Cadiz, Spain, May 12, 1946.
[Document filed at Ellis Island, New York]

List **17**

STATES IMMIGRANT INSPECTOR AT PORT OF ARRIVAL

Aliens, or a port of another insular possession, in whatever class they travel, MUST be fully listed and the master or commanding officer of each vessel carrying such passengers must upon arrival deliver lists thereof to the immigrant inspector

SECOND-CABIN PASSENGERS ONLY

26

Arriving at Port of N E W - Y O R K , May 12th, 19 40

Detail inset (bottom of page):

| 11 | My sister Matilde Marki | Ware. | Was.Seatle | do My Brother | do do | D O | 807- 30th Ave. South Seattle-Washington | NO Perm. Yes | DO DO |
| 12 | My brother | do | | do do | do My Uncle | do do | D O | My friend Luke Myshuba 327 | NO Perm. Yes | DO DO |

273

WESTERN UNION (May 17, 1946)

RALPH CAPELUTO—SEATTLE CURTAIN MFG. CO.

807 30 AVE SEATL—PREFONTAINE BLDG.

WILL ARRIVE MONDAY 8 AM PENNSYLANIA RAILROAD STATION, JACK

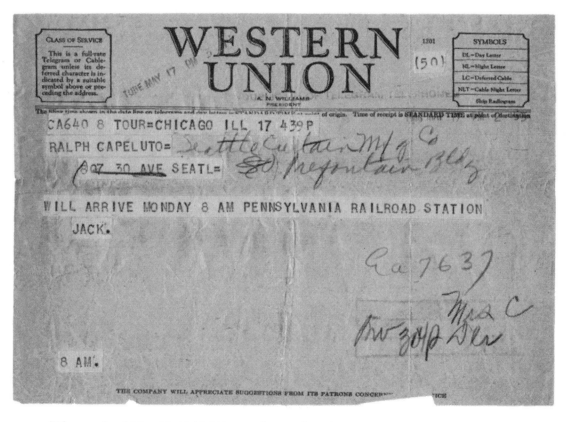

Telegram dated May 17, 1946. Telegram from Jack Barkey to Ralph Capeluto announcing anticipated arrival time in Seattle, Wash.

WESTERN UNION

RALPH CAPELUTO

SEATTLE CURTAIN MANUFACTURING CO—THIRD AND YESLER WAY

SEATTLE, WASH.

NO NEED TO CABLE SINCE QUOTA SET IN STATE DEPARTMENT HERE. ADVISE YOUR RELATIVES TO COME AHEAD SINCE TURKISH QUOTA GREATLY OVERSUBSCRIBED. REGRETABLY WILL NOT BE REOPENED FOR A YEAR OR LONGER.

HUGH DE LACY, MC[84]

---

[84] This wire dated May 24, 1946.

WESTERN UNION

RALPH CAPELUTO

SEATTLE CURTAIN MANUFACTURING CO=THIRD AND YESLER WAY

SEATTLE, WASH

RE: TELEPHONE CALLS PLEASE WIRE ME DATA ON AGES PLEASE OF BIRTH ETC. FOR MAURICE AND HIME BARKC. ALSO INFORMATION AS TO WHY THEY MAY NOT HAVE RECEIVED VISAS UNDER ITALIAN QUOTA AS DID OTHERS. HAS PASSAGE BEEN ARRANGED FOR THEM IS IT DESIRED THAT I CABLE CONSUL IN TANGIERS OR WILL LETTER THROUGH DIPLOMATIC POUCH SERVE=

HUGH DE LACY, MC[85]

---

[85] This wire dated May 25, 1946.

May 26, 1946

Hon. Hugh De Lacy

House of Representatives

Washington, DC

Dear Mr. De Lacy:

I acknowledge receipt of your wire of May 25th in regards to inquiry about data and ages and birth-place of Maurice and Haim Barki. As per our telephone conversation, I wish to inform you that my single sister Esther Capeluto and a nephew Jack Barki have been here in Seattle with me since May 20th, and I was awaiting their arrival before writing you.

It seems that they all have received Italian visas except, of course, my brother-in-law and the twin boys, Maurice and Haim Barki. It is very obvious that my brother-in-law, who is born in Turkey, would naturally come under the Turkish quota, but we are at a loss to see why they consider the twins, Maurice and Haim, under the Turkish quota when they were born and raised and always lived in the Isle of Rhodes, Italy, until they were forced to leave in 1939.

I am enclosing a copy of the schedule of persons for whom I made application so that you may get information from that.

I hope and pray that you will succeed in obtaining visas for the boys. Then we are in hopes of bringing the father in as a tourist until the time comes for him to enter under the Turkish quota.

I want to thank you most sincerely for what you have done in this matter. I feel sure that with your help the family will be reunited and become good law-abiding citizens. You ask me in your wire if you should cable or write a letter through diplomatic pouch. I will leave that to your good judgment. If you feel that a cable is better, please spare no expense as I am anxious to see this through.

Thanking you again from the bottom of my heart, and with kindest personal regards,[86]

---

[86] This letter is from Ralph Capeluto.

(Attachment to letter on previous page)

SCHEDULE OF PERSONS FOR WHOM APPLICATION IS MADE

NAME	DATE OF BIRTH	PLACE OF BIRTH	PRESENT ADDRESS	RELATIONSHIP
Esther Capeluto	March 10, 1909	Isle of Rhodes	Tangiers, Mor.	Sister
Abraham Barki	Feb. 20, 1891	Aidin, Turkey	"	Bro.-in-law
Mathilda Barki	March 5, 1895	Isle of Rhodes	"	Sister
Claire Barki	March 14, 1921	"	"	Niece
Rachel Barki	March 5, 1923	"	"	Niece
Haim Barki (twins)	March 27, 1925	"	"	Nephew
Maurice Barki	March 27,1925	"	"	Nephew
Jacques Barki	March 3, 1928	"	"	Nephew
Regina Barki	Jan. 9, 1932	"	"	Niece

HUGH DE LACY

First District of Washington

136 House Office Building

Home Address:

Seattle, Washington

H. Richard Seller, Secretary

Member:

COMMITTEE ON NAVAL AFFAIRS

CONGRESS OF THE UNITED STATES
HOUSE OF REPRESENTATIVES
WASHINGTON, DC

May 29th, 1946

Mr. Ralph Capeluto

Seattle Curtain Manufacturing Company

Third and Yesler

Seattle 4, Washington

Dear Mr. Capeluto:

Thank you for your letter of May 26 and for the further information regarding Maurice and Haim Barki.

Apparently there have been a number of misunderstandings with the consul in Tangiers as to the desires of the various members of your family. The Visa Division here tells me that the Consul informed them that Haim and Maurice desired to remain with their father until he is eligible to come to this country under the Turkish quota. Since they were minors, it was therefore necessary for them to be given numbers under the Turkish quota.

There is no reason, however, to prevent their accompanying their mother, and if they wish to do this, they can come under the Italian quota. Since their father may have to wait a long time to enter this country, this seems the best thing for them to do, and they should immediately make their desires known to the consul and apply for visas under the Italian quota.

I am writing to the consul today and advising him of the desire of these two boys to accompany their mother to this country. If you wish, you might cable your family to the effect that it would be advisable for Haim and Maurice to apply to the consul again for their visas so that they can be allotted Italian quota numbers at the earliest possible date.

If you feel that further action is advisable, please let me know.

With best wishes,

Sincerely yours,

HUGH DE LACY, MC

hd:br

TRANSLATION

WIRE

Dated MAY 29 (1946)

SENT FROM CADIZ, SPAIN, TO UNCLE RALPH

WE LEAVE TODAY ON THE "MAGALLANES" WILL ARRIVE AT NEW YORK JUNE 8. PLEASE NOTIFY HARRY __ HUGS FROM MAMA, RACHEL, REGINA.

CLAIRE[87]

---

[87] Harry Benatar was Mazaltov's cousin who lived in Brooklyn. He met the travelers in NY as well as Vic and Morris some time later. He and his wife Rita were very good friends of Auntie Rae Capeluto.

ADDRESS OFFICIAL COMMUNICATIONS TO
THE SECRETARY OF STATE
WASHINGTON 25, D. C.

DEPARTMENT OF STATE
WASHINGTON

June 18, 1946.

In reply refer to
DF-A/C
811.111 Barki, Abraham

Mr. Ralph Capeluto,
Seattle Curtain Mfg. Company,
Prefontaine Building,
Third and Yesler Way,
Seattle, Washington.

Sir:

The following expenses have been incurred for telegrams sent at
your request, and for which reimbursement is requested as required by
Section 169 of Title 5 of the United States Code:

Date	To or from	In regard to	Cost
4/17/46	To Tangier	visas, Ester Capelluto, Matilde, Claire, Rachel, Jacques and Regina Barki	$20.90
4/19/46	From Tangier	" " " "	5.56
		Total.........	$26.46

Please make the remittance payable to the order of "The Secretary
of State of the United States" and forward it, together with this statement, to the "Chief, Division of Finance, Department of State". When
your remittance is received this statement will be receipted and returned
for your files.

This statement covers only the charges for the telegrams described,
and if other telegrams are necessary to comply with your request an additional statement will be rendered for the cost thereof.

Very truly yours,

For the Secretary of State:

Louis F. Thompson
Chief, Division of Finance

By _N.E. Talley_

Letter dated June 18, 1946. Letter from the U.S. State Department to Ralph Capeluto
requesting remittance for expenses.

List 12

LIST OR MANIFEST OF ALIEN PASSENGERS FOR THE UNITED

ALL ALIENS arriving at a port of continental United States from a foreign port or a port of the insular possessions of the United States, and all aliens arriving at a port of said insular possessions from a foreign port, a port of continental United This (yellow) sheet is for the listing of

-SPANISH- S.S. "MAGALLANES" Passengers sailing from CADIZ SPAIN , May 30 th , 1946

No. on List	HEAD TAX STATUS	Family name	Given name	Age (Yrs. Mos.)	Sex	Married or single	Calling or occupation	Able to — read	Able to — lang.	Nationality (Country of which citizen or subject)	Race or people	Place of birth — Country	Place of birth — City or town, State, Province or District	Immigration Visa	Issued Place	Issued Date	Data concerning verification of landings, etc.	Last permanent residence — Country	Last permanent residence — City or town, State, Province or District
1		PADILLA RUEDA	Maria	40	F	W	Home	Yes	Spanish	Yes	Spanish	Spanish	Spain	Sevilla	HIV-247	Madrid	Apr-9/46	Spain	Madrid
2		BRITO PADILLA	Alicia de	8	F	S	-.-	None	do	None	do	do	do	Madrid	do	do	do	do	do
3		BORROGAN ROJAS	Maria Teresa	32	F	M	Home	Yes	do	Yes	do	do	do	Amusco	HC-245	do	May-21/46	do	do
4		FERNANDEZ FARRA	German	22	M	S	Clerk	do	do	do	Mexican	do	Mexican	Mexico	HC-247	do	May-24/46	do	do
5		PIQUE CASTELLS	Juan	46	M	M	Merchant	do	do	do	Spanish	do	Spain	Barcelona	HC-49	Barcelona	May-16/46	Colombia	Bogotá
6		PIQUE TOVAR	Juan	7	M	S	Student	do	do	do	do	do	Colombia	Bogotá	do	do	do	do	do
7		BERNAT FERRER	Miguel	49	M	M	Owner Farmer	do	do	do	do	do	Spain	Soller	HC-131	do	May-21/46	Spain	Soller
8		BAUZA BERNAT	Juan	63	M	S	do	do	do	do	do	do	do	do	HC-132	do	do	do	do
9		GONZALEZ RAMIREZ	Juan	45	M	M	Merchant	do	do	do	do	do	do	San Fernando	HIV-3	Tenerife	Apr-26/46	do	La Laguna
10		PAGES-TELAIDO	Manuel	32	M	M	Salesman Uphols-	do	do	do	do	do	Porto Rico	Ponce	HC-11	Barcelona	May-9/46	do	Barcelona
11		GARCIA VERA	Jose	28	F	S	terer	do	do	do	do	do	Spain	La Orotava	HC-7	Tenerife	May-23/46	do	La Orotava
12		TOSCO GONZALEZ	Juana	25	F	M	Home	do	do	do	do	do	do	Los Silos	HC-10	do	May-23/46	do	Los Silos
13		JIMENEZ MEDINA	Andrés	35	M	M	Farmer	do	do	do	do	do	do	Santiago del Teide	HC-9	do	do	do	Buenavista
14		JIMENEZ MARTIN	Fernanda	35	F	M	Home	do	do	do	do	do	do	Buenavista	HC-8	do	do	do	do
15		JIMENEZ JIMENEZ	Elisa A.	9	F	S	Student	do	do	do	do	do	do	do	do	do	do	do	do
16		JIMENEZ JIMENEZ	Fernando	6	M	S	-.-	None	do	None	do	do	do	do	do	do	do	do	do
17		JIMENEZ JIMENEZ	Maria Cristina	1	F	S	-.-	-.-	do	do	do	do	do	do	do	do	do	do	do
18		CAPOLLUTO BARKI	Mathilde	50	F	M	Home	Yes	Sp.Ita.	Yes	Italian	Hebrew	Italy	Rodi	QIV-1694	Tangier	Apr-22/46	Marocco	Tangier
19		BARKI	Regina	14	F	S	Student	do	Spa.Fr.	do	do	do	do	do	QIV-1906	do	do	do	do
20		BARKI	Clara	25	F	S	Bookeeper-typist	do	do	do	do	do	do	do	QIV-1695	do	do	do	do
21		BARKI	Rachel	23	F	S	Dressma-ker	do	do	do	do	do	do	do	QIV-1696	do	do	do	do

---

18	UNDER 16 SEC. 105.J(a)	CAPOLLUTO BARKI	Mathilde	50	F	M	Home	Yes	Sp.Ita.	Yes	Italian	Hebrew	Italy	Rodi
19		BARKI	Regina	14	F	S	Student	do	Spa.Fr.	do	do	do	do	do
20		BARKI	Clara	25	F	S	Bookeeper typist	do	do	do	do	do	do	do
21		BARKI	Rachel	23	F	S	Dressma-ker	do	do	do	do	do	do	do

Manifest from the Spanish ship S.S. Magallanes, which brought Matilda, Claire, Rachel and Regina Barkey to the United States from Tangier via Cadiz, Spain, June 8, 1946.
[Document filed at Ellis Island, New York]

STATES IMMIGRANT INSPECTOR AT PORT OF ARRIVAL

States, or a port of another insular possession, in whatsoever class they travel, MUST be fully listed and the master or commanding officer of each vessel carrying such passengers must upon arrival deliver lists thereof to the immigrant inspector
SECOND-CABIN PASSENGERS ONLY

Arriving at Port of ___ NEW YORK N.Y. _____ 19 46 JUN 8 1946   371

No. on List		Final destination										Purpose of coming to United States											Height	Color of		Marks of Identification
1	My bro. Rafael Padilla Testanos 1 Sevilla	Madrid	-.-	P.C.	Lon	Yes	Husband	Yes	NO	-.-	c/o Husband Delfin de Grito 1019-67th Street Brooklyn N.Y.	Yes	NO	NO	NO	NO	NO	NO	GOOD	NO	5 3	fair blk	blk	none
2	do	do	-.-	do	do	do	Father	do	do	-.-	do	do	do	do	do	do	do	do	do	do	3 4	do	br.	br.	do
3	My bro. Isidro Borrogan Puebla 12 Madrid	MEXICO	-.-	do	yself	do	do	-.-	-.-	A HOTEL IN NEW YORK IN TRANSIT TO MEXICO	do	do	do	do	do	do	do	do	do	do	5 5	do	blonde	br.	do
4	My father Eduardo Fernandez Juan Bravo 44 Madrid	MADRID	-.-	do	do	do	Yes 8ds, N.Y.			Jan. 1946	do	do	do	do	do	do	do	do	do	do	5 9	do	blk	br.	do
5	My mother Eugracia Castells San Fernando 50 Igualada COLOMBIA	-.-	do	do	do	do 16ds	do	-.-	927. 1946	A HOTEL IN NEW YORK IN TRANSIT TO COLOMBIA	do	do	do	do	do	do	do	do	do	do	5 5	dk. grey	br.	do
6	do	do	do	-.-	-.-	do	Father	do	do	do	do	do	do	do	do	do	do	do	do	do	do	3 7	do	br.	br.	do
7	My wife Catalina Frosters Santa Teresa Soller	-.-	P.R. Lares	do	yself	do do	-.-	P.R. 940	P.O.Box 184 Lares P.R.	do	do	do	do	do	do	do	do	do	do	5 7	dk. grey	br.	white db
8	My mother Carina Bernal Jose A. 108 Soller	-.-	do	Carican	do do	do	-.-	-.-	do	Carican Puerto Rico c/o Rosa Marrero	do	do	do	do	do	do	do	do	do	do				scar on back
9	c/o Benito Marrero Barrio Mirasol Lares P.R.	-.-	do	Lares	do	do	No	-.-	-.-	Barrio Mirasol Lares	do	do	do	do	do	do	do	do	do	do	5 5	do	dk.	br.	of neck
10	My wife Angeles Cahue Rabasa 38 Barcelona	-.-	do	S.Juan	do	yself	do	Yes 11	P.R. 024	Adjuntas P.R.	No	Ply	do	do	do	do	do	do	do	do	5 7	do	br.	br.	none
11	La Castana 12 La Orotowa Tenerife Canary Island VENEZUELA	-.-	do	do	do	No	-.-	-.-	HOTEL IN NEW YORK IN TRANSIT TO VENEZUELA	Yes	do	do	do	do	do	do	do	do	do	5 7	do	br.	br.	scar on wrist right hand
12	My husband Pascacio Perez Caracas Venezuela	-.-	do	-.-	do	Husband	do	do	-.-	-.-	do	do	do	do	do	do	do	do	do	do	5 5	mei	blk	br.	do
13	Buenavista Tenerife C.I.	do	-.-	-.-	do	yself	do	do	-.-	-.-	do	do	do	do	do	do	do	do	do	do	5 5	do	fair	blue	none
14	do	do	do	-.-	-.-	do	Husband	do	do	-.-	do	do	do	do	do	do	do	do	do	do	5 2	fair	cheanut	br.	scar on forehead
15	do	do	do	do	-.-	do	Father	do	do	-.-	do	do	do	do	do	do	do	do	do	do	4 2	do	br.	br.	none
16	do	do	do	do	-.-	do	do	do	do	-.-	do	do	do	do	do	do	do	do	do	do	3 2	do	br.	br.	do
17	do	do	do	do	-.-	do	do	do	do	-.-	do	do	do	do	do	do	do	do	do	do	2 2	do	br.	brn.	do
18	My niece Vida Capelluto Rome Italy	-.-	Wass. Seattle	do	Brother	do	do	-.-	-.-	My bro. Ralph Capelluto 807 30th Ave.S.Seattle	No	Ply	do	do	do	do	do	do	do	4 1	ldk.	br.	blk	Several warts on nose and face
19	do	do	do	-.-	do	do	do	Uncle	do	do	-.-	do	do	do	do	do	do	do	do	5 2	do	br.	br.	none brun-
20	do	do	do	-.-	do	do	do	do	do	-.-	do	do	do	do	do	do	do	do	5 2	do	br.	br.	Mole on right side of neck
21	do	do	do	-.-	do	do	do	do	do	-.-	do	do	do	do	do	do	do	do	5 4	do	br.	br.	Two pockmarks above right eye brow
22																									
23																									
24																									
25																									
26																									
27																									

18	My niece Vida Capelluto Rome Italy		-.-	Wass. Seattle	do	Brother	do	do	-.-	-.-	-.-	My bro. Ralph Capelluto 807 30th Ave.S.Seattle	No	Ply	do		do	
19	do	do	do	-.-	do	do	do	Uncle	do	do	-.-	-.-	-.-	do	do			do	do	do
20	do	do	do	-.-	do	do	do	do	do	-.-	-.-	-.-	do	do		do	do	do
21	do	do	do	-.-	do	do	do	do	do	-.-	-.-	-.-	do	do		do	do	do

DEPARTMENT OF STATE
WASHINGTON
June 18, 1946
In Reply refer to
DF-A/C
811.111 Barki, Abraham
Mr. Ralph Capeluto
Seattle Curtain Mfg. Company
Prefontaine Building
Third and Yesler Way
Seattle, Washington
Sir:

The following expenses have been incurred for telegrams sent at your request, and for which reimbursement is requested as required by Section 169 of Title 5 of the United States Code:

Date	To or From	In regard to	Cost
4/17/46	To Tangier	Visas, Esther Capeluto. Matilde, Claire, Rachel, Jacques and Regina Barki	$20.90
4/19/46	From Tangier	"	5.56
		TOTAL	$26.46

Please make the remittance payable to the order of "The Secretary of State of the United States" and forward it, together with this statement, to the "Chief, Division of Finance, Department of State." When your remittance is received, this statement will be receipted and returned for your files.

This statement only covers the charges for the telegrams described. And if other telegrams are necessary to comply with your request, an additional statement will be rendered for the cost thereof.

Very truly yours,

For the Secretary of State

Louis F. Thompson

Chief, Division of Finance

by [signed] H. L. Talley

LEGATION OF THE

UNITED STATES OF AMERICA

Tangier, Morocco, June 21, 1946

The Honorable Hugh de Lacey

House of Representatives

Washington, DC

Sir:

In reply to your letter of May 29, 1945, concerning the immigration visa status of Haim and Maurice (Moses) Barki, sons of Abraham Barki, I take pleasure in informing you that on June 13, 1946, the Legation requested of the Department of State numbers under the Italian quota in order to enable them to proceed to the United States to join their mother, Mrs. Mathilde Barki, and the other members of the Barki family who were born in Italy and to whom visas under the Italian quota were issued during the month of April. As Mr. Abraham Barki was born in Turkey and thus comes under the quota for that country, he must, as you state, await his turn in the new quota year beginning July 1, 1946, numbers under the Turkish quota having been exhausted for the year ending June 30.

You may be assured that every consideration consistent with United States immigration laws and regulations will be given the cases of those members of the Barki family who have not yet received visas when quota numbers for them are received.

Very truly yours,

Paul H. Alling

Diplomatic Agent

HUGH DE LACY   Member:

First District of Washington   COMMITTEE ON NAVAL AFFAIRS

136 House Office Building

Home Address:

Seattle, Washington

H. Richard Seller, Secretary

CONGRESS OF THE UNITED STATES

HOUSE OF REPRESENTATIVES

WASHINGTON, DC

July 5, 1946

Mr. Ralph Capeluto

Seattle Curtain Manufacturing Company

Third and Yesler Way

Seattle 4, Washington

Dear Mr. Capeluto:

In the absence of Mr. De Lacy, who is in Seattle this week, I am enclosing a letter we have received from the United States Legation at Tangier, Morocco, with regard to Haim and Maurice Barki. You will be pleased to know that they have been given numbers under the Italian quota in order to enable them to proceed to the United States.

Sincerely yours,

ISABELLA SAVERY

Secretary

is:hl

Encl.

TRANSLATION

Wire from Tangier, July 27, 1946

TO: Ralph Capeluto

5th Floor, Prefontaine Building

Seattle, Wash.

"VISA HAIM, MOISE OBTAINED—WILL TRY TO LEAVE SOON=WIRE EVENTUAL OB-JECTIONS—INFORM YOURSELVES IMMEDIATELY QUOTA PAPA _ HUGS

BARKI[88]

---

[88] This wire is date stamped incorrectly, and should be "1946 Jul 28."

WESTERN UNION

TB06   1946 Aug 17 PM 151

T.C. DU353 INTL (SUBJECT TO CORRECTION 121 WDS)=CD CADIZ VIA RCA 13 FR 17 1100

RALPH CAPELUTO=

FIFTH FLOOR PREFONTAINE BLDG SEATTLE (WASH) =

LEAVE CADIZ TODAY MARQUES COMILLAS LOVE=

BARKI[89]

---

[89] This wire was sent by Vic (Haim) and Morris (Moise).

Application for a Certificate of Arrival and Preliminary Form for a Declaration of Intention

Take or mail this application to-

Immigration and Naturalization Service,

New Post Office and Courthouse Building,

Pittsburgh, PA

Date: October 7, 1946

I, Esther Capeluto, residing at 807—30th Avenue South, Seattle, King, Washington, and desire to declare my intention to become a citizen of the United States in accordance with the naturalization law, in the _____ Court at Seattle, Washington. I submit herewith a statement of facts to be used in making such declaration and three photographs of myself, each of which I have signed.

1) I arrived in the United States through the port of New York, New York under the name of Esther Capeluto on May 12, 1946 on the vessel SS "Marques de Camilla".

2) I have _____ been absent from the United States as follows: _____ _____. I have _____ been absent at any other time.

3) I have _____ used another name in this country than that given above. (If so) It was _____. I used that name because _____.

4) The full name of the person shown on my steamship ticket was Esther Capeluto.

5) I was born in Rhodes, Italy on _____.

6) My father's full name was Mussani Capeluto.

7) My mother's maiden name was Rachel Capeluto.

8) (If a married woman) My maiden name was _____.

9) My last foreign residence was Tangier Morocco.

10) The place where I took the ship or train which landed me in the United States was Cadiz, Spain.

11) The ticket on which I came to this country was bought at Madrid, Spain.

12) (If arrival by ship) Name of steamship line was Transatlantic, third cabin. I arrived as a passenger.

13) I traveled on an immigration visa and a passport.

14) I paid $10.00 head tax at Tangier Morocco on _____.

15) I was _____ examined by United States immigration officers at Tangier, Morocco.

16) (If not examined, state why, and give the circumstances of your entry) _____
_____.

17) The person in the United States to whom I was coming was my brother, Ralph Capeluto.

18) The place in the United States to which I was going was Seattle, Washington.

19) The names of some of the passengers or other persons I traveled with and their relationship to me, if any, are my nephew, Jack Barki.

20) (If married) My wife or husband is _____ of foreign birth. (S)he was _____ naturalized on _____ at _____ Certificate No. _____ or became a citizen by _____.

21) Have you ever been deported from the United States or are deportation proceedings now pending against you? _____ If so, state all facts: _____

22) Was your father or mother ever a citizen of the United States? _____ If so, give full particulars _____ _____.

23) Did you register under the Alien Registration Act, 1940? _____ If so, state the number of your Alien Registration Receipt Card _____.

24) Did you yourself fill out this form? <u>No</u>. If not, who filled out this form for you? <u>My niece, Claire Barki</u>.

I certify that the foregoing statements are true to the best of my knowledge and belief.

_____

STATEMENT OF FACTS TO BE USED IN MAKING MY DECLARATION OF INTENTION

1) My full name is Esther Capeluto.

2) My place of residence is 807—30th Avenue South, Seattle, King, Washington.

3) My occupation is _____.

4) I am 37 years old.

5) I was born on _____ in Rhodes, Italy.

6) My personal description is as follows: Sex _____; color white; complexion clear; color of eyes brown; color of hair brown; height 5 feet, 2 inches; weight 122 pounds; visible distinctive marks _____; race white; present nationality Italian.

7) I am not married.

8) I have _____ children.

9) My last place of foreign residence was Tangier Morocco.

10) I emigrated to the United States from Tangier Morocco.

11) My lawful entry for permanent residence in the United States was at Seattle, Wash. under the name of Esther Capeluto on May 20, 1946 on the Milwaukee train.

12) Since my lawful entry for permanent residence I have not been absent from the United States, for a period or periods of six months or longer, as follows:

14) It is my intention in good faith to become a citizen of the United States and to reside permanently therein.

15) I will, before being admitted to citizenship, renounce forever all allegiance and fidelity to any foreign prince, potentate, state, or sovereignty of whom or which at the time of admission to citizenship I may be a subject or citizen.

16) I am not an anarchist; nor a believer in the unlawful damage, injury, or destruction of property, or sabotage; nor a disbeliever in or opposed to organized government; nor a member of or affiliated with any organization or body of persons teaching disbelief in or opposition to organized government.

17) I certify that the photographs attached to this application are a likeness of me and were signed by me.

I certify that the above statement of facts is true to the best of my knowledge and belief.

NOTE-Have you enclosed (if required) THREE

PHOTOGRAPHS OF YOURSELF?

_____

Signature of Applicant

807—30th Avenue South

The Consulate General of Italy

TANGIER

COPY

UNITED SERVICE FOR NEW AMERICANS INC.

105 Nassau St.

New-York 7 N.Y.

Oct. 24, 1946

RE. BARKI, Abraham

Case #A 38812

Tangiers, Morocco

Washington Emigre Bureau, Inc.

Seattle, 4 Wash.

Dear Miss Peck.

With regard to Mr. Abraham Barki, our liaison with government made inquiry at the visa Division of the State Department and was advised that there was a request from the consul in Tangiers in July 1946 for a quote number.

Mr. Barki has been put on the waiting list. He has a priority as of August 1944, the date on which documents were filed with the State Department.

We have cabled to our committee in Morocco requesting present status of the case and will keep you advised of further developments.

Sincerely yours,

Signature

Migration Department

Reply to.

Jean Lifschutz.

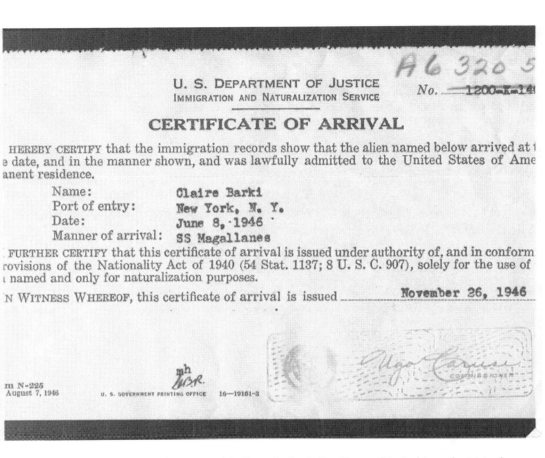

A 6 320 5

U. S. DEPARTMENT OF JUSTICE
IMMIGRATION AND NATURALIZATION SERVICE

No. ___1200-K-14

CERTIFICATE OF ARRIVAL

HEREBY CERTIFY that the immigration records show that the alien named below arrived at
e date, and in the manner shown, and was lawfully admitted to the United States of Ame
anent residence.

Name: **Claire Barki**
Port of entry: **New York, N. Y.**
Date: **June 8, 1946**
Manner of arrival: **SS Magallanes**

FURTHER CERTIFY that this certificate of arrival is issued under authority of, and in conform
rovisions of the Nationality Act of 1940 (54 Stat. 1137; 8 U. S. C. 907), solely for the use of
named and only for naturalization purposes.

N WITNESS WHEREOF, this certificate of arrival is issued _____ **November 26, 1946**

m N-225
August 7, 1946   U. S. GOVERNMENT PRINTING OFFICE   16—19161-3

Certificate issued November 26, 1946. Claire Barkey's Certificate of Arrival into the United
States on June 8, 1946.

Form N-300
U. S. DEPARTMENT OF JUSTICE
IMMIGRATION AND NATURALIZATION SERVICE
(Edition of 1-13-41)

No. _____

Application for a Certificate of Arrival and Preliminary Form for a Declaration of Intention

For use in searching records of arrival:

RECORDS EXAMINED	RECORD FOUND
Card index _____	Place _____
Index books _____	Name _____
Manifests _____	
_____	Date _____
_____	Manner _____
Use Form N-210 in issuing certificate of arrival on this application.	Marital status _____
	(Signature of person making search)

TO THE APPLICANT: DO NOT WRITE ABOVE THIS LINE. READ CAREFULLY AND FOLLOW THE INSTRUCTIONS ON LAST PAGE HEREOF

☞ *Take or mail this application and your money order to—*
IMMIGRATION AND NATURALIZATION SERVICE,   Date ___August 6___, 19 46
New Post Office and Courthouse Building,
Pittsburgh, Pa.

I, __Claire Barki__, residing at __2008 - 33rd. So.__

__Seattle__ __King__ __Wash.__ , desire to declare my intention to become a
(City or town) (County) (State)
citizen of the United States, in accordance with the naturalization law, in the _____ Court at __Seattle__
(Name of court) (City or town)
__Wash.__ I submit herewith a statement of facts to be used in making such declaration, and three photographs of myself,
(State)
each of which I have signed.

I hereby apply for a Certificate of Arrival (if required) showing my lawful entry into the United States for permanent residence and enclose money order
No. _____ for $2.50, payable to the order of the "Commissioner of Immigration and Naturalization, Washington, D. C.," in payment therefor. (See reference to "money order," page 4.)

(1) I arrived in the United States through the port of __New-York__ __New-York__
(City or town) (State)
under the name of __Claire Barki__, on __June__ __8__ __1946__
(Month) (Day) (Year)
on the vessel __S/s. "Magallanes"__
(If otherwise than by vessel, show manner of arrival)
(If arrival was through Canada or Mexico, I arrived at the port of _____, Canada or Mexico,
on _____ on the vessel _____)
(Month) (Day) (Year)

(2) I have _____ been absent from the United States as follows: _____
(Date of departure and return, ports of entry, and names of vessels or other means)
_____ I have _____ been absent at any other time.

(3) I have __no__ used another name in this country than that given above. (If so) It was _____
I used that name because _____

(4) The full name of the person shown on my steamship ticket was __Claire Barki__

(5) I was born in __Rhodes__ __Italy__ on __March__ __14__, __1921__
(City or town) (Country) (Month) (Day) (Year)

(6) My father's full name is/was __Abraham Barki__

(7) My mother's maiden name was __Matilde Capeluto__

(8) (If a married woman) My maiden name was _____

(9) My last foreign residence was __Tangier__ __Morocco__
(City or town) (Country)

(10) The place where I took the ship or train which landed me in the United States was __Cadiz__ __Spain__
(City or town) (Country)

(11) The ticket on which I came to this country was bought at __Madrid__ __Spain__
(City or town) (Country)

(12) (If arrival by ship) Name of steamship line was __Trasatlantica__
first, second, or third cabin __Third cabin__ I arrived as a passenger, stowaway, seaman, member of crew, or
(State which)
otherwise __as a passenger__
(State which, giving particulars)

(13) I traveled on (an immigration visa, a passport, or permit to reenter) __An immigration visa and a passport__
(State which)

(14) I paid $ __10.00__ head tax at __Tangier__ __Morocco__ on __April__ __22, 1946__
(City or town) (State or country) (Month) (Day) (Year)

(15) I was _____ examined by United States immigration officers at __Tangier__ __Morocco__
(City or town) (State or country)

(16) (If not examined, state why, and give the circumstances of your entry) _____

(17) The person in the United States to whom I was coming was __My uncle Ralph Capeluto__

(18) The place in the United States to which I was going was __Seattle__ __Wash.__

(19) The names of some of the passengers or other persons I traveled with and their relationship to me, if any, are __My mother Matilde__
__and my sisters Rachel and Regina.__
[OVER]

16—11312   (1)

Claire Barkey's Application for a Certificate of Arrival, filed Aug. 6, 1946.

2

(20) (If married) My wife or husband is _____ of foreign birth. (S)he was _____ naturalized on _____

(Month)   (Day)   (Year)

at _____ _____ _____ certificate No. _____ ;

(City or town)   (County)   (State)

or became a citizen by _____

(21) Have you ever been deported from the United States, or are deportation proceedings now pending against you? _____ If so, state all facts _____

(22) Was your father or mother ever a citizen of the United States? No. _____ If so, give full particulars _____

(23) Did you register under the Alien Registration Act, 1940? Yes. _____ If so, state the number of your Alien Registration Receipt Card 6326548

(Yes or no)   (Registration number)

(24) Did you yourself fill out this form? Yes _____ If not, who filled out this form for you? _____

I certify that the foregoing statements are true to the best of my knowledge and belief.

(Show whether Mr.
Mrs. or Miss)   _____

(Original signature of applicant, without abbreviation; also alias, if used)

2008 - 33rd. Ave. So.

(Address at which applicant receives mail)

16—11312   U. S. GOVERNMENT PRINTING OFFICE

295

3

No. _____

STATEMENT OF FACTS TO BE USED IN MAKING MY DECLARATION OF INTENTION

(1) My full name is __Claire Barki__

(2) My place of residence is __2008 - 33rd. Ave.So. Seattle__ __King__ __Wash__

(3) My occupation is __Office work__ (4) I am __25__ years old.

(5) I was born on __March 14 ,1921__, in __Rhodes__ __Italy__

(6) My personal description is as follows: Sex __female__, color __white__, complexion __clear__, color of eyes __brown__ color of hair __brown__, height __5__ feet __2__ inches; weight __116__ pounds; visible distinctive marks _____; race __white__; present nationality __italian__

(7) I am __not__ married; the name of my wife or husband is _____

we were married on _____ at _____

he or she was born at _____ on _____

and entered the United States at _____ on _____

for permanent residence in the United States, and now resides at _____

(8) I have _____ children; and the name, sex, date, and place of birth, and present place of residence of each of said children who is living are as follows:

_____

(9) My last place of foreign residence was __Tangier__ __Morocco__

(10) I emigrated to the United States from __Tangier__ __Morocco__

(11) My lawful entry for permanent residence in the United States was at __Seattle__ __Wash__

under the name of __Claire Barki__ on __June 16,1946__ on the __Milwaukee train__

(12) Since my lawful entry for permanent residence I have __no__ been absent from the United States, for a period or periods of 6 months or longer, as follows:

DEPARTED FROM THE UNITED STATES			RETURNED TO THE UNITED STATES		
PORT	DATE (Month, day, year)	VESSEL OR OTHER MEANS OF CONVEYANCE	PORT	DATE (Month, day, year)	VESSEL OR OTHER MEANS OF CONVEYANCE

(13) I have _____ heretofore made declaration of intention number _____, on _____ at _____, in the _____

(14) It is my intention in good faith to become a citizen of the United States and to reside permanently therein. (15) I will, before being admitted to citizenship, renounce forever all allegiance and fidelity to any foreign prince, potentate, state, or sovereignty of whom or which at the time of admission to citizenship I may be a subject or citizen. (16) I am not an anarchist; nor a believer in the unlawful damage, injury, or destruction of property, or sabotage; nor a disbeliever in or opposed to organized government; nor a member of or affiliated with any organization or body of persons teaching disbelief in or opposition to organized government. (17) I certify that the photographs attached to this application are a likeness of me and were signed by me.

I certify that the above statement of facts is true to the best of my knowledge and belief.

NOTE—Have you enclosed (if required) THREE PHOTO-GRAPHS OF YOURSELF? MONEY ORDER FOR $2.50?

_____ (Signature of applicant)

__2008 - 33rd.Ave.So.__ (Address at which applicant receives mail)

NOTE TO CLERK OF COURT.—For facts of arrival, use data in Form N-210 A, N-225 A, or N-310, whichever is attached hereto. Form N-210 A, N-225 A, or N-310 and this statement of facts form should be attached to the duplicate declaration and returned at end of month to the immigration and naturalization office at the address given on the first page of this form.

16—11312

4

INSTRUCTIONS TO THE APPLICANT

Pages 1, 2, and 3 of this form must be completely filled out (preferably on the typewriter)

When Declaration Not Required.—You are not required to file a declaration of intention to become a citizen of the United States if you are:

(a) An alien who has served honorably for 3 years in the United States Army, Navy, Marine Corps, or Coast Guard, or for 5 years on board any vessel of the United States Government other than the Navy, Marine Corps, or Coast Guard, or on board vessels of more than 20 tons burden which are not foreign vessels and whose home port is in the United States; or

(b) An alien who married a citizen of the United States or whose spouse was naturalized on or subsequent to September 22, 1922; or

(c) A woman who prior to September 22, 1922, lost your American citizenship by: (1) marriage to an alien or through the loss of American citizenship by your husband, or (2) by marriage to an alien ineligible to citizenship after September 22, 1922.

Immigrant Identification Cards and Alien Registration Receipt Cards.—Every alien who entered the United States for permanent residence on the basis of an immigration visa on or after July 1, 1928, and prior to August 27, 1940, should be in possession of an Immigrant Identification Card. Every alien in the United States should be in possession of an Alien Registration Receipt Card. You need not forward either card with this application. However, you will be required to present these cards when you appear to file your petition for naturalization and to surrender them at the time you are admitted to citizenship. You should therefore carefully save your Immigrant Identification Card and your Alien Registration Receipt Card.

Photographs.—You must send with this application three photographs of yourself taken within 30 days of the date of this application. These photographs must be 2 by 2 inches in size, must not be pasted on a card or mounted in any other way, must be on thin paper, have a light background, and clearly show a front view of your face without hat. Snapshots, or group or full-length portraits will not be accepted. Each of these photographs must be signed by you on the margin and not on the face or clothing.

Money Order.—If you arrived in the United States after June 29, 1906, you must get a money order in the sum of $2.50, payable to the order of the "Commissioner of Immigration and Naturalization, Washington, D. C." This money order, which is in payment for the issuance of a certificate of your arrival in the United States, must be attached to this application when you send or take it to the Immigration and Naturalization office at the address given on the first page of this form.

Date of Your Arrival.—If you do not know the exact date of your arrival in the United States, or the name of the vessel or port, and you cannot obtain this information by consulting your family or friends who came over with you, give the facts of your arrival as you remember them in the appropriate blank spaces on the first page of this form. Your Immigrant Identification Card or your passport, ship's card, or baggage labels, if you have them, may help you to answer these questions.

Absence from the United States.—In statement No. 2 on page 1 of this form, show ALL of your absences from the United States, regardless of how long you were away. In statement No. 12 on page 3, show only your absences which were for 6 or more months. Absence from the United States for more than 6 months but less than 1 year during the periods of continuous residence required in the United States may break the continuity of your residence for naturalization purposes. An absence from the United States of 1 year or more during such periods will break the continuity of your residence for naturalization purposes, except that after you have resided in the United States for at least 1 year and have filed a declaration of intention, if your absence abroad is made necessary because you are an employee of the United States Government, an American institution of research, or an American firm or corporation engaged in foreign trade and commerce of the United States, you may prevent a break in the continuity of your residence for naturalization purposes by making an application on Form N-470. For complete information you should address the office of this Service nearest to you, or the "Commissioner of Immigration and Naturalization, Washington, D. C."

Nationality and Race.—Nationality in statement No. 6, page 3, refers to the country of which you are a citizen or subject. As to "race" in the same statement, Section 303 of the Nationality Act of 1940 provides that only white persons, persons of African nativity or descent, and descendants of races indigenous to the Western Hemisphere are eligible for naturalization. There are certain exceptions, in the case of native-born Filipinos who have served honorably in the United States Army, Navy, Marine Corps, or Coast Guard for a period of at least 3 years, and in the cases of women who have lost citizenship through marriage.

As stated above, the following races are eligible for naturalization:

White	Indian
African or African descent.	Eskimo.
Filipino.	Aleutian.

State to which of these classifications you belong.

PENALTY FOR FALSELY SWEARING IN NATURALIZATION CASES

It is a felony, punishable by a fine of not more than $5,000 or imprisonment for not more than 5 years, or both, for an alien or other person, whether an applicant for naturalization or citizenship, or otherwise — (1) Knowingly to make a false statement under oath either orally or in writing, in any case, proceeding, or matter relating to, or under, or by virtue of any law of the United States relating to naturalization or citizenship. (Nationality Act of 1940, Sec. 346(a) (e).)

U. S. GOVERNMENT PRINTING OFFICE   16—11312

DUPLICATE

The Consulate General of Italy at Tangier

CERTIFIES

THAT, FROM A JUDICIAL ATTESTATION, issued by the District Court of Rhodes on December 28, 1938, it follows that Mr. Barchi, Abramo of the late Haim and the late Lea Clara Alagem, is an Italian citizen and was born at Aidin on the 20th of February, 1891 (twenty February, eighteen hundred ninety-one).

Mr. Barchi, Abramo, who now resides at Tangier, is in possession of Passport No. A/2588282/1529-IV, issued by this Consulate General on the 14th of April, 1944.

This certificate is issued at the request of the concerned as a practical document for the purpose of obtaining a visa of entry into the United States of America.

Tangier, December 6, 1946

for THE CONSUL GENERAL

(signature)

No. 618 R P

Art 6 T.C.

Pts GRATIS

FINALLY — THE USA!

After so many years of writing letters, pleading and waiting, the Barkeys had to move with extreme speed once they received the okay to enter the United States.

Rather than traveling together, the family was split up and came in four different groups. Jack and Esther were the first to leave, on April 26, 1946. They had only one week to prepare after getting their visas.

They first traveled for about a day to Spain by boat and train. Jack had $10 (U.S.) in his pocket, plus bread, cheese and cookies that his mother had packed. They waited two or three days at the port of Cadiz, Spain, for the ship they would take to America. The Marques de Comillas was a converted cattle ship that carried cargo and passengers to the United States and South America. Most were immigrants or travelers. There were no others from Rhodes. Esther had a cabin down below and Jack slept forward under the anchor on lumber in a big hold.

He ate something around 5 p.m. the first night, then the ship hit rough water out of Cadiz. The anchor below was making so much noise he couldn't sleep and became quite seasick.

Instead he found a cot on deck, wrapped himself in a blanket and slept there for three days. The trip from Spain to New York took ten days.

Once in New York, the Barkey's cousin, Harry Benatar, met Jack and Esther. Jack, then 18 years old, heard the stevedores handling cargo speaking English with a Brooklyn accent and wondered if he would ever learn that foreign tongue.

Benatar, a cigar-smoking boxing aficionado, bribed a custom agent so they could go through more quickly, even though they had all the legal papers and nothing to declare.

They stayed at Benatar's New York house for one week then caught the Empire Builder train to Seattle. On the way they stopped in Chicago, where they waited seven hours.

Although Jack was afraid to leave the train station for fear he couldn't find his way back, the station provided a novel treat for him. Smelling something he had never smelled before, a salty, buttery aroma, he was drawn to a concessionaire where five or six people had lined up.

"I gave him $1. He gave me 90 cents back. He gave me a big jumbo popcorn. It was so good I came back for a second one. Today my weakness is popcorn," Jack said.

Jack and Esther shared a Pullman sleeping car on the train as it rumbled through huge expanses of land Jack never imagined.

"I thought we would never get there," he said.

Finally they arrived at Seattle's King Street Station on May 20, and were greeted by their uncle Ralph Capeluto.

They stayed at his home for a week, then moved into the Seattle home Ralph had purchased for the Barkey family.

During the week at Ralph's house, Jack met a man who helped him get a job. Although he spoke no English, he was hired as a stock boy at Leed's shoe store. He started the next day and attended Broadway Technical School at night.

The next group to leave was Mathilda and her three daughters. They hired a seamstress in Tangier to make a couple of outfits each for the journey. Ralph told them not to bring anything with them, so they packed lightly, not really having much to bring anyway.

Although they were desperate to get to America, the girls—especially 14-year-old Regina—still had a tough time leaving their friends behind.

"I wanted to come in a way, but it was hard leaving my friends. I had already made one move and everything was new, with a new language and a new way of life," she said.

The four left Tangier on May 19, headed for Cadiz. There, they boarded the ship Magallanes and headed for America. They had a cabin on the ship, which was filled mainly with immigrants and others returning to the United States.

Harry Benatar met the four in New York and took them to a hotel. "It was unbelievable. The taxis, the cars, the buildings. We had never seen such tall buildings," Regina said.

While in New York they left the hotel to shop. They saw a Coca-Cola sign, something they had never seen before. Thinking it would be a good landmark, they remembered that their hotel was near the sign.

Then they set out on their walk. On every block, they saw another Coca-Cola sign. Little did they know what they were seeing, or what a poor landmark they had chosen. With some luck, they finally made it back to their hotel.

They were in New York for three days before boarding a train to Seattle. On the train Mathilda wouldn't let her daughters out of her sight. She was afraid something would happen to Claire, 25, Rachel, 23 and Regina, 14.

As with Jack and Esther, the four found a treat while waiting for the train in Chicago. Hungry, and not knowing what to eat, the girls stood in line with others waiting for a drink. Regina tasted her first chocolate malt at that Chicago train station.

Back on the train, Mathilda again kept a careful eye on her daughters. "She would hardly let us stand up," Regina said. "When we got to Seattle, our legs were swollen from sitting so long. We were exhausted. It seemed like eternity."

Ralph and Rachel Capeluto met them at the train station and were joined by Jack and Esther. Then they showed the four their new house. It had been completely furnished and looked so big.

In her new country, Regina felt somewhat isolated because she did not know English. She was held back in school so she could be with her cousin Betty Capeluto, Ralph and Rachel's daughter. Everyone thought Betty would know Spanish and could interpret for Regina, but Betty knew less Spanish than Regina hoped.

She graduated from Garfield High School in 1951 and at age 18, she met Victor Amira. They got married less than three years later.

On Aug. 12, Victor and Morris Barkey left Tangier, taking a boat to Algeciras, Spain. They rode a bus to Cadiz. Because they didn't want their baggage disturbed, they gave the guards a couple packages of cigarettes and went through.

They stayed at a hotel a few days before embarking on Aug. 17 on the Marques de Comillas to New York, the same ship their brother Jack and Aunt Esther had taken to America four months earlier. This time there were other people from Rhodes and Tangier on the boat, which was filled mainly with immigrants heading to the United States, Cuba and Mexico.

A representative from the Hebrew Sheltering and Immigrant Aid Society (HIAS) met them in New York when they arrived Aug. 27. Eventually they, too, connected with Harry Benatar.

"Oh boy, those tall buildings," Morris recalled. "I had seen them in the movies, but you get a stiff neck (looking at them)."

The United States was so foreign to the Barkey boys that the American dollars they carried were no longer in circulation. They had to exchange their old, large size $20 bills for the newer, smaller ones then circulating in the United States.

Despite New York's reputation as a tough town, the pair witnessed human kindness from a man who asked to borrow money. Victor gave the stranger $20 of the $22 he had in his pocket. Benatar told him he would never see the money again. But to his surprise, the man—who needed the money to get his luggage off the ship as he headed for Mexico—sent him the money a few months later.

During their few days in New York, Benatar took the two to a movie and to a variety show where they saw Gene Krupa. They also saw a boxing match and went to Coney Island, where they had a big milkshake.

They boarded the train to Seattle and stopped in Chicago, where they walked and walked and walked around the city, visiting a museum. On the train to Seattle they admired the gorgeous views of Montana in the American West.

When they arrived in Seattle, a distant relative, Rosie Alhadeff, met them at the train station. Within two weeks, on Sept. 10, 1946, they had landed jobs at Lee & Estes, an auto freight company, where they were each hired for 77.5 cents an hour to type up the bill from bills of lading.

Victor completed his high school requirements in 1948 and 1949 and entered the University of Washington, where he earned a bachelor's degree in business administration, majoring in accounting.

Morris studied English, composition and history at Edison Technical School and later entered the University of Washington.

Abraham Barkey, because he was born in Turkey, had to remain in Tangier for three more years as he waited for his visa to be approved. The United States had a very low quota for the number of Turkish immigrants it would grant visas to, much lower than the Italian quota, which had allowed for the other family members to enter the country. Abraham's family corresponded with him regularly and sent him money once a month. He finally arrived in Seattle by airplane in 1949 and found a job dying shoes to match women's dresses at Leed's shoe store.

REGNO D'ITALIA

Dati e connotati del Titolare
Professione [illegible]
figli a di Abramo
e di Capelluto Matilde
nat a Rodi
il 14 - 3 - 1921
domiciliat a Rodi
Prov. di id
statura media
occhi castani
capelli id
barba —
baffi —
colorito roseo
segni particolari —
Colonna riservata ai connotati della moglie

Figli

Nome	Data di nascita	Visto

Fotografie
Spazio riservato alla fotografia della moglie
Firma del Titolare [illegible]
Autenticazione della firma della titolare
Firma dell' Autorità
R. CONSOLE GENERALE
Dato Tangeri
Firma della moglie
14 APR 1944

Claire Barkey's passport.

JACK BARKI

THE BOY FROM TANGIERS[90]

Jack Barki, the Boy from Tangiers
For U.S. has nothing but cheers
In five months of time
He stands third in line,
At Leeds Train Quiz -

This Boy from Tangiers!

Jack Barki landed in Seattle from Tangiers just five months ago at the age of 18 years. Two days later he applied for, was accepted, and reported for work at Leed's Shoe Store as roustabout. He has not missed a day, has been interested in his work which he has done exceptionally well, trustworthy, willing to learn, eager for more education, and today is doing service on the main floor. He is friendly, polite, courteous, never oversteps his position, and that smile of his is so captivating it would soften the hardest of hearts! To hear him speak one would think he had studied English before coming to this country, but when confronted, he says, "No," he has learned it all since coming here.

After Manager Moore had held his training quiz with his sales force, this boy, being so desirous of development, asked why he could not take this test. Seeing great possibilities in this young lad and wanting to assist him in any way possible in his future welfare, Mr. Moore gave him the test the following morning. Can one ever visualize this boy's learning in so short a time when he passed this test with a grade of 92%? Could any of our American born boys have done better?

Here is a chance for all EDISONIANS to do our bit in helping a deserving lad climb to the top of the ladder with a foundation as strong as the "Rock of Gibraltar" from whence he came, and before a foremost leading citizen, fellow countryman, and above all else, an acknowledged asset, and brother, in the largest of satisfied families in the United States—E.B.S.

So, let's help, let's all help
This boy all down through the years,
To always be true
To red, white and blue,
Our prodigy -
Jack, from Tangiers!
Abe Landau—by
Tom Moore
Fannie Jordan

October 16, 1946

---

[90] This tribute was written about Jack Barkey by his co-workers at Leed's shoe store.

TRANSLATION

Seattle, March 6, 1947

[Letter from Claire to the Rhodian Community of Belgian Congo]

FROM: Claire Barkey

2008—33rd Avenue South

Seattle 44, Wash.

Dear Sirs:

First of all, I make it my duty of introducing myself to those who do not know me, entreating those to whom my name rings a bell to make an effort and try to remember me as it may be possible.

The introduction must be brief, the object of this letter dealing with nothing concerning my person.

My name is Claire Barkey (or Barki) originally from Rhodes, a place where the majority to whom this letter is addressed, were born and spent the best years of their lives. My present residence is Seattle (Wash.) since June 1946 after having spent seven years in Tangier (Morocco) from June 1939, at which time the famous decree was issued inviting (so to speak) all the Jews of foreign origin residing in Italy since the year 1919 to depart.

My father, having arrived at Rhodes from Turkey in February 1919, we were compelled to seek refuge in the first country accepting us. How many times during the bad moments experienced in our new residence we wished for the worst days spent in our native land, but later on, we became aware that we were the most fortunate of those struck by that decree, as nothing can be compared with the tragic fate that befell those left in that prison, the only name that can be given to that island.

It is precisely of these unlucky people who have been unjustly persecuted, and have unjustly sacrificed their lives to satisfy the unjustified hate of some tyrants, that I take the liberty of speaking in this letter. Not of them, but rather of the few survivors of this catastrophe that I precisely wish to address, requesting you to pay attention to my brief and explicit appeal.

I believe that like me and all those who have been deprived of many of our dear beings who resided in that land, you are all acquainted about this matter. This spares me the unpleasant times of remembering again this tragedy. Unfortunately, the past is something irremediable, although so many sad recollections will never be erased from our memory, and we will always remember those who have disappeared if only for the kindness and innocence that characterized them and that so wisely were able to inculcate us.

For these inherited qualities and for eternal remembrance that we will keep, I pray you pay attention to the contents of this letter.

As you are aware, there remain in Italy some of the few survivors of our community from Rhodes. I do not know if you ever wondered whether these people were safe there and how they must be living, morally more than materially, because in what concerns the latter, everyone in his own way is contributing to the best of his ability and for the moment they do not lack help from whichever way it comes. They can be deprived of this help from one moment to the next, and poverty is a bad counselor. Although this is a great danger, all the more is the moral condition of these people.

Based on the contents of some letters that I keep receiving from some female friends from Italy, these people are completely demoralized, especially at the thought that there is a no way out of there. The majority have been claimed by relatives and already is reunited with them, ready, as it is natural, to forget the whole past. But these few who remain there, why don't they have someone to send for them? How will they ever forget all the sad past? Living always in the same environment, struggling to be able to live, they will never be able to take this step. Besides, we must foresee the consequences that it can cause or more exactly is causing.

In plain truth, although many among you may have understood what these words involve, I must say that many of these young ladies have already alienated themselves from our community, getting married with people who always have hated us or keep on hating us.

For this only reason, to avoid the worsening of the conditions of these few helpless ones, and to help them regain faith in the future, I ask all my compatriots to help this cause in any way they can.

Immigration to the Congo, although it entails difficulties, is not impossible. Being a matter of a special case and insignificant numbers and with the getting together of the Community, I am very certain that this cause can be brought to a favorable conclusion.

I, on my part, would have liked to do something within my possibilities, but you know what difficulties prevent the immigration to these regions. (I can vouch for that from experience. My uncle Ralph Capeluto succeeded to bring us here after endless difficulties, my family arriving here in three groups and leaving my father, still in Tangier waiting his turn in the Turkish quota and God only knows when he will join us.)

Seeing enough people who have succeeded in entering Belgian Congo and bearing in mind the importance of our Community there, I thought that it would be the best idea and more fruitful. Now, the only thing that I could undertake is to do my best to have the local Jewish community contribute to the expenses that these steps require and to participate in the traveling expenses that I suppose will not be small.

I have been thinking for some time to lay bare this case, but I was completely convinced that it had been suggested by the recent arrivals to the Congo from Italy. As days went by and with no result, I think it advisable to take this step before it is too late.

I do not know how to thank you in anticipation of the attention you will give my letter, and wishing you a favorable outcome in your efforts for which God will reward you, I remain, respectfully yours,

Claire Barkey

P.S. I count on the collaboration of those recently arrived from Italy to provide all the details that you may need, their being up-to-date more than anyone else.

ABRAMO BARCHI.
Paseo Cenarro, 33.
TANGER.

TANGER, a 26 de Septiembre de 1947.

Republica Dominicana,
Secretaria del Estado de relaciones Exteriores.
CIUDAD TRUJILLO.

Exelentisimo Sr:

Barchi Abramo, de nacionalidad Italiana, con pasa-
porte nº 223409, expedido por este Consulado General de Italia en
Tanger, nacido en Aidin, en fecha de 20 Febrero de 1891 de profesion Zapatero y con un capital de 2.000 Dolares y una renta mensual
de 100 Dolares que recibo de mi familia que reside actualmente en
SEATTLE, America del Norte, Sra. BARCHI, 2008. 33rd. Av. SO SEATTLE
U.S.A.

Es por lo que tengo el honor de solicitar de su
Exelencia, permiso de Immigracion a la Republica Dominicana y que el
objeto de mi viaje es instalarme para ejercer mi profesion.

En caso de ser favorecido por su Exelencia, suplico
encarecidamente, me facilite visado via Argel.

En espera de una contestacion favorable, quedo de
Ud. suyo affmo. y atto. s. s. q.e.s.m.

Su humilde servidor,

Letter dated September 25, 1947. Letter from Abraham Barkey (still in Tangier) to Dominican
Republic seeking permission to immigrate there.

TRANSLATION

Tangier, September 26, 1947

Abramo Barchi

Pase Cenarro 33

Tangier

Dominican Republic

Foreign Relations—Secretary of State

Ciudad Trujillo

Honorable Sir:

[I am] Abraham Barchi, of Italian nationality, with Passport No. 223409, issued by the General Consulate of Italy in Tangier, born in Aidin on February 20, 1891, shoemaker by trade, and with a capital of $2,000 and a monthly income of $100, which I receive from my family residing presently in Seattle, North America, Mrs. Barchi, 2008—33rd Avenue South, Seattle, USA.

I hereby have the honor of requesting from Your Excellency a permit to emigrate to the Dominican Republic and that the object of my trip is to settle there in order to exercise my trade.

In case of being favored by Your Excellency, I highly entreat you to grant me a visa via Algiers.

Awaiting your favorable response, I remain,

Yours truly,

Humbly at your service[91]

---

[91] It is unclear whether Claire prepared this letter for her father to sign or he was able to find someone to assist him locally.

TRANSLATION FROM FRENCH

Tangier, October 24, 1947

Answer to the note of the International Social Service, communicated to Mr. Abraham Barki:

Within the remarks which precede the questionnaire to which the undersigned answers below, mention is made of the conditions of immigration by refugees on grounds of nationality and of the quota of each for admittance into the United States.

Now, the party concerned was refused authorization under the pretext that he was born in Turkey, which does not mean that he is Turkish. And according to identity documents, his passport, and the statement by the Italian Minister in Tangier, statement which was turned over to the Minister of the United States in this city, it unquestionably results that the undersigned is without a doubt of Italian nationality and not of Turkish nationality, and as a matter of fact, his wife and his children, who can be nothing but of the nationality of her husband, and father, respectively, were able to enter the United States while, in spite of the repeated steps and the unquestionable proofs provided by him, they opposed him under the pretext that he was born in Turkey. The remarks set forth in the note by the International Social Service take up again the same excuse, that is to say, a basis absolutely false, that of nationality.

Having said that, we hereby answer the questions asked as follows:

1) The family lived in Tangier from July 1, 1939 and the head of the family until now.

2) Clarice (Claire) born on March 14, 1921 at Rhodes.

   Rachel born on March 5, 1923 at Rhodes.

   Haim and Moise, twins, born on March 27, 1925 at Rhodes.

   Jacques born on March 3, 1928 at Rhodes.

   Regina born on January 1, 1932 at Rhodes.[92]

3) The husband supported his family by working and thanks to the assistance of the Jewish community.

4) It is the brother of the wife concerned who is in a very good position who has taken the whole immigrant family under his charge. His name is Mr. Ralph Capeluto, 807—30th Avenue South, Seattle, Washington.

5) The family left in three groups:

---

[92] Regina was born on January 9.

Jacques on May 12, 1946

The mother with the three girls on June 9, 1946.

The other two children on August 27, 1946.

6) It is obviously true that thanks to the relative above mentioned this family has settled and was able to live in Washington.

7) The husband was never advised that he had to wait several years; on the contrary, they informed him that it was a matter of some months; otherwise, he would never have consented to separate himself from his family for such a long period.

8) The undersigned has no possibility of helping his own, he does not work but the latter are secure from want and his only wish is to join them.

9) The family has always been united and would be naturally happy to be united. The absence of the father casts a shadow over the family happiness.

We hope that this exile will not last and that thanks to the intervention of the International Social Service, Mr. Barki will be finally authorized to emigrate to the United States where a numerous and interesting family waits for him. They live at 2008 33rd Avenue South, Seattle, Washington.[93]

---

[93] It is clear from the correspondence here that Avraham Barki and his family doggedly pursued his quest to emigrate by contacting a variety of agencies. Whoever wrote this reply on Avraham's behalf to an International Social Service questionnaire was not acquainted with the laws in effect at that time. What counted then was the place of birth, not the citizenship. Avraham's bureaucratic nightmare was created by the lack of recognition of his Italian passport as proof of citizenship, combined with a 1921 U.S. law limiting immigration from a given country to three percent of the number of people from that country living in the U.S. in 1910. The Turkish population in the U.S. at the time was minimal, ergo, the small contingent allowed.

Additional sources:
http://en.wikipedia.org/wiki/List_of_United_States_immigration_legislation;
http://www.ushmm.org/wlc/en/article.php?ModuleId=10007094

SEATTLE - FIRST NATIONAL BANK

Established 1970

– – –

Seattle 14, Washington

October 31, 1947

W.H. Berry

Vice President

American Consul General

Tangiers

Morocco

Dear Sir:

We are writing to you on behalf of our highly valued client, Mr. Ralph M. Capeluto, who is making application for entry into the United States for Mr. Abraham Barki as a visitor.

Mr. Ralph M. Capeluto has been known to this Bank for a number of years. He is an American citizen, is principal owner of a large manufacturing plant, and enjoys a net work in excess of $50,000. His income is amply sufficient to provide Mr. Abraham Barki's financial requirements while in this country.

We do not hesitate to recommend Mr. Capeluto as to honesty, reliability and dependability. We have had many business dealings with him and have always found him prompt in meeting his commitments.

Yours truly,

WHB/FB   (signed)

Vice President

On letterhead for Worldwide Travel Service)

George V. Wachtin

218 Vance Building

Seattle 1, Washington

Phone Main 5696

     November 5 1947

Mr Abraham Barki

Paseo Cenarro 33

Tangier,

Marocco

     Dear Mr Barki:-

     At the request of Mr and Mrs Ralph Capeluto we are enclosing herewith Affidavits of Support signed by Mr Capeluto and Charles D Alhadeff and you will present the affidavits and supporting evidence consisting of bank letters and Mr Capeluto's copy of income tax to the American Consulate and apply for a six month visa. Your transportation will be arranged from here either on plane or ship.

     Should other documents be required by the Consulate please contact Mrs Capeluto at once.

          Very truly yours,

          (signed)

GVW/L

SEATTLE-FIRST NATIONAL BANK

SEATTLE 14, WASHINGTON

December 31, 1947

Mr. Ralph Capeluto

Seattle Curtain Manufacturing Co.

Seattle, Washington

Dear Ralph:

For your information, following is a copy of a letter just received from the Legation of the United States of America, Tangier, Morocco, dated December 2, 1947:

"Receipt is acknowledged of your letter of October 30, 1947 concerning the desire of Mr. Abraham Barki to proceed to the United States in order to visit his family for approximately six months.

It is regretted that it is not possible in view of the circumstances surrounding Mr. Barki's case, to consider him a <u>bona fide</u> applicant for temporary visitor's status.

Before visas were issued to Mr. Barki's wife and children to enable them to proceed to the United States, great pains were taken to explain to Mr. Barki that a visa for himself would not be available until his turn under the Turkish quota was reached and that there would doubtless be a period of some years before he could expect such an eventuality.

Mr. Barki has been informed of the decision of this office in connection with this desire to be considered a potential temporary visitor to the United States."

This is not very encouraging news. However, I am sure you would like to know what response was made to our letters written on Mr. Barki's behalf.

Wishing you and your family a very Happy and Prosperous New Year, I am,

Sincerely yours,

Vice President

WHB/FB

AFFIDAVIT of SUPPORT

UNITED STATES OF AMERICA)

STATE OF WASHINGTON (s s

COUNTY OF KING)

Ralph Capeluto being duly sworn, deposes and says:

That he is 47 years of age, that he was born at Rhodes, that he has resided continuously in the United States since 1920

That his present address is 807 - 30th Avenue, South, in the City of Seattle, County of King in the State of Washington

That he is a citizen of the United States and holds Certificate of Naturalization # 2393226 issued at New York City on February 21, 1927 by the United States District Court, Southern District of New York

That he is and always has been a law abiding resident; that he does not belong to nor is in anywise connected with any group or organization whose principles are contrary to organized government nor does the undermentioned relative belong to any such organization nor has he ever been convicted of any crime

That the following relative, his brother-in-law ABRAHAM BARKI, age 56, born at Aidin, Turkey, February 20, 1891, and at present residing at Paseo Cenarro #33, Tangier, Marocco, desires to come to the United States for a temporary visit not to exceed six months and that he is able and willing to furnish a bond to the United States Immigration Authorities to insure the departure at the expiration of such period, should bond be required, of said Abraham Barki. That the affiant will maintain and support him in the United States

That the prospective visitor is in good health, mentally and physically

That his present dependents consist of wife and four children: Morris age 16, Betty age 14; Marlene age 11 and Amelia age 8

That his regular occupation is manager and principal owner of Seattle Curtain Company, located at Prefontaine Building at Seattle, Wash. and his yearly earnings amount to $29,219.03 and his net worth is in excess of $50,000. He owns his home located at above address free and clear, and valued at over $10,000.

That he is willing and able to receive, maintain and support said relative and hereby assumes such trust guaranteeing that at no time will he allow him to become a burden on the United States or on any state, county, city, village or township of the United States

Deponent further states that this affidavit is made by him for the purpose of including the American Consul to vise the passport of said Abraham Barki and the Immigration Authorities to admit him into the United States for a temporary visit

<u>   Ralph Capeluto   </u> (signed)

Subscribed and sworn to before me a Notary Public in and for the said county and state this 1st day of November AD 1947

<u>   (signed)   </u>

Notary Public

My commission expired June 29 1948

File this return with Collector of Internal Revenue on or before March 15, 1947. Any balance of tax due (item 9, below) must be paid in full with return. See separate instructions for filling out return.

Page 1

FORM 1040
Treasury Department
Internal Revenue Ser...

U. S. INDIVIDUAL INCOME TAX RETURN
FOR CALENDAR YEAR 1946

1946

or fiscal year beginning .... 1946, and ending 1947

Do not write in these spaces

File Code

Serial No.

District

(Cashier's Stamp)

EMPLOYEES.—Instead of this form, you may use your Withholding Statement, Form W-2, as your return, if your total income was less than $5,000, consisting wholly of wages shown on Withholding Statements or of such wages and not more than $100 of other wages, dividends, and interest.

Name **Ralph Capeluto**
(PLEASE PRINT. If this return is for a husband and wife, use both first names)

ADDRESS **Prefontaine Bldg. Yesler Way**
(PLEASE PRINT. Street and number or rural route)

Seattle 4 **King** **Washington**
(City or town, postal zone number) (County) (State)

Occupation **Curtain Manufacturer** Social Security No. ....

	List your own name. If married and your wife (or husband) had no income, or if this is a joint return of husband and wife, list name of your wife (or husband).	Relationship	List names of other close relatives (as defined in Instruction 1) with 1946 incomes of less than $500 who received more than one-half of their support from you. If this is a joint return of husband and wife, list dependent relatives of both.	Relationship
Your Exemptions	Your name **R Capeluto**	x x x x x x x x	**Amelia**	**Daughter**
	Morris	**Son**		
	Betty	**Daughter**		
	Marlene	**do.**		

Enter your total wages, salaries, bonuses, commissions, and other compensation received in 1946, BEFORE PAY-ROLL DEDUCTIONS for taxes, dues, insurance, bonds, etc. Members of armed forces and persons claiming traveling or reimbursed expenses, see Instruction 2.

	Print Employer's Name	Where Employed (City and State)	Amount
2.			$
		Enter total here →	$

Your Income

3. Enter here the total amount of your dividends ....

4. Enter here the total amount of your interest (including interest from Government obligations unless wholly exempt from taxation) .... 752 | 00

5. If you received any other income, give details on page 2 and enter the total here ...... 28,460 | 03

6. Add amounts in items 2, 3, 4, and 5, and enter the total here ...... $ 29,219 | 03

How to Figure Your Tax

IF YOUR INCOME WAS LESS THAN $5,000.—You may find your tax in the tax table on page 4. This table, which is provided by law, automatically allows about 10 percent of your total income for charitable contributions, interest, taxes, casualty losses, medical expenses, and miscellaneous expenses. If your expenditures and losses of these classes amount to more than 10 percent, it will usually be to your advantage to itemize them and compute your tax on page 3.

IF YOUR INCOME WAS $5,000 OR MORE.—Disregard the tax table and compute your tax on page 3. You may either take a standard deduction of $500 or itemize your deductions, whichever is to your advantage.

HUSBAND AND WIFE.—If husband and wife file separate returns, and one itemizes deductions, the other must also itemize deductions.

Tax Due or Refund

7. Enter your tax from table on page 4, or from line 12, page 3 .... $ 3,089 | 04

8. How much have you paid on your 1946 income tax?
(A) By withholding from your wages ...... $
(B) By payments on 1946 Declaration of Estimated Tax ...... 3,334 | 50
Enter total here → 3,334 | 50

9. If your tax (item 7) is larger than payments (item 8), enter **BALANCE OF TAX DUE** here ...... $

10. If your payments (item 8) are larger than your tax (item 7), enter the **OVERPAYMENT** here ...... $ 245 | 46
Check (√) whether you want this overpayment: Refunded to you ☐ or Credited on your 1947 estimated tax ☒

If you filed a return for a prior year, what was the latest year? **1945**

Is your wife (or husband) making a separate return for 1946? **Yes** ("Yes" or "No")
If "Yes," write below:

To which Collector's office was it sent? **Tacoma 2 Washington**
Name of wife (or husband) **Tacoma 2 Washington**

To which Collector's office did you pay the amount claimed in item 8 (B), above? **Tacoma 2 Washington.**
Collector's office to which sent **Tacoma 2 Washington.**

I declare under the penalties of perjury that this return (including any accompanying schedules and statements) has been examined by me and to the best of my knowledge and belief is a true, correct, and complete return.

3-10-47

(Signature of person (other than taxpayer or agent) preparing return) (Date)   (Signature of taxpayer) (Date)

(Name of firm or employer, if any)   (If this is a joint return of husband and wife, it must be signed by both)

16—48254-1

Tax return dated March 10, 1947. Ralph Capeluto's 1946 tax return.

Do not use this page if your income is wholly from salaries, wages, dividends, and interest

Schedule A.—INCOME FROM ANNUITIES OR PENSIONS

1. Cost of annuity (total amount you paid in)	$	4. Total amount received this year	$
2. Amount received tax-free in prior years		5. Excess, if any, of line 4 over line 3	
3. Remainder of your cost (line 1 less line 2)	$	6. Enter line 5, or 3 percent of line 1, whichever is greater (Attach separate schedule for each additional annuity or pension)	$

Schedule B.—INCOME FROM RENTS AND ROYALTIES

1. Kind of property	2. Amount of rent or royalty	3. Depreciation or depletion (explain in Schedule F)	4. Repairs (explain in Schedule G)	5. Other expenses (itemize in Schedule G)
	$	$	$	$
Net profit (or loss) (col. 2 less sum of cols. 3, 4, and 5)	$	$	$	$

Schedule C.—PROFIT (OR LOSS) FROM BUSINESS OR PROFESSION. (Farmers should obtain Form 1040F)

(State (1) nature of business _____; (2) business name _____)

1. Total receipts _____ $

COST OF GOODS SOLD		OTHER BUSINESS DEDUCTIONS	
(To be used where inventories are an income-determining factor) (Enter the letters "C" or "C or M" on lines 2 and 8 if inventories are valued at either cost, or cost or market, whichever is lower)		11. Salaries and wages not in line 4	$
		12. Interest on business indebtedness	
2. Inventory at beginning of year	$	13. Taxes on business and business property	
3. Merchandise bought for sale		14. Losses (explain in Schedule G)	
4. Labor		15. Bad debts arising from sales or services	
5. Material and supplies		16. Depreciation, obsolescence and depletion (explain in Schedule F)	
6. Other costs (explain in Schedule G)		17. Rent, repairs, and other expenses (explain in Schedule G)	
7. Total of lines 2 to 6	$	18. Amortization of emergency facilities (attach statement)	
8. Less inventory at end of year		19. Net operating loss deduction (attach statement)	
9. Net cost of goods sold (line 7 less line 8)	$	20. Total of lines 11 to 19	$
		21. Total of lines 9 and 20	
10. Gross profit (line 1 less line 9)	$	22. Net profit (or loss) (line 1 less line 21)	

Schedule D.—GAINS AND LOSSES FROM SALES OR EXCHANGES OF CAPITAL ASSETS, ETC.

1. Net gain (or loss) from sale or exchange of capital assets (from separate Schedule D)		1,259 39
2. Net gain (or loss) from sale or exchange of property other than capital assets (from separate Schedule D)		

Schedule E.—INCOME FROM PARTNERSHIPS, ESTATES AND TRUSTS, AND OTHER SOURCES

1. Name and address of partnership, syndicate, etc. **Seattle Curtain Co.**	Amount	$	27,200 64
2. Name and address of estate or trust	Amount		
3. Other sources (state nature)	Amount		
4. Total			27,200 64

Total income from above sources (Enter as item 5, page 1) $ 28,460 03

Schedule F.—EXPLANATION OF DEDUCTION FOR DEPRECIATION CLAIMED IN SCHEDULES B AND C

1. Kind of property (If buildings, state material of which constructed)	2. Date acquired	3. Cost or other basis (do not include land or other nondepreciable property)	4. Assets fully depreciated in use at end of year	5. Depreciation allowed (or allowable) in prior years	6. Remaining cost or other basis to be recovered	7. Estimated life used in accumulating depreciation	8. Estimated remaining life from beginning of year	9. Depreciation allowable this year
		$	$	$	$			$

Schedule G.—EXPLANATION OF COLUMNS 4 AND 5 OF SCHEDULE B, AND LINES 6, 14, AND 17 OF SCHEDULE C

1. Column or Line No.	2. Explanation	3. Amount	1. Column or Line No.	2. Explanation	3. Amount
		$			$

16—49564—1 ☆ GPO

Do not itemize deductions if—(1) You determine your tax from the tax table on page 4, or
(2) Your total income is $5,000 or more and you claim the $500 standard deduction.
If husband and wife living together at end of year file separate returns and one itemizes deductions, the other must file
his or her return on Form 1040, and must also itemize deductions.

DEDUCTIONS

Describe deductions and state to whom paid. If more space is needed, list deductions on separate sheet of paper and attach to this return.		Amount
Contributions	$	
	Allowable Contributions (not in excess of 15 percent of item 6, page 1)	$
Interest	$	
	Total Interest	
Taxes	$	
	Total Taxes	
Losses from fire, storm, shipwreck, or other casualty, or theft.	$	
	Total Allowable Losses (not compensated by insurance or otherwise)	
Medical and dental expenses	$	
	Net Expenses (not compensated by insurance or otherwise) $	
	Enter 5 percent of item 6, page 1, and subtract from Net Expenses	
	Allowable Medical and Dental Expenses. See Instruction for limitation	
Miscellaneous (See Instructions)	$	
	Total Miscellaneous Deductions	
	TOTAL DEDUCTIONS	$

TAX COMPUTATION—FOR PERSONS NOT USING TAX TABLE ON PAGE 4

1. Enter amount shown in item 6, page 1. This is your Adjusted Gross Income. **Community half** ... $ 14,609 52
2. Enter DEDUCTIONS (if deductions are itemized above, enter the total of such deductions; if adjusted gross income (line 1, above) is $5,000 or more and deductions are not itemized, enter the standard deduction of $500) ... 500 00
3. Subtract line 2 from line 1. Enter the difference here. This is your Net Income ... $ 14,109 52
4. Enter your exemptions ($500 for each person whose name is listed in item 1, page 1) ... 2,500 00
5. Subtract line 4 from line 3. Enter the difference here ... $ 11,609 52
6. Use the tax rates in instruction sheet to figure your combined tentative normal tax and surtax on amount entered on line 5. Enter the tentative tax here. (If line 3 above includes partially tax-exempt interest, see Tax Computation Instructions) ... $ 3,251 62
7. Enter here 5 percent of amount entered on line 6 ... 162 58
8. Subtract line 7 from line 6. Enter the difference here. This is your combined normal tax and surtax. (If alternative tax computation is made on separate Schedule D, enter here tax from line 12 of Schedule D) ... $ 3,089 04

IF YOU USED THE $500 STANDARD DEDUCTION IN LINE 2, DISREGARD LINES 9, 10, AND 11, AND COPY ON LINE 12 THE SAME FIGURE YOU ENTERED ON LINE 8.

9. Enter here any income tax payments to a foreign country or U. S. possession (attach Form 1116) ... $
10. Enter here any income tax paid at source on tax-free covenant bond interest ...
11. Add the figures on lines 9 and 10 and enter the total here ...
12. Subtract line 11 from line 8. Enter the difference here and in item 7, page 1. This is your tax ... $ 3,089 04

16—58251-1

Schedule D (Form 1040)

U. S. TREASURY DEPARTMENT
Internal Revenue Service

SCHEDULE OF GAINS AND LOSSES

FROM SALES OR EXCHANGES OF (1) CAPITAL ASSETS AND (2) PROPERTY OTHER THAN CAPITAL ASSETS

(TO BE FILED WITH THE COLLECTOR OF INTERNAL REVENUE WITH FORM 1040)

For Calendar Year 1946

Or fiscal year beginning _____, 1946, and ending _____, 1947

(See Instructions on other side)

Name of taxpayer __Ralph Capeluto__

Address __Seattle Curtain Co. Prefontaine Bldg. Seattle 4 Washington.__

(1) CAPITAL ASSETS

1. Kind of property (if necessary, attach statement of descriptive details not shown below)	2. Date acquired Mo. Day Year	3. Date sold Mo. Day Year	4. Gross sales price (contract price)	5. Cost or other basis	6. Expense of sale and cost of improvements subsequent to acquisition or March 1, 1913	7. Depreciation allowed (or allowable) since acquisition or March 1, 1913 (attach schedule)	8. Gain or loss (column 4 plus column 7 less the sum of columns 5 and 6)	9. Percentage	10. Amount
SHORT-TERM CAPITAL GAINS AND LOSSES—ASSETS HELD NOT MORE THAN 6 MONTHS									
			$	$	$	$	$	100	$
								100	
								100	
								100	
Total net short-term capital gain or loss (enter in line 1, column 3, of summary below)									$
LONG-TERM CAPITAL GAINS AND LOSSES—ASSETS HELD FOR MORE THAN 6 MONTHS									
			$	$	$	$	$	50	$
								50	
								50	
								50	
Total net long-term capital gain or loss (enter in line 2, column 3, of summary below)									$

SUMMARY OF CAPITAL GAINS AND LOSSES

1. Classification	2. Capital loss carry-over (attach statement)	3. Net gain or loss to be taken into account from column 10, above (a) Gain	(b) Loss	4. Net gain or loss to be taken into account from partnerships and common trust funds (a) Gain	(b) Loss	5. Total net gain or loss taken into account in columns 2, 3, and 4 of this summary (a) Gain	(b) Loss
1. Total net short-term capital gain or loss	$	$	$	$	$	$	
2. Total net long-term capital gain or loss		$	$	1,259 35		1,259 35	
3. Net gain in column 5, lines 1 and 2. (Enter on line 1, Schedule D, page 2, Form 1040)						1,259 35	x x x x x x
4. Net loss in column 5, lines 1 and 2. (The amount to be entered on line 1, Schedule D, page 2, Form 1040, is (1) this item or (2) net income, or adjusted gross income if tax is computed by use of the tax table on page 4, Form 1040, computed without regard to capital gains or losses, or (3) $1,000, whichever is smallest).						x x x x x x x	$

COMPUTATION OF ALTERNATIVE TAX

Use only if you had an excess of net long-term *capital gain* over net short-term *capital loss*, and line 5, page 3, Form 1040, exceeds $18,000

1. Net income (line 3, page 3, Form 1040)	$	6. Combined tentative normal tax and surtax on amount on line 5. (See Tax Computation Instructions on page 4 of Form 1040 Instructions)	$
2. Excess of net long-term capital gain over net short-term capital loss (line 2, column 5 (a), less line 1, column 5 (b), of summary above)		7. Less: 5 percent of line 6	
		8. Partial tax (line 6 less line 7)	
3. Ordinary net income (line 1 less line 2)	$	9. 50 percent of line 2	
		10. Alternative tax (line 8 plus line 9)	
4. Less: Exemptions (line 4, page 3, Form 1040)		11. Total normal tax and surtax (line 8, page 3, Form 1040)	$
5. Balance	$	12. Tax liability (line 10 or line 11, whichever is the lesser). (Enter on line 8, page 3, Form 1040)	$

(2) PROPERTY OTHER THAN CAPITAL ASSETS

1. Kind of property	2. Date acquired	3. Gross sales price (contract price)	4. Cost or other basis	5. Expense of sale and cost of improvements subsequent to acquisition or March 1, 1913	6. Depreciation allowed (or allowable) since acquisition or March 1, 1913 (attach schedule)	7. Gain or loss (column 3 plus column 6 less the sum of columns 4 and 5)
		$	$	$	$	$
Total net gain (or loss) (enter on line 2, Schedule D, page 2, Form 1040)						$

If any item in this schedule was acquired by you otherwise than by purchase, attach a statement explaining how acquired.

UNITED STATES OF AMERICA)

STATE OF WASHINGTON (s s

COUNTY OF KING)

    Ralph Capeluto swear that the attached Income tax return for the calendar year of 1946 is a true and correct copy of the return filed with the Collector of Internal Revenue at Tacoma, Washington and to the best of my knowledge and belief is a true and corrrect and complete return for that taxable year

<u>   Ralph Capeluto (signed)   </u>

Subscribed and sworn to before me

Notary Public this November 1 1947

<u>   (signed)   </u>

My commission expires June 29 1948

UNITED STATES OF AMERICA)

STATE OF WASHINGTON   (s s

COUNTY OF KING   )

Charles D Alhadeff being duly sworn, deposes and says:

That he is 38 years of age, that he was born at Rhodes, that he was born in Seattle and has resided continuously in the United States and has always maintained his American Citizenship

That his present address is 1350 Lakeside Avenue South, in the City of Seattle, County of King in the State of Washington

That he is and always has been a law abiding resident; that he does not belong to nor is in anywise connected with any group or organization whose principles are contrary to organized government nor does the undermentioned friend belong to any such organization nor has he ever been convicted of any crime

That on account of friendship and affection he holds for Mr and Mrs Ralph M Capeluto, whose affidavit is attached herewith, he is willing, should it become necessary, to maintain and support the prospective visitor, listed below, and is able and willing to furnish a bond to the United States Immigration Authorities to insure the departure after a six month visit of

ABRAHAM BARKI, age 56, born at Aidin, Turkey, February 20, 1891, at present residing at Paseo Cenarro #33, Tangier, Marocco

That the prospective visitor is in good health, mentally and physically

That his present dependents consist of wife and three children

That his regular occupation is wholesale fish dealer and is a part owner of Whiz Fish Products Company, located at 2000 Alaskan Way at Seattle, Washington and his yearly income amounts to over $10,000 and his net worth is over $100,000

That he is willing and able to receive, maintain and support said friend and hereby assumes such trust guaranteeing that at no time will he allow him to become a burden on the United States or on any state, county, city, village or township of the United States

Deponent further states that this affidavit is made by him for the purpose of including the American Consul to vise the passport of said Abraham Barki and the Immigration Authorities to admit him into the United States for a temporary visit

_____Charles D Alhadeff_____ (signed)

Subscribed and sworn to before me a Notary
Public in and for the said county and state this
1st day of November AD 1947

_____(signed)_____

Notary Public

My commission expired June 29 1948

Annex 2

Information Sheet for North America

Departure date: February 26, 1949

Part A to be completed by all passengers

According to your nationality, use section 1 or 2

1   <u>American citizens</u>

Last name:

Given name(s):

Address in the U.S.A.:

Passport No.:

Place of Birth:

2   <u>Passengers without American nationality</u>

Last name: Barki

Given name(s): Abraham

Address in the U.S.A. (1): Seattle 44 WASH. c/o Barkey

2008 33nd Ave So.

The passenger has in his/her possession:

   a "Re-entry-Permit" – Form I-I32 No. (2)

   a "Foreign Service" – Form 256 A No. (3) I 562026

   a "Foreign Service" – Form 257 No. (4)

Indicate in the following order of preference:

the address where the passenger will stay over the course of his or her visit to the U.S.A. with the exception of any hotel address

for business men, the address of the company they will visit or for tourists, the address in the U.S.A. of the travel agency with which they have a relationship

for passengers in transit <u>only</u>, the address of their hotel

The number can be found in the right corner of the preceding form by the words "Permit No."

The number is preceded on the form by the letter "I"

The number is preceded on the form by the letter "V"

Passenger Ticket

and

Baggage Check

Issued by

AIR FRANCE

Member of International Air Transport Association

Headquarters: 2 Rue Marbeuf – Paris (8th)

R.C. Seine 258.463 B

Commercial Division: 119-121 Avenue des Champs-Élysées – Paris-8th

Wagons – Lits/Cook

World Travel Service

TANGIER

See Conditions of Contract Inside   PAGE 1   Place of Issue

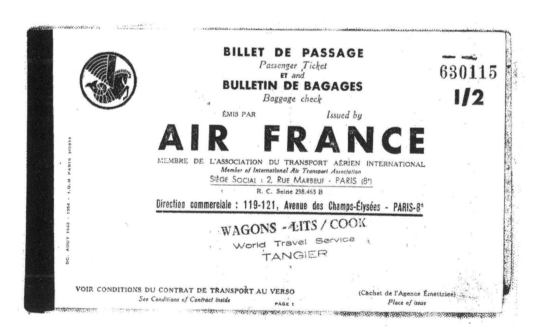

Abraham Barkey's airline ticket and baggage claim ticket from Air France. By waiting three years in Tangier, Abraham was able to come to the United States via airplane instead of by slow boat, like the rest of his family before him.

(page 2)

AFNY-C9

AIR FRANCE

FRENCH NATIONAL AIRLINE

No. 4883

Date   Feb. 27, 1949

Plane No. F-BZ2L   Flight No. 009142

Received from BARCHI

the sum of Eighty Dollars ($80.00)

Collected for the Collector of Customs, Port of New York, in payment of Alien Head Tax for the account of Immigration and Naturalization Service.

AIR FRANCE

By (signed)

EPILOGUE: THE BARKEYS IN SEATTLE

Once the family arrived in the United States, they immediately joined the workforce and eventually became U.S. citizens. They maintained their connection to their Sephardic Jewish heritage through their synagogue, but they also became Americans, and participated fully in the new country they called home.

In 1949, Abraham Barkey finally joined his family in Seattle. He worked at Leed's shoe store dying women's shoes for many years. He and Mathilda (Mazaltov) Barkey moved from their house to a small apartment in the 1960s and he eventually moved into the Carolyn Kline Galland Home for Seattle's aging Jewish residents, where he was known as a fun-loving elder gentleman. He died in 1981, at age 91.

Mathilda Barkey, the consummate mother and grandmother, kept house and carried on the Sephardic traditions at home. She was a wonderful cook and matriarch. She lived until 1977, dying at age 82.

Claire Barkey married Philip Flash in 1960 and they had two children, Cynthia and Edward. She worked various jobs as an accountant and Spanish teacher and prided herself in keeping a beautiful Northwestern style home filled with art and artifacts that she and Phil collected. She spent her time knitting and crocheting beautiful items for her family and she honored her past by proudly continuing to speak Spanish, Italian and French—along with English. Claire died in 1991 at age 70. After Claire's death, Phil lived an active and productive life as a historian and artist and died in 2015 at age 96.

Rachel Barkey married Merle Erdrich in 1950 and had three children, Roberta, Harry and Michele. She is remembered for her love of music, which was always playing in the house, her facility with languages, and her creativity, which she joyfully shared with others. Her talents in sewing, knitting and crocheting allowed her to make beautiful, one-of-a-kind clothing for herself and her family. She died of cancer in 1968 at age 45. Merle died in 1987 at age 68.

Victor Barkey married Ruth Delores Druker in 1956 and they had one daughter, Myrna. Prior to his marriage, Victor graduated with a degree in accounting from the University of Washington and became a CPA. He spent his working career doing both public and private accounting, first working for others and then opening his own practice. Victor was an active volunteer for Seattle's Jewish community, serving as president of Congregation Ezra Bessaroth, Seattle Sephardic Brotherhood, and the Hebrew Free Loan Society. He utilized his musical talents by singing in the Seattle Chorale and the Seattle Opera chorus, and by directing Ezra Bessaroth's high holiday choir. Ruth died in 1998 at age 79 and Victor died in 2004 at age 79.

Morris Barkey was drafted into the U.S. Army in September 1950, only four years after he arrived in the United States. He fought in the Korean War and 13 months later returned to Seattle in 1952. In Seattle, he completed a degree in English and Spanish from the University of Washington. He later moved to Los Angeles, where he worked 30 years for a freight and shipping company. In 1977 he married Flory Gabay, and they had four children, Illana, Sarina, Avraham and Yemina. He remains an active volunteer at his local synagogue. He is fluent in seven languages, always continuing to study.

Jack Barkey worked as an accountant at The Boeing Co. and devoted many years to volunteering at nursing homes, hospitals and his synagogue in Seattle. He had no children, but was a favorite uncle to his nieces and nephews. He died in 2006 at age 78.

Regina Barkey married Victor Amira in 1952 and worked for 30 years as a high school secretary. They had three children, Susan, Marcelle and Rozanne. Regina is very active in her synagogue kitchen, spending many hours preparing traditional Sephardic dishes. She keeps the Sephardic cooking tradition alive at her home with large family meals that always include the special Rhodesli dishes, which she is teaching the next generation to prepare.

Ralph Capeluto, who with Rachel had four children—Morris, Betty, Marlene and Mimi—continued to run his successful curtain business and was active in his synagogue. He eventually passed his business on to his son Morris and Morris' wife Jewel, who ran it with their children. Ralph died in 1984 at age 84.

Rachel Capeluto helped with the business and raised the couple's children. She graciously entertained the family for Jewish holidays in the couple's home and was active in her synagogue. She died in 1994 at age 87.

Esther Capeluto married Joseph Huniu and worked at the Capeluto's curtain factory. Through her kindness and thoughtfulness, she unofficially adopted the Barkey children and grandchildren and looked over them, especially after her sister Mathilda died. She was active in her synagogue and died in 1994 at age 85.

More than 50 descendants of the Barkey family are alive today, thanks to Claire's perseverance and unwavering commitment to ensure her family escaped from Rhodes.

APPENDIX

SONG FOR THE SUFFERING OF THE BELLY

Too many fights we had
For we wanted them to show us the figures [money]
It was not to the advantage of the threesome,
They closed the door on us.

The refugees to eat
They go to the mess hall.
They eat sticky rice,
and the medicine follows.

A lot is spent without getting any value
for there is no kitchen.
It is better to eat in the street
and not in the mess hall.

Laredo is already fed up!
He went for a walk,
seeing that there is no reason
to take revenge upon us.

A lady bearing a child had a toothache.
To see Sagues she went running, and
she was given an aspirin.

Two groups in front of the Colon [popular restaurant]
keep on arguing.
Cohen-Levy are the stool pigeons,
and are being beaten.

We are out of clothing and shoes,
keeps saying Sagues.
Nor is there any money left.
"Go and see Laredo."

It is a pity to see
these refugees eat;
after a stomachache
to the hospital they are taken.

Many meetings were held
by Cohen, Sagues, Laredo.
They satisfy everyone
except the shoemaker [the author].

We were healthy and strong.
Toothless we are left
from eating soggy pasta.
Sick we became.

They gave us new mattresses.
They appear to be two years old
made out of local straw [actually "crin," a vegetable fiber].
What a deception!

Exceptions were made
in distributing the clothing,
Some of good quality,
Others to fit the local porters.

Clothing, shoes are being given.
"Run to the mess hall."
But to heal the sores
there is no cure.

By Chelibon Maish[94]

Tangier, 1943

---

[94] This ballad, written in a mélange of Ladino and Spanish, is the work of Chelibon Maisch, husband of Mazaltov's and Ralph's sister Sarina. It concerns the family's refugee experience 1939 through 1946 in Tangier. Financial aid was being sent by Jewish organizations from the U.S. and a local committee was in charge of distributing food, clothing, etc. Unfortunately, the predominately Ashkenazi committee members gave preference to the Ashkenazi refugee families, and claimed the Sephardic families were not refugees. "I am glad to say that the Barkey family did not want nor would accept any help," writes Morris Barkey.

FAMILY PHOTOGRAPHS

Mussani Capeluto on the job peddling notions.

Taken in Rhodes Circa mid-1920s

Mathilda's parents and sisters (Capeluto family), (back row, left to right) Joya, Sarina Maish, Chelibon and Esther (front row) Mussani Capeluto (father), Rachel Capeluto (mother).

Taken in Rhodes Circa 1927

The Barkey family and Aunt Esther. Claire (extreme back),
(back middle left to right) Esther Capeluto (Mathilda's sister),
Rachel, Mathilda (Middle row, left), Morris (right), Victor
(front row), Regina and Jack.

Taken in Rhodes Circa 1936

The Barkey family (back row, left to right) Victor, Mathilda (mother), Morris, Abraham (father), Claire, Rachel, (front row, left to right) Regina, Jack.

Taken in Rhodes Circa 1939

The Barkey family and Aunt Esther (back row, left to right) Esther Capuleto (Mathilda's sister), Mathilda (mother), Abraham (father), Claire (middle), Jack (front row, left to right), Victor, Regina, Morris.

Taken in Rhodes Circa 1937

Mathilda and Abraham Barkey.

Taken in Rhodes Circa 1920

Ralph Capeluto on his wedding day.

Taken in Seattle, Wash. Circa 1930

Claire Barkey (third woman from left) working as a nurse's aide with the British Red Cross.
Taken in Tangier, Morocco. Circa mid-1940s.

The Barkey family and Aunt Esther. (Back row left to right) Esther
Capeluto, Claire, Mathilda, Abraham, Rachel and Jack, (front row, left to
right) Morris, Regina, Victor Barkey.

Taken in Tangier, Morocco, Circa 1945.

THE SEATTLE TIME

TRAVELING FAMILY REUNITED HERE

* * *   * * *   * * *   * * *

Group From Rhodes Happy in 7 Languages

Left to right (rear row), VICTOR, JACK and MORRIS BARKI, and (front row) CLAIR, REGINA, MATHILDA (MAMMA) and RACHEL BARKI and ESTHER CAPELUTO

They were happy to be together again—and in the U. S.

In five languages seven members of the Barki family were telling each other today how happy they are to be together again and to be in the United States of America.

With the recent arrrival of the 21-year-old twins, Morris and Victor Barki, the family, which started traveling toward the United States seven years ago, will be a complete circle whenever the father arrives from Tangier.

"When that will be," Victor shrugged sadly, "no one knows. It depends on the quota."

First to come, in May, were the "pioneers," 18-year-old Jack Barki and his aunt, Miss Esther Capeluto, to stay with Miss Capeluto's brother and sister-in-law, Mr. and Mrs. Ralph Capeluto, 807 30th Ave. S. Next were the children's mother, Mathilda, Capeluto's sister, and three daughters, Clair, 25, Rachel, 23, both of whom immediately got jobs in a department store, and Regina, 14.

Family Has Home

Capeluto, who came to the United States in 1920, has been trying since to get his relatives over here. He lost five relatives in German crematories.

Capeluto bought a home for the family at 2008 33rd Ave. S.

"We are so grateful to our

uncle," the twins said, their eyes shining.

The Barkis, mother and children, were born on the island of Rhodes, where they lived until 1939. The father, a shoemaker, was born in Turkey, although, like the others is an Italian Jew. In 1939, they had to leave Rhodes, because of their father's Turkish birth, and traveled across North Africa to Tangier, off Morocco, facing the Rock of Gibraltar.

"All the time, though," said Morris, "we wanted to come to the United States."

They were lucky to leave Rhodes when they did, because after the Germans entered, Capeluto explained, the Jews still remaining there were taken in cargo ships either to forced labor in Poland or to crematories.

Some Have Taken Papers

"We're going to take the whole bunch of them to get their citizenship at once," said Mrs. Capeluto, who came as a baby to the United States from Rhodes. "Those who came first already have taken out their first papers."

The Barki twins, who talk in a spontaneous duet, also are ambitious to become citizens of the United States and to apply for military service. Both are interested in continuing their educations and making languages their career.

The family speaks Italian, French, Spanish, Hebrew and, with the exception of "Mamma," English.

Words tumble from the twins when they tell what they like best about America:

"Freedom, first," they said, "and the atmosphere of welcome, and everybody is equal, even if some are rich and some are poor. Since we were little boys, we have desired to come here."

The twins landed in New York last Tuesday aboard the Spanish liner Marques de Comillas and surprised a social worker who, thinking the Barkis were small children, had met the boat to "take care of cute little twins."

"Cute!" shouted the twins, in a burst of laughter.

The article that appeared in the Seattle Times in the summer of 1946.

The Capeluto Family: Back row: Morris, Ralph,
Betty, Rachel. Front row: Mimi and Marlene.

Taken in Seattle, Wash. Circa 1940

The house that Ralph and Rachel
Capeluto acquired for the Barkey family
at 2008 33rd Ave. South, Seattle, Wash.

(Left to right) Esther (Capeluto) Huniu, Abraham Barkey, Mathilda Barkey, Rachel Capeluto and Ralph Capeluto on the occasion of the Barkey's 50th wedding anniversary.

Taken in Seattle, Wash. Circa 1970

Clara Barki graduation certificate from Scuole Israelitiche Italiane, 1932.

Clara Barki graduation certificate from Scuole Israelitiche Italiane, 1934.

EL BOLETIN   3

Una otra dama respectable viene de desparecer ,es la defunta LEA CAPELLUTO (Nacida Menasche) hermana del sin. Maurice D. Menasche de Paris, tia de los siniores Giuseppe y Elia Menasche y madrina de los siniores Celibon y Reuben Capelluto, todos ellos notables de nuestra Comunidad.

Era una de estas creaturas que el destino persigue sin estanco y que suportava todo con resignacion. Bivda y dedichada aioda en la flor de la edad, ella inspirava siempre estima y compasion. Ella tuve la consolacion de verse sostenida y conortada siempre por todos sus parientes.

Presentamos a todos ellos nuestras sinceras condohenzas y rogamos que la alma de la defunta repose en el lugar reservado a los justos.

EN EL COLEGIO RABINICO

Viernes, 21 junio, verso la tadre, el Comm. Ascher Alhadeff, uno de los primeros sostenidores de nuestro grande instituto, se reunia alli acompagnado del Sin. Hizkia Franco, Presidente de nuestra Comunidad y del Sin. Moise Alaluf su cercano, por asistir al uficio de Kabalat Shabat y de Arvit, en el oratorio del Colegio.

El Comm. Vitalis, digno presidente del Consiglio Directivo, asistia igualmente al uficio. Un elevo del establicimiento, aiudado de sus compagneros inchia el rolo de uficiante. El caracter solemnel de la oracion y las bozes agradables de estos bravos joyenes, impresionaron profondamente todos los fieles.

El Comm. Alhadeff y todos los asistentes se retiravan de alli despues de aversen congratulado con el Sin. Rector y con todo el personel del establicimiento de la dulce impresion que se llevavan de alli en esta solemnel ocasion.

Partencias

El prof. Renato Cohen, ex-director de nuestras escuelas y su siniora vienen de partir definitivamente por Italia despues de una estancia aqui de dos anios. Son motivos de salud que han determinado la demision y la partencia del prof. Cohen.

Le deseamos buen viaje y completo restablicimiento.

***

Con la partencia del Sin. Cohen, el posto de la direccion de nuestras escuelas resta vacante. Pueden pero estar siguros que el consilio de esta Comunidad esta hasiendo pasos y esfuersos en vista de un buen remplasamiento. El es ya en correspondencia por el escojimiento del personal menesteroso a nuestras escuelas y esto en vista de relevar ainda mas el nivel de los estudios y la importancia de estos establicimientos.

A la atencion de nuestros lectores

Atiramos la atencion de nuestros lectores sovre dos ovrajes recientemente publicados y ya anunciados, dos ovrajes interesantes que cada uno de ellos devria procurarse. Se trata del hermoso livro de oraciones con traslado en italiano de S. Em. Rebi David Prato, Gran Rabino de Alexandria, y la Historia de los judios de Rodes de nuestro amigo el prof. Abraham Galante. Pueden procurarsen estos ovrajes cerca la Cancleria de nuestra Comunidad.

El livro de oraciones vale Lit. 20.

Historia de los judios de Rodes vale Lit. 25.

EN NUESTRAS ESCUELAS

Notamos con plaser los nombres de los elevos de nuestras escuelas que se distinguieron particolarmente en los examenes de cavo de anio que vienen de tomar fin:

Nombre	Paternidad	Clase	Premio
Clara Barki	Abraham	3ª Tecnica	1º
Sara Benatar	Nissim	»	2º
Rica Capuia	Isacco	»	2º
Sara Hasson	Bohor	»	3º
Sami Hanan	Hanoh	2ª	1º
Fortune Capuia	Isacco	»	2º
Giacomo Levi	Bension	»	3º
Rosa Israel	Mair	1ª	1º
Clara Gabriel	Mosè	»	2º
Rachele Hugnù	Isacco	»	3º
Elsa Pacifici	Renato	5ª Element. Fem.	1º
Virginia Alhadeff	Mosè	»	2º
Estella Cohen	Rahamin	»	2º
Estella Surnahy	Giacomo	»	3º
Anna Cohen	Giuseppe	»	3º
Elisa Franco	Hizkia	4ª	1º
Dolly Menasche	Isacco	»	1º
Estella Sigura	Isacco	»	2º
Graziella Begas		»	3º
Giuditta Vital	Mosè	2ª	1º
Estella Amato	Rahamin	»	2º
Matilde Levi	Giacomo	»	2º
Isacco Alhadeff	Giacobbe	5ª Elem. Maschile	1º
Davide Menasche	Giuseppe	»	2º
Leon Menasche	Abraham	»	3º
Enrico Hanan	Isacco	4ª	1º
Bension Menasche	Giuseppe	»	2º
Giuseppe Turiel	Michele	»	3º
Roberto Hasson	Abramo	3ª	1º
Salvo Alcana	Celebi	»	2º
Giuseppe Vital	Mosè	2ª	1º
Isacco Cordoval	Giuseppe	»	1º
Rabina Franco	Isacco	»	2º
Scemaia Israel	Boaz	1ª	1º
Vittorio Habib	Bohor	»	1º
Mercada Ferera	Samuele	»	1º
Sara Israel	Benjamin	»	1º
Matilde Rahamin	Haim	»	1º
Marco Algranti	Giuseppe	»	2º
Mordehai Levi	Nissim	»	2º
Lucia Capelluto	Nissim	»	3º
Isacco Levi	Isider	»	3º

Obtuvieron menciones especiales el elevo Scemaia Israel de Boaz de la 1ª Elementare, Giuseppe Vital de Mosè de la 2ª Elm. y Isacco Alhadeff de la 5ª Elem.

Article from Rhodes newspaper, 1935, listing Clara Barki number one in her class. This was her last year in the Jewish school. She went to work as a secretary after that at age 14.

4   EL BOLETIN

En los Institutos Reales

En estos ultimos dias tomaron fin los examenes de cavo de anio en los Reales Institutos superiores y medios de nuestra ciudad. Tuvimos el plaser de constatar que los elevos judios que los frequentan se distinguieron en modo particolar dando provas de inteligencia y de aplicacion a los estudios. He aqui la lista de los elevos que obtuvieron notas brilantes:

Nombre	Paternidad	Clase	Medalla
Moisè Amato	Sadic	4° Inst. Super.	oro
Daniele Capelluto	Giuseppe	» » »	plata
Michele Levi	Moisè	3° Liceo	oro
Giacomo Capuia	Ioda	» » »	bronzo
David Benalar	Muwa	2° Inst. Super.	plata
Giacomo Franco	Hizkia	» » »	plata
Nissim Alhadeff	Comm. Isacco	2° Liceo	oro
Moisè Buenavida	Hizkia	1° Inst. Super.	plata
Giuseppe Notrica	Masliah	4° Gimnasiale	plata
Maurizio Galante	Elia	» »	bronzo
Maurizio Turiel	Michele	» »	bronzo
Giuseppe Hasan	Boaz	3° »	oro
Giuseppe Hasson	Nathan	1° »	oro
Rodolfo Habib	Salomone	1° »	oro
Salvatore Hasson	Bohor	» »	plata
Boaz Alhadeff	Comm. Isacco	» »	bronzo

Nuestras felicitaciones.

UNA MIRADA A LA PRENSA

Estranias mentalidades

La interesante revista italiana conocida bacho el nombre de « Critica » publica un interesante articulo intitulado « Estranio germanismo ». Destacamos de alli las lineas que siguen que nos parecen dignas de ser retenidas:

« A cualo valio la persecucion que en Almania se hiso y se hase de los judios? A embezarnos que una muy grande y muy eficaz parte de aquella obra que admiravamos como el resultado de un esfuerze alman en critica, historia, filosofia, filologji, en sciencias naturales y matematicas, en tecnica, en medecina, en literatura, en musica y en pintoria no era que ovra judia? No lo saviamos ni nos apercuiamos mismo de la cosa; pero la persecucion, apartando el grano de la planta venenosa, nos hiso avrir los ojos y nos induxo a contar y las cifras se munchiguan cada dia y cada dia se descuvre un nuevo judio entre las personas que hasta ahora consideravamos almanes » porque escrivian en « alman ».

Ninguno pensava que los sean dichos arianos de Almania havrian tenido menester de tanto ayudo de los ajenos y havrian aceptado tantas ovras de los non arianos (de los judios)! Que verguenza

de utilizar tantas ovras ajenas y adorar de ella la historia como la hicieron hasta ahora.

Y que alma dignitosa, desdignosa y fiera es aquella de Julius Streicher (capo de la prensa antisemitica almana) que ahora viene demandando que no se hagan cuidar los malados christianos por celebridades medicales judias tales que los Wassermann, los Neisser, los Frankel etc., que los dechos antes una que de aceptar el ayudo judial Bravo! En una renunciacion heroica digna de un verdadero ariano a la cuala se pudria solamente objectar que de esta manera la palavra « ario » escapara con tomar el sentido de « imbecile » (necio).

Superfluo de ajuntar que aquellos hombres que servian a lo vero y a lo bello (los servian judios) y que nosotros admiravamos tanto no eran puro ni judios ni almanes y sus ovra tenia origen non en sus nacionalidad, pero en sus humanidad comun, en esta humanidad comun que ahora es en estos y por estos ofendida en nosotros todos ».

A tales judicios luminosos partiendo de una mente sana como aquella de los dirigentes de « La Critica » se pasan de todo comentario. No se puede ajuntar a ellos que una sola palavra: Bravo.

El retorno de S.E. el Governador

Al momento de meter soto pensa embezamos con plaser que domingo (alhad) 7 julio a las oras 11 arivaran en nuestra ciudad de retorno de Italia Sus Excelencias el Governador y Donna Ottavia Lago. Sus Exelencias seran recividas uficialmente con los onores merecidos.

Les auguramos disde hoy la entrabuena.

Comunicados uficiales

Sigun ordinanzas de la honorable Podesteria de nuestra ciudad es defendido:

1.o — Sacudir y despolvar en las calles publicas de las ventanas y de los balcones de las moradas tapetes y otras semejantes ropas.

2.o — De espander hogos y blanquerias en las terazas y en los campos de las moradas sovre postos que dan sovre las vias publicas de las oras 8 de la manana hasta el encerarse del sol.

3.o — De entretener dientro la ciudad carneros, cavras y puercos. El termino por el alochamiento de la ciudad de estos animales tomara fin el 30 Novembre proximo.

Aquellos que contraviendran a estas ordinanzas seran apenados sigun la ley.

Donos

Los donos siguientes fueron hechos en favor del Patronato Escolar:

4 bancos de parte de la siniora Sarina de Victor Menasche en memoria de su defunto padre Elia Fintz.

50 Livetas de parte de la siniora Regina de Semah Franco.

Vilegiantes

Entre los vilegiantes que este anio venieron vijitar nuestra isla tuvimos el plaser de conocer el sin. David Aboulafia, abogado bien conocido en Jerusalem. Es un profesionista distinguido que se dedica cuerpo y alma a la causa judia.

Le deseamos la enrabuena.

Director responsable : **HIZKIA FRANCO**

TIPOGRAFIA RODIA—RODI

UNITED STATES OF AMERICA

DECLARATION OF INTENTION

No. 50528

(Invalid for all purposes seven years after the date hereof)

United States of America
Western District of Washington   ss.

In the _____ U. S. District _____ Court
of W. Dist. of Wash. Seattle, Washington

(1) My full, true, and correct name is CLAIRE BARKI also known as CLAIRE BARKEY

(2) My present place of residence is 2008 33rd Ave. So., Seattle, King, Washington

(3) My occupation is Clerk (4) I am 25 years old. (5) I was born on March 14, 1921

in Rhodes, Italy (6) My personal description is as follows: Sex female color white complexion medium, color of eyes brown, color of hair brown, height 5 feet 2 inches, weight 116 pounds, visible distinctive marks none, race white, present nationality Italian

(7) I am not married; the name of my wife or husband is _____

(8) I have no children; and the name, sex, date and place of birth, and present place of residence of each of said children who is living, are as follows:

(9) My last place of foreign residence was Tangier, Morocco (10) I emigrated to the United States from Tangier, Morocco (11) My lawful entry for permanent residence in the United States was at New York, New York under the name of Claire Barki on June 8, 1946 on the S.S. Magallanes

(12) Since my lawful entry for permanent residence I have not been absent from the United States, for a period or periods of 6 months or longer, as follows:

DEPARTED FROM THE UNITED STATES			RETURNED TO THE UNITED STATES		
PORT	DATE (Month, day, year)	VESSEL OR OTHER MEANS OF CONVEYANCE	PORT	DATE (Month, day, year)	VESSEL OR OTHER MEANS OF CONVEYANCE

(13) I have not heretofore made declaration of intention: No. _____ on _____ in the _____

(14) It is my intention in good faith to become a citizen of the United States and to reside permanently therein. (15) I will, before being admitted to citizenship, renounce absolutely and forever all allegiance and fidelity to any foreign prince, potentate, state, or sovereignty of whom or which at the time of admission to citizenship I may be a subject or citizen. (16) I am not an anarchist; nor a believer in the unlawful damage, injury, or destruction of property, or sabotage; nor a disbeliever in or opposed to organized government; nor a member of or affiliated with any organization or body of persons teaching disbelief in or opposition to organized government. (17) I certify that the photograph affixed to the duplicate and triplicate hereof is a likeness of me and was signed by me.

I do swear (affirm) that the statements I have made and the intentions I have expressed in this declaration of intention subscribed by me are true to the best of my knowledge and belief: SO HELP ME GOD.

Claire Barki   Claire Barkey

Subscribed and sworn to (affirmed) before me in the form of each shown above in the office of the Clerk of said Court, at Seattle, Washington this 2nd day of January anno Domini 47. I hereby certify that Certification 1200 K 1404 from the Commissioner of Immigration and Naturalization, showing the lawful entry for permanent residence of the declarant above named on the date stated in this declaration of intention, has been received by me, and that the photograph affixed to the duplicate and triplicate hereof is a likeness of the declarant.

[SEAL]

MILLARD P. THOMAS
Clerk of the U. S. District Court.
By Marion Miller Deputy Clerk.

Claire Barki
Claire Barkey

A 6 320 548

Form N-315
U. S. DEPARTMENT OF JUSTICE
IMMIGRATION AND NATURALIZATION SERVICE
(Edition of 11-1-41)

Claire Barki's naturalization application to become a U.S. citizen, 1947.

344

4408 Q.

AFFIDAVIT OF WITNESSES

The following witnesses, each being severally, duly, and respectively sworn, depose and say:

My name is **Germaine Louise Ferrari** my occupation is **Housewife**

I reside at **1900 - 23rd Ave. South** **Seattle, Washington**

My name is **Sidonie Mary Dugue** my occupation is **Housewife**

I reside at **Box 36** **Medina, Washington**

I am a citizen of the United States of America; I have personally known and have been acquainted in the United States with **Raymonde Eugenie Duet** , the petitioner named in the petition for naturalization of which this affidavit is a part, since **January 9, 1951** to my personal knowledge the petitioner has resided, immediately preceding the date of filing this petition, in the United States continuously since the date last mentioned, and I have personal knowledge that the petitioner is now and during all such period has been a person of good moral character, attached to the principles of the Constitution of the United States, and well disposed to the good order and happiness of the United States, and in my opinion the petitioner is in every way qualified to be admitted a citizen of the United States.

I do swear (affirm) that the statements of fact I have made in this affidavit of this petition for naturalization subscribed by me are true to the best of my knowledge and belief. SO HELP ME GOD.

Germaine Louise Ferrari ✓ *Sidonie Marie Dugue*
(Signature of witness) (Signature of witness)

Subscribed and sworn to before me by the above-named petitioner and witnesses, in the respective forms of oath shown in said petition and affidavit

the Clerk of said Court at **Seattle, Wash.** this **10th** day of **January** Anno Domini 19 **52**

RAYMONDE EUGENIE DUET
RAYMONDE DUET **DESIGNATED EXAMINER**

10th **January,** A. D. 19 **52** and that Certificate of Arrival **a6 260 036**

MILLARD P. THOMAS Clerk by *B. Erickson* Deputy Clerk

OATH OF ALLEGIANCE

I HEREBY DECLARE, on oath, that I absolutely and entirely renounce and abjure all allegiance and fidelity to any foreign prince, potentate, state, or sovereignty of whom or which I have heretofore been a subject or citizen; that I will support and defend the Constitution and laws of the United States of America against all enemies, foreign and domestic; that I will bear true faith and allegiance to the same; that I will bear arms on behalf of the United States or perform noncombatant service in the Armed Forces of the United States when required by law; and that I take this obligation freely without any mental reservation or purpose of evasion—So Help Me God. In acknowledgment whereof I have hereunto affixed my signature.

Raymonde Eugenie Duet
Raymonde Duet
(Signature of petitioner)

MAY 13 1952

Sworn to in open court, this day of A. D. 19.

MILLARD P. THOMAS
Clerk.

By *Emo Bell*
Deputy Clerk.

NOTE.—In renunciation of title or order of nobility, add the following to the oath of allegiance before it is signed: "I further renounce the title of (give title or titles) which I have heretofore held," or "I further renounce the order of nobility (give the order of nobility) to which I have heretofore belonged."

Petition granted: Line No. **10** of List No. **2450** and Certificate No. **7022687** issued.

Petition denied: List No.

Petition continued from to Reason

U. S. GOVERNMENT PRINTING OFFICE 16—19680-1

ORIGINAL
(To be retained by
Clerk of Court)

UNITED STATES OF AMERICA

INDEXED

No. 4 4 0 8 1

PETITION FOR NATURALIZATION
[Under General Provisions of the Nationality Act of 1940 (Public, No. 853, 76th Cong.)]

To the Honorable the ___U. S. District___ Court of ___W. Dist. of Wash.___ at ___Seattle, Washington___

This petition for naturalization, hereby made and filed, respectfully shows:

(1) My full, true, and correct name is ___CLAIRE BARKI aka CLAIRE BARKEY___

(2) My present place of residence is ___2008 - 33rd South, Seattle, King, Wash.___ My occupation is ___Office Clerk___

(4) I am ___30___ years old. (5) I was born on ___March 14, 1921___ in ___Rodi Island of Rhodes, Italy___

(6) My personal description is as follows: Sex ___female___, color ___white___, complexion ___medium___, color of eyes ___brown___, color of hair ___brown___, height ___5___ feet ___2___ inches, weight ___112___ pounds, visible distinctive marks ___none___, race ___white___,

present nationality ___Italian___ (7) I am ___not___ married; the name of my wife or husband is _____

we were married on _____

he or she was born at _____

and entered the United States at _____ for permanent residence in the United States

and now resides at _____ and was naturalized on _____

at _____ certificate No. _____ or became a citizen by _____

(8) I have ___no___ children; and the name, sex, date and place of birth, and present place of residence of each of said children who is living, are as follows:

(9) My last place of foreign residence was ___Tangier, Morocco___

___Cadiz, Spain___ (10) I emigrated to the United States from

(11) My lawful entry for permanent residence was

at ___New York, New York___ under the name of ___Claire Barki___

on ___June 8, 1946___ on the ___SS Magallanes___

as shown by the certificate of my arrival attached to this petition.

(12) Since my lawful entry for permanent residence I have ___not___ been absent from the United States, for a period or periods of 6 months or longer, as follows:

DEPARTED FROM THE UNITED STATES			RETURNED TO THE UNITED STATES		
PORT	DATE (Month, day, year)	VESSEL OR OTHER MEANS OF CONVEYANCE	PORT	DATE (Month, day, year)	VESSEL OR OTHER MEANS OF CONVEYANCE

(13) I declared my intention to become a citizen of the United States on ___January 2, 1947___ in the ___U. S. District___ Court of ___W. Dist. of Wash.___ at ___Seattle, Washington___ (14) It is my intention in good faith to become a

citizen of the United States and to renounce absolutely and forever all allegiance and fidelity to any foreign prince, potentate, State, or sovereignty of whom or which at this time I am a subject or citizen, and it is my intention to reside permanently in the United States. (15) I am not, and have not been for the period of at least 10 years immediately preceding the date of this petition, an anarchist; nor a believer in the unlawful damage, injury, or destruction of property, or sabotage; nor a disbeliever in or opposed to organized government, nor a member of or affiliated with any organization or body of persons teaching disbelief in or opposition to organized government. (16) I am able to speak the English language (unless physically unable to do so). (17) I am, and have been during all of the periods required by law, attached to the principles of the Constitution of the United States and well disposed to the good order and happiness of the United States. (18) I have resided continuously in the ___read and write___

United States of America for the term of 5 years at least immediately preceding the date of this petition, to wit, since ___June 8, 1946___

and continuously in the State in which this petition is made for the term of 6 months at least immediately preceding the date of this petition, to wit, since ___June 16, 1946___ (19) I have ___not___ heretofore made petition for naturalization. No. _____ in the _____

Court, and such petition was dismissed or denied by that Court for the following reasons and causes, to wit: _____

and the cause of such dismissal or denial has since been cured or removed.

(20) Attached hereto and made a part of this, my petition for naturalization, are my declaration of intention to become a citizen of the United States (if such declaration of intention be required by the naturalization law), a certificate of arrival from the Immigration and Naturalization Service of my said lawful entry into the United States for permanent residence (if such certificate of arrival be required by the naturalization law), and the affidavits of at least two verifying witnesses required by law.

(21) Wherefore, I, your petitioner for naturalization, pray that I may be admitted a citizen of the United States of America, and that my name be changed to ___CLAIRE BARKEY (No middle name or initial)___

(22) I, aforesaid petitioner, do swear (affirm) that I know the contents of this petition for naturalization subscribed by me, that the same are true to the best of my own knowledge, except as to matters therein stated to be alleged upon information and belief, and that as to those matters I believe them to be true, and that this petition is signed by me with my full, true name: SO HELP ME GOD.

Claire Barki
(Full, true, and correct signature of petitioner, without abbreviation)

Form N-405
U. S. DEPARTMENT OF JUSTICE
IMMIGRATION AND NATURALIZATION SERVICE
(Edition of 1-31-41)

AR 6 320 548

ABOUT THE AUTHOR

Cynthia Flash Hemphill is a journalist and publicist. She owns Flash Media Services, a media relations firm based in Bellevue, Wash. During her long media career, Flash worked for United Press International, *The Scottsdale Progress, Hayward Daily Review*, and *Tacoma News Tribune*. Her articles have appeared in *People Magazine*, *The Seattle Times*, the *Puget Sound Business Journal*, and dozens of other magazines, newspapers and online media sources. As a first-generation American, she became interested in this important immigration story after being surrounded by the Sephardic Jewish culture of her mother's large family. She is proud to be able to preserve and pass on this story for others to enjoy. Reach her at cynthia@flashmediaservices.com.

BOOK GROUP QUESTIONS

Author

Was Claire a hero?

General

What is the book's greatest strength or most serious flaw?

Did this book shock or disturb you?

If you had to describe this book in just one word, what would it be?

What other books that you have read could this one be compared to?

Would you recommend this book to someone else?

Characters

Which character(s) did you identify with most and why?

Did you feel the main character was sympathetic?

Did you love her or hate her?

What choices do the main characters face?

How do their decisions affect their own lives and the lives of other characters?

Why does a character make a particular choice?

Style

Does the author's writing style/use of language add to the book or make it more difficult to read?

Read a paragraph from the book to illustrate the author's style or special use of language.

Is this book believable?

Theme

What is the book about?

What ideas drive the story?

Is the theme relevant today?

Compare/contrast this time period with today. How might the book's feel (tone, urgency) be different/ same if it were written today?

What do we learn about the Holocaust from this book?

Title

Why do you think the author chose the title?

Was it a good choice?

How does it relate to the story?